THE CEO LIFE

A HOLISTIC BLUEPRINT TO SCALE YOUR BUSINESS & YOUR LIFE

T. RENEÉ SMITH

FOREWORD BY DR. FELICIA PHILLIPS, PRESIDENT & CEO, PPICW

PREFACE BY DR. KARMETRIA BURTON, DELTA AIR LINES

The CEO Life: A Holistic Blueprint to Scale Your Business and Your Life

ISBN-13: 978-0-578-49779-2

T. Reneé Smith
c/o iSuccess Consulting, Inc.
3645 Marketplace Blvd., Suite 130-51
Atlanta, Georgia 30344
www.treneesmith.com / www.isuccessconsulting.com / www.theceo.life

Cover design by Nicole Mitchell (www.nikmitchell.com)
Editing by Candice L. Davis (www.candiceldavis.com)
Book design by Elena Reznikova (www.DTPerfect.com)

DEDICATION

This book is dedicated to every small business owner who has sacrificed, wondered how they were going to grow their business, quit in their head no less than a hundred times, fought with their spouse about their business, and yet gets back up every day to share their skills and talents with the world.

You no longer have to take this journey by yourself. Here's a holistic blueprint to light your path.

Table of Contents

Contents

Contents

"Four keys determine success: mindset, skill, strategy, and accountability."

— T. Reneé Smith

Acknowledgments

WRITING AND PUBLISHING THIS BOOK was like delivering a baby. It seemed like the contractions got stronger the closer I got to the book deadline. Unexpected events happened: clients were demanding, there were kids' birthday parties to plan, teacher conferences to attend, an anniversary to celebrate, and business as usual. Growing a business, staying happily married, raising healthy children, and remaining sane in the process requires a village and a strong support system. Through the years, my family tribe and inner circle have expanded to include blood family, relatives, extended family, sister-girlfriends, neighbors, teachers, therapists, and the list goes on.

First, I must thank the most amazing husband in the world, Anthony Smith Sr. He is a strong and confident man who loves and supports me unconditionally and allows me to truly be me and walk in my calling. He has been patient as I learned how to be the boss in the boardroom and the helpmate at home. Keep praying for me because that's still a work in process. I am strong-willed, opinionated, and love to be in control, but I am learning every day how to strike a healthy balance. My business would not be where it is without you, Anthony. You are an amazing man of God, husband, father, and role model. Big hugs and kisses to my boys, who keep me young, dreaming, and living on the edge. Anthony Jr. and Jalen, Mommy loves you.

To my mom, dad, and brother (aka the best uncle in the world), thank you for always supporting me, loving me, and encouraging me to reach for the stars and go after my dreams. Also, thank you for the amazing Sunday dinners with black-eyed peas, collard greens, and candied yams. You keep my belly happy.

To my rock-star, always-have-my-back business sister, Dr. Felicia Phillips, your work ethic and giving heart inspire me. Thank you for the amazing opportunity to partner with you on Delta Air Lines Supplier Development Academy (SDA) and so many other wonderful projects. Dr. Karmetria Burton, Kimberly Coffman, Sandra Duckworth, Reggie Williams, and Vic Bolton, it is my joy to work with you on SDA and helping to scale small businesses globally.

To my sister-girlfriends, thank you for allowing me to do life with you: Stephanie Roberts, Linda Williams, Shannon Doyle Bell, and Angel Parks. To my Romar family crew, we have been going strong since our boys met in the Pre-K2 class so many years ago, and we are still going strong: Tabitha Jeffcoat, Candace Sabino, and Lashonta Drinks, thank you for being a part of the crew.

To my extended family and angels to my kids, Kaneesha Alford, Kay Tillery (momma bear), Ajah Myers, Wayne Stuart, Chelse Moore, and Dr. Jennifer Poulos, thank you because I couldn't do what I do without your rock-solid support for my family. To Spirit with T2S Enterprises, thank you for giving me a safe space and the tools to step into my power. You are gifted at what you do and changing lives around the world. Thank you for helping me to live my most authentic life.

Nicole Warren and Randi Okray, my business right and left hands, thank you for making me look good. Your passion, excellence, and commitment are invaluable. Thank you for helping me to execute my vision. To all of my consultants, strategic partners, and vendors, you are too many to name, but all of you are appreciated and loved. Thank you for everything you do for our team and clients on a daily business. To all of my amazing clients, you motivate me to keep doing what I believe God has called me to do, and it is my honor to serve you. There would be no iSuccess Consulting without you.

Vickie Irwin-Avery, you have such a big heart and a love for small businesses. Thank you for your sacrifice and all the things you do behind the scenes to help small businesses. You truly are a powerful advocate and an amazing mentor. Sally Wilson, thank you for holding my feet to the fire when I say I am going to do something and pushing me farther than I ever thought I could go. Your mentorship helps keep me accountable to my goals. Greater Women's Business Council (GWBC), Roz Lewis, and Lissa Miller, thank you for providing an amazing mentoring program that provides access and training to women business owners. I am truly humbled to be a part of it. I have had so many coaches, mentors, and trainers help me along the way, and they have cut my learning curve in half, identified my blind spots, and provided timely advice to help me scale smartly.

Candice L. Davis my editing fairy, book coach, cheerleader, and "talk me down off the ledge sister" when I wanted to give up, what can I say? We did it! Thank you for pushing me to publish with excellence. All of the rewrites and research were worth it. This book is part of my legacy to the small business community. Nicole Mitchell, thank you for a beautiful book cover and amazing graphic design work. Elena Reznikova, this book would not be complete without your beautiful book design. Thank you for creating an interior layout that was easy to navigate. It is always a joy working with you.

Finally, to every small business whose path I have crossed, thank you for believing in yourself, inspiring me, and sharing your gift with the world. Your talent is needed, so keep doing what you're doing.

Foreword: A Note from the Trenches

WHO WANTS TO BE A MILLIONAIRE? Most small business owners would answer that question with a resounding, "I do!" They want to get beyond the mom-and-pop stage, beyond fulfilling their own orders, struggling as a solopreneur, or putting themselves last on the payroll. Unfortunately, most of those entrepreneurs don't yet have the resources, the skills, or the systems to scale to that size, sustain that growth, and keep growing. They don't have the business strategy that can take them from great at what they do to great at running a business. That's the missing link T. Renee Smith provides her clients and which she has captured here in *The CEO Life*.

As a serial entrepreneur, master business strategist, and founder of PPICW, a business development and creative consulting firm, I've seen businesses large and small from every angle. I know how important it can be for a small business to have the right guidance in order to survive, and even more so to grow. Of course, in the digital age, it's easy for almost anyone to put up a website and call themselves a business strategist. However, if you look behind the copywriting and the branding, you'll find many of these people are also new to business. That isn't to say they don't have an intellectual understanding of how to start, grow, and scale a business. Some of them very well may, but that's very different from the knowledge that comes from real-world, hands-on experience. Experience creates an understanding that goes not just wide but also deep. T. Renee has that experience, and it informs everything she does. That's why

I knew from the very beginning that I wanted her to partner with me to develop and manage Delta's Supplier Development Academy.

There's a reason why corporations and organizations closely examine a potential supplier's experience and past performance. That performance matters. It paints a picture of what a business is capable of doing in the future. T. Renee's track record demonstrates that she knows how to succeed. Fortunately for her clients though, her record hasn't been perfect. Early in her role as a business owner, she made mistakes and suffered losses, and because of those setbacks and the lessons they taught her, she's able to dramatically shorten the learning curve for her clients. She shows them her own missteps so they can avoid them.

I'm no stranger to business losses either. With a background in real estate and finance, I was right in the middle of the housing crisis. I watched people make millions, and I watched them lose millions. I watched people go from riding high to falling low. During that time, I observed the differences between those people who gave up and those who bounced back to rebuild or create something new. The entrepreneurs who had the resilience to start over brought with them a wisdom they couldn't have earned any other way. T. Renee has that same kind of resilience and that same kind of wisdom. Her experience has also taught her that a businessperson is still a whole person, and the rest of your life can't be ignored as you pursue the next deal. To truly succeed in business, you have to succeed in life. The holistic approach to business she shares in these pages will help you keep your priorities in front of you as you seek to align your business goals with your life goals.

When T. Renee and I met a decade ago, I saw in her a vibrant woman who would become a lifelong friend. I also found a collaborator with skills complementary to my own. She had already been in business for years, and her enthusiasm for helping small businesses grow immediately won me over. Her passion for excellence and her attention to the details make a real difference for her clients, making her stand out in a crowded market. A teacher at heart, T. Renee breaks down big concepts into small, actionable steps her clients can implement. She meets small business owners where they are, and she fully invests in their success. That investment is what you'll find in these pages.

Dr. Felicia Phillips

PPICW and U.S. Business Women's Network

Preface: A Note from the Other Side of the Desk

ACCESS IS EVERYTHING to the small business owner. The ability to be considered for and secure corporate contracts can transform a business from a fledgling entrepreneurial venture into a thriving enterprise. However, as the General Manager for Supply Chain Management and Supplier Diversity at Delta Air Lines, I've discovered something that many of the small business owners I interact with are unaware of when they seek those contracts. *Access is just the beginning.*

Many entrepreneurs dream of landing a contract as a supplier for a major corporation, and it's certainly a dream worth pursuing. A successfully executed contract with just one major corporation can pull your business out of the "small" category, launching you to new levels of revenue and profitability. It can also lead to new contracts with other corporations, so that first successful relationship is crucial. However, the only way to secure the deal and successfully execute on it is to be corporate ready. This is a different world from selling direct to consumer or business to business. Your business must be ready to scale to the level required of the vendors who work with some of the biggest companies in the world. Fortunately, positioning your business to scale to meet demand is doable, especially if you have a mentor to guide you along the way.

That's where T. Renee Smith and *The CEO Life* come in. I first met T. Renee when she came on board during the developmental stages of Delta's Supplier Development Academy. The program is designed to help small business owners master the strategies required to position themselves for sustainability and to be ready to scale when the opportunity presents itself. Through our work with these suppliers, T. Renee and I reached the same conclusion. Most small business owners need to stop working *in* their business and start working *on* their business. They need to step out of their role as baker, marketer, caterer, or software developer, and step more fully into their role as CEO. It's the only way to take your business to the next level.

I'm committed to helping more small business owners make that leap, a passion I developed early in my career. After securing my degree, I was shocked to find that no one was waiting to hand me a job. When my father offered me a position in his business, along with the rare benefits of free room and board, I took it. My time spent cold calling companies taught me a lot about the value small businesses can and do bring to our communities, our economy, and our nation. It also taught me exactly what kind of work it takes to get in front of the right person, to show up and network effectively, and to be prepared when opportunity presents itself. I was delighted to discover in T. Renee Smith a passion for helping small businesses grow that matched my own.

Initially, I found it hard to believe someone so vibrant had been an entrepreneur for more than two decades, but it quickly became clear that T. Renee has a wealth of experience earned by doing. She brings to the table an uncommon willingness to share the lessons she's gleaned from her wins and her losses alike. As a business strategist, she helps small businesses develop and implement plans to grow and increase profitability. Her passion is so contagious that working with her naturally becomes a fun, invigorating experience.

More and more, large corporations are recognizing how they can boost their bottom line by diversifying their suppliers. T. Renee is committed to ensuring more small businesses are ready to jump in and make the most of those opportunities. She's on a mission to help entrepreneurs think like CEOs, position themselves to scale, and strategize for the long-term health of the business. In *The CEO Life*, she gives you exactly what you need to do all of that and more.

DR. KARMETRIA BURTON

DELTA AIR LINES

Introduction

"STRIVE FOR WORK-LIFE BALANCE," many of the experts say, "because you can have it all." Is that a myth, or is it a realistic goal that we, as busy women, wives, moms, and business owners, should work hard to achieve? (I speak from the perspective of a woman in business, but men, this elusive balance is just as much a factor in your lives as it is in ours. Stay with me.) In my more than twenty-five years of business ownership, twelve years of marriage, and eleven years of parenting, this has been an ongoing struggle for me. On the one hand, I want to be a dedicated wife and mom, who caters to the needs of my husband and children, and on the other hand, I want to be a boss, running a successful company and fulfilling my purpose. I want it all. I want them both, but often, these two worlds collide. I know you see all the pictures on social media where every hair is in place, the kids are dressed in their Sunday best, and the savvy businesswoman's office has everything neatly organized and in place. However, my day-to-day world looks totally different and could provide some juicy video bites for one of the *Real Housewives* television shows.

I searched high and low for a book that could show me how to be successful in both worlds *at the same time*. I found some great books on how to grow your business, whether you're a man or a woman, and some very intriguing books on women's empowerment, but nothing gave me the exact steps to keep my marriage spicy, ensure my kids are thriving, and keep my business growing, all while I remain true to myself and sane in the process.

I've had the pleasure of meeting some amazing businesswomen and corporate executives. Regardless of their background, line of business, or ethnicity, one common thread runs through their stories: there's no such thing as balance. I have seen successful businesswomen who feel lonely in their marriages because their husbands don't support them and seemingly perfect couples who struggle behind closed doors because the wife secretly resents that she's not pursuing her purpose and feels like she's sacrificing her life for her kids and marriage. I have been on both ends of the spectrum, and neither end feels good.

I've also met men who run successful businesses but go home to an empty house because they've destroyed their marriage by giving their life to work. They're lucky to see their kids every other weekend, and some of them bounce from one marriage to another, hoping to find a woman who can put up with the fact that she'll essentially be a single mom in the marriage. Others manage to stay married, but the relationship is a shell of what they dreamed it would be. Many of these men sacrifice their health on the altar of business success, only making a change—if it isn't too late—when they suffer a heart attack or receive a life-threatening diagnosis.

As for me, my journey has been filled with the highest of highs and lowest of lows. The same day I was featured in *Entrepreneur* magazine, the sheriff served me notice of a lawsuit. While I was filing business bankruptcy, I was evicted from my plush 10,000-square-foot office space. My business bank account was overdrawn, and my dreams were crumbling right in front of my eyes. What was happening to my American dream of small business ownership?

Through it all, I learned that you can create the life that you want, but it requires effort, transparency, surrender, and a whole lot of prayer. In reflecting on what I wanted to share in this book, I thought back to a conversation my husband and I had many years ago. He told me he was tired of me coming to bed in a black bonnet and my red lumberjack-plaid pants (oversize sweats) and that he and the kids were tired of getting the leftovers from me after I'd poured into my business all day. I meticulously argued my point. I was working to build an empire, a legacy for our family, and I didn't understand why he didn't support me. Those words fell on deaf ears. Finally, my husband said one thing that stopped me in my tracks. "How is it going to feel," he asked me, "to be a successful businesswoman and a single mom?" That moment started my quest to figure out how to have it all without sacrificing myself, my marriage, or my family in the process.

Months after that conversation, I realized I had been cheating on my husband. I wasn't cheating with another man, but I was emotionally cheating with my business. My business provided me with validation, love, affection, and adoration from others, financial security, and the opportunity to pursue my purpose, so I no longer sought those things from my husband. I had placed my business on a pedestal. I thought about it when I was awake, dreamed about it when I was asleep, and longed to get back to it when I was away from it. My business consumed me. It had taken priority over my marriage and sometimes over my kids. I had to take a really long look in the mirror and at the direction my life was moving in. I was headed for a divorce and breaking up my family without even realizing it. Yes, I wanted a successful business, but at what cost?

In another conversation, my husband pointed out that it was funny how I was often too tired and worn out to practice my "marriage ministry," but if a client called, I was up and ready to go. Catering to the needs of my husband wasn't as important as catering to the needs of my business. When I was spending time with the kids, I would often be on my phone or my laptop. My oldest son complained about how much I read my email while I was supposed to be playing with him and his brother. I might have been physically present, but my mind definitely wasn't there. (I know I wasn't the only one acting like I was going to the bathroom and sneaking upstairs to check email and text messages during family time. Can you relate?)

Not only was my business taking over my marriage and family, but it was also taking over my life. I worked so hard that my body, mind, and spirit didn't get the attention they needed. I found myself getting sick more often, I was tired, and one fateful day, my back went completely out while I was walking down the stairs. When I went to the chiropractor, she said I was simply stressed and overworked. So not only was my marriage falling apart, but I was also headed to an early grave. The more I argued and thought my husband didn't support my business, the more we grew apart. The more I poured into my business, the more an emotional wall went up with my husband. The journey of entrepreneurship I had started more than twenty years earlier definitely wasn't turning out how I'd expected.

Business owners often start a business to create flexibility, financial security, and the freedom to pursue their dreams. Entrepreneurship requires individuality, breaking away from the crowd, and accomplishing goals. It can be hard to turn off that independent drive and aggressiveness and turn on partnership and union, the foundations of marriage. It can be difficult to switch hats from the boss at work to a loving partner at home. Sometimes the pursuit of building a business overshadows the things we hold so dear–family relationships.

I've been at the point of breakdown, near divorce, at my wits' end with my kids, and considering closing my business and walking away from everything just to find a little bit of peace. My breakthrough came when I decided to do something different and then actually did it. Do you want to know what that something is? Read on. In *The CEO Life*, I share with you my journey of learning to have success as a wife, mother, and businesswoman all at the same time. The strategies I use can work for you whether you're single or married, a woman or a man, a parent or not. Simply put I'll show you how to grow a business that allows you to have a life. Sometimes the words on these pages will make you laugh, cry, or do a reality check about what's really going on in your own life.

As business owners, it's important for us to share our successes but also our failures, mishaps, and painful truths. If you learn from my experiences, you may be able to avoid some of those same struggles. Let's get rid of the façade that we have it all together and speak the truth. Every hair isn't in place, our house isn't as spotless as we claim, our children don't always listen, our marriage isn't as perfect as it seems, our business isn't always doing as well as we say it is, and sometimes, when we get a moment of peace, we realize there's a scared little girl or a scared little boy inside of us, trying to figure out how our life, family, or business ended up the way it did.

It doesn't matter how much outward success we have if it isn't matched by our internal peace. I finally burned the superwoman cape and stopped trying to have it all at the same time. I realized that I don't have to be perfect, I don't have to live up to anybody else's expectations, and the only approval that really matters is God's and mine. From bankruptcy and failed businesses to being incarcerated and on the brink of divorce, life has definitely thrown me some curve balls.

I have finally accepted that, on Monday, I may nail it by making a home-cooked meal, finishing client projects on time, and ensuring my children do their homework. Then I can wake up on Tuesday, and the kids barely make it to school on time, I take a nap while I'm supposed to be working, and the kids take a quick wash-up instead of a bath before bed. Instead of balance or perfection, I strive for work-life integration. I now endeavor to find joy and peace in all areas of my life regardless of what season of life I am in. I have embraced the ebbs and flow of life and realize that sometimes I'll crush it as a wife, mom, and business owner, and other times I'll question if I even have what it takes to be successful. Life is an emotional journey, and I have learned to give myself compassion when I fail, when I'm afraid, and when I question myself.

Learning how to be authentically me has been a journey of self-discovery. I've found a safe place inside of myself that offers me all the acceptance and love I need. I have learned to speak in terms of "and" instead of "or." I now realize I have the power to redefine my success and set boundaries so I can be successful as a wife, an engaged mother, and a rock-star business owner—without having to choose one over the others. I want to share this wonderful gift with you.

Throughout the pages of this book, I will share my personal stories and teach you my CEO Life System, which shows you the exact five steps you must master to grow and scale your business:

Business Strategy

Unique Branding

Integrated Marketing and Sales

Leveraged Systems

Decisive Leadership

Are you ready to burn your superhero cape, stop trying to live up to the expectations of others, and admit that you can't do it all by yourself? This is your time. If not today, then when? I invite you to learn how to scale up the quality of your business and personal life at the same time. Let the journey begin.

From the Desk of the Decision-Maker

Kimberly Coffman

Manager, Supplier Diversity, Supply Chain Management

Delta Air Lines

THE BIGGEST MISTAKE I see small businesses make when they want to do business with corporations like mine is forgetting that corporations have their own policies, procedures, and standard practices that employees must adhere to as corporate representatives. I recommend small businesses follow the guidance and direction provided by corporate representatives. This will ensure that all steps required to do business with the corporations are fulfilled based on their unique needs and expectations and your company's opportunity to market to them won't get delayed or missed.

> "There is no such thing as work-life balance. Everything worth fighting for unbalances your life."
>
> — ALAIN DE BOTTON

CHAPTER ONE

The CEO Struggle

01	**Forgiveness** ▶ Forgiving yourself ▶ Forgiving others
02	**Intentional Living** ▶ Self-reflection ▶ Belief system and mindset ▶ Priorities and boundaries
03	**Embrace Each Season** ▶ Sowing (planting and reaping season) ▶ Watering season ▶ Harvesting season
04	**Recognize Your Purpose** ▶ Personality type & unique experiences ▶ Resonating with a cause ▶ Passions and strengths ▶ Spiritual gifts & empowering yourself
05	**Cultivate a Spiritual Practice** ▶ Mind ▶ Body ▶ Spirit
06	**Execute in Spite of Fear** ▶ Effective decision making ▶ Rules of life

The CEO Struggle

RUNNING YOUR OWN BUSINESS is supposed to give you the freedom to do what you want with your life. However, for many business owners, growing a business consumes far more time than any conventional job ever would. You don't get to spend time with your family like you want to, you frequently feel like you're one day away from burn out, you take work home, and you get stuck in the trenches of day-to-day work instead of being the creative visionary for your company. This situation ruins the joy and personal freedom of business ownership, and a lack of strategy, structure, and systems prevents your business from scaling.

What's the magic formula to succeed as a spouse, parent, and business owner at the same time? There is no magic formula; it's all about priorities, boundaries, and striving for harmony instead of balance. Based on the season of life you're in, sometimes you will focus more on your family, and other times you will focus more on your business. Understanding this truth helps to relieve some of the guilt you may feel when you aren't giving your all to your spouse, kids, business, or self-care routine. Instead of striving for balance, work towards creating harmony in each area.

I'll be the first to admit that it requires heart, determination, and pure resilience to build a successful business while keeping your family intact. I've found it's essential to take time to focus on what I need, personally and spiritually, to ensure that my cup is full before I start to pour into my family and business. You're supposed to pour into others with your overflow, not your reserves, but too often, we run ourselves into the ground trying to be everything to everybody. We say yes to other people when we should say no. We say no to ourselves when we should say yes. I love Shonda Rhimes's book, T*he Year of Yes*. In it, she reveals how saying yes to herself for one year totally changed her life in a positive way. One of the best things I learned from the book is that "no" is a complete sentence. To give our all to others or our business, we first have to make sure that we are whole in our mind, body, and spirit.

There are several facets to creating success in all areas of her life. You have the woman/man, wife/husband, mother/father, business owner, and all the other roles we play. In order to have authentic success, we must address the needs of each area and not just one.

I speak from a woman's perspective in this section because I want to share my experience. However, in my many years of working with male business owners and executives, I have come to realize that they experience many of the same challenges that we do. They struggle with how to be an involved and understanding husband, father, son, and friend while aggressively growing a business. They sacrifice their health in pursuit of their dreams and forget that self-care is just as important for them as it is for us. They sometimes feel left out because women have magazines, conferences, support groups, and sisterhoods, and the men are left to figure things out on their own. Well, not on my watch. Men, the strategies I share in *The CEO Life* are just as relevant to helping you on your journey to achieve success in your business and life as it is to women. The advice works equally as well for men as it does for women as long as you follow the steps.

Man or woman, your wholeness—mind, body, and spirit—is the foundation of your success. It's impossible to sustain success, over the long haul, in your marriage, your relationships with your kids, and your business, if you're not whole and happy with who you are as a person. Resentment, unforgiveness, fear, and insecurity will always creep up when you least expect it if you don't have a solid foundation.

As I started to mature and grow as a woman, I realized I was the common denominator in my problems. Frequently, when there was conflict in my marriage, I had brought insecurity, selfishness, or emotional baggage from previous relationships into the situation. As a mother, when I was yelling, screaming, and losing patience, it was often because I saw a reflection of myself in my kids. (Moms and dads, don't tell me you've never yelled at your kids because they were acting like you.) I was trying to discipline them for something I'd yet to discipline myself to do in my own life. In my business, when I wasn't reaching my revenue goals or attracting the right clients, insecurity, perfectionism, low self-esteem, and fear had crept in. There were times when I wasn't being the best friend I could be because I was on empty and not pouring back into myself with prayer, exercise, meditation, eating right, or taking some "me" time. The results showed up differently in each area of my life, but the root of it all was a shaky foundation.

I've done many things to help me on this path of self-discovery, to start pulling back the layers and shifting my mindset to replace old beliefs that no longer serve me. One of the most important things I did was go to therapy. In minority communities, we often look at therapy as a bad thing. We're raised to believe what goes on in the house stays in the house. We are told not to share our secrets and to take them to the grave with us. This mentality causes preventable illnesses, premature deaths, divorces, rifts between families, overall unhappiness, and unfulfilled dreams.

What I know for sure is all the secrets you keep will prevent you from living an abundant and authentic life. Now, don't get me wrong. Holding a mirror up to yourself and being real and honest about who you are is no walk in the park. It has taken me years—and I mean many years—of struggle, denial, blame, projection, grief, tears, tantrums, and the full gamut of emotions to start accepting the real me and having compassion for myself.

As women, it's much easier for us to have compassion for

others—your kids, your husband (well, when you're not pissed off with him), your parents, your boss, and everyone else—but we are so hard on ourselves. As men, you're often told that your emotions don't matter and forbidden to show yourself any compassion at all. Throughout my evolution, I've learned how to be compassionate with myself, which is a true game-changer.

I use the word evolution instead of change because change sounds like such a daunting process. Evolution, on the other hand, is an unfolding, a process of growth and expansion in a desirable direction. It requires you to look at the areas of your life that aren't going the way you want them to and take responsibility for changing them. Evolution means no longer blaming other people for where you are in life and taking your power back by focusing your energy on the things you want instead of complaining about the things you don't. When you focus your energy on being grateful, you call into your life more of what you want.

The world and those closest to us will often beat us down without even knowing they're doing it. In my process of evolution, I've had to learn how to focus inwardly instead of outwardly. That means my happiness, joy, and peace come from inside me and not from what someone else does or doesn't do or what someone says or doesn't say. I have learned how to validate myself. Now, that doesn't mean I don't like to receive validation from others. It means I don't base my happiness in life on anyone else's approval. It's a value-add, not a requirement.

As small business owners navigating the fine line between maintaining a thriving business and keeping commitments to family, community, friends, and self, it is important to develop a CEO Mindset. That simply means you have to go from toiling in your business to leading with the decisiveness of a chief executive. This all starts with shifting your mindset to focus on the intangibles required to grow a successful business just as much as you focus on the business fundamentals, like marketing and sales. One mantra

I often use to stay motivated and moving in the right direction is "I am F.I.E.R.C.E." I don't say this in a conceited way at all. I say it in a self-care way, one that helps me to remember who I am. I say it in the same way I want you to say it to yourself.

F.I.E.R.C.E. stands for:

Forgive yourself and others.

Intentional living is a daily choice.

Embrace each season.

Recognize your purpose.

Cultivate a spiritual practice.

Execute in spite of fear.

Forgiveness

Forgiveness is such a powerful concept because it requires you to humble yourself, get out of your own way, and realize that everything is not about you. For most of my life, I didn't understand what forgiveness truly meant. At some point, you've probably thought, "I'm not going to forgive her because she wronged me, he stole from me, she betrayed me, or he did something unforgivable." You think that, by holding this grudge, you're going to make the other person pay. In actuality, when you hold a grudge, you pay. You pay in the amount of success you can achieve, the amount of happiness and joy you can experience, and the amount of stress you will have in your life. When you practice forgiveness, you're not saying what the other person did was okay. You're simply releasing yourself from the pain and burden of carrying the weight of unforgiveness. I love this quote from Martin Luther King Jr.: "Forgiveness is not an occasional act; it is a permanent attitude."

Learning to forgive is a process and will take time to cultivate. The wake-up call for me was when I realized I was married to my husband but was making him pay for the negative things I perceived my ex had done to me during our ten-year relationship. In therapy, I learned that the words and actions from my husband that triggered me were actually unresolved issues from my past. When I was able to look at those issues head-on, I was able to start forgiving myself and others so the healing process could begin.

Here are the ten steps I used to start my forgiveness process.

Step 1. Realize that forgiveness is an ongoing process, not a one-time event.

Step 2. Decide not to wait until you are ready to forgive and make a decision to forgive now.

Step 3. Remove yourself from having to be the judge and executioner, and do not seek revenge.

Step 4. Allow yourself to feel whatever emotion you are feeling at the time (hurt, pain, betrayal, anger, resentment, etc.). Your feelings will probably need time to catch up with your decision to forgive.

Step 5. Recognize that you can't be a victim and victorious at the same time, and choose not to be a victim.

Step 6. Shift your mindset to stop asking, "Why me?" Instead ask, "What lesson do I need to learn in this situation?" Then ask, "What's next?"

Step 7. Seek the help of a therapist, an advisor, or a trusted friend to help you see your blind spots. They will help you realize that the story you're telling yourself is continuously replaying the issue in your mind and keeping you stuck.

Step 8. Take action and apply everything you learn from the person helping you.

Step 9. Share your process of forgiveness with others so they can release themselves from their past and begin healing. You don't want to be the only one in your friend circle or family who's getting healed and healthy.

Step 10. Complete this process daily. Remember forgiveness takes consistent practice to cultivate.

For deeper insight and knowledge about forgiveness, read a relevant book that you resonate with or watch videos that walk you through the steps to forgiveness. I've read several great books on the topic. A few to check out are *Let It Go: Forgive So You Can Be Forgiven*, by T. D. Jakes, *The Book of Forgiving: The Fourfold Path for Healing Ourselves and Our World*, by Desmond Tutu and Mpho Tutu, and *Total Forgiveness*, by R. T. Kendall.

Forgiveness is one of the greatest gifts you can give yourself. It opens up the gateway to healing, which is the path to abundance, peace, and joy in every area of your life. Take a minute to think about the people in your life who you need to focus on forgiving. This is one of the intangible things that affect whether or not business owners reach their highest possible level of success. Your business growth is directly tied to your mindset. Shift your mindset; shift your business and your life.

Intentional Living

Oprah Winfrey has had a profound impact on my life. She really is my mentor; she just doesn't know it yet. I recently watched her *Super Soul Sunday* interview with Gary Zukav, author of *The Seat of the Soul.* During the interview, Oprah stated, "The number one principle that rules my life is intention." She reminded me of a quote I've read and heard in different places and which really resonates with me: "There are only three kinds of people in the world. Those who make things happen, those who watch things happen, and those who say what happened." One thing I know for sure is that I want to be a person who makes things happen. To do and achieve everything I want in my life and business, I have to live every day with intention.

It is so easy to get distracted with things like social media, go with the flow of what's going on around us, or focus on whatever the most pressing issue is in our lives. At certain times and in certain seasons of life, we have to respond to impactful situations, such as emergencies, unexpected events, losses, or things outside of our control. However, living without intention on a daily basis pushes us farther from achieving our goals in business and life.

So what is intention? Intention is living every day with an aim, a purpose, or a destination. It is a choice to deliberately pursue what is important over the long term rather than the short term. It's about doing the things today that will yield you results tomorrow and making sound decisions that move you closer to your goal rather than farther away from it.

Writing this section is so timely for me because of an experience I had just this morning when I was working out. So I was minding my own business, and I overheard one gentleman talking with another about the SEC game the University of Georgia played against the University of Alabama over the weekend. Now, I am not a big sports fan, but my husband is a huge Alabama fan–Roll Tide! So whenever

I hear someone talking about Nick Saban, the head coach, my ears perk up. After this man finished his conversation, he turned and started talking to me.

Remember I was minding my own business, focused on getting my thirty minutes of cardio in, considering I hadn't worked out at the gym for the last six months, but he felt I needed to hear his opinion. He went on to say how Nick Saban and Alabama were lucky, and then I broke down that luck had nothing to do with it. I started to school him (in a positive and loving way) about how Nick Saban had clear intentions to achieve his goals and a team and strategy in place to execute on those intentions.

Needless to say, after our conversation, this stranger was very curious about what I did. I told him I was a business strategist and asked about his profession. I learned he'd been in business for eight years and that he was very stressed and felt like he was at the point of a breakdown. He also said he was looking to open another business with his son in the next thirty days. As I listened, it became more and more obvious that he wasn't clear about his intentions for his business or his personal life. His pattern of being stressed out, leaving money on the table with clients, and being unproductive will continue unless he does something different.

The moment I started being more intentional in my life, maintaining my health, enjoying my marriage, raising my kids, and running a business became easier. Don't mistake the term easier for "not requiring a lot of time and effort." It took a lot of work, but now I understand the purpose, the why, or the reasons behind what I do, which makes it easier for me to overcome setbacks, delays, or disappointments.

I recently watched a video of Simon Sinek, author of *Start with Why: How Great Leaders Inspire Everyone to Take Action*. (The book is a must-read for every leader and entrepreneur.) In his video, Simon talks about the necessity of understanding your destination. He gives this example. If you're in a crowded room and you tell everyone to go in a straight line to the door with the red exit sign at the back of the room, they will continue to walk to the door even if you put a chair in their way. They will see the chair as an obstacle, move it out of the way, and continue to go towards the door with the red sign over it in the back of the room. However, if you tell the same group of people to wander around the room and end up wherever they want to go, and you put a chair in front of them, they will stop and stand there because they have no clear final destination. The same is true in your life and your business. If you have no clear intention or end goal, you will continue to wander around aimlessly and often give up if something gets in your way.

In order to truly understand where you want to go, you have to understand where you came from and identify the thinking that could derail you from reaching your goals.

Here is my five-step ladder system for self-discovery that will help you start being more intentional in your life and business.

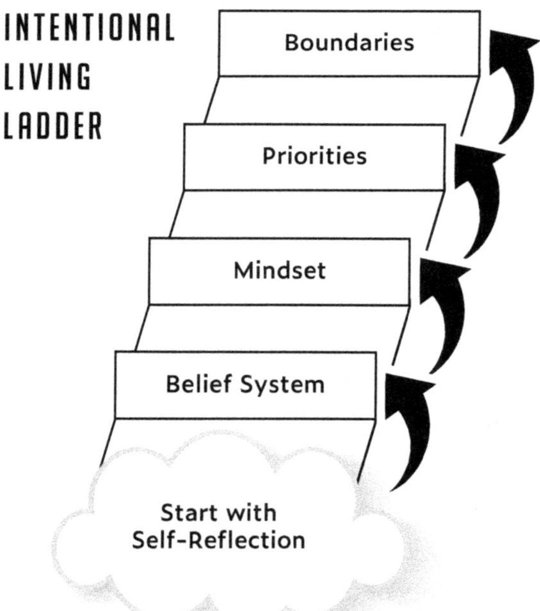

Start with self-reflection. The very first step in living an intentional life is to be honest with yourself about what you want in life. What do you value most? Be selfish for a moment. Stop thinking about what everyone else wants or expects you to do. Tap into that place inside of yourself where your dreams reside and ask yourself: "What do I really want out of life?" Give yourself permission to dream again. Get rid of the negative thoughts, like I'm too old, I need to lose weight, I'm not pretty enough, I'm not smart enough, I'm not rich enough, and all the other "I'm not enough" statements that that keep you stuck.

Ask yourself a couple more questions: "What is my purpose, passion, or the burning desire I have inside myself that I want to fulfill? What does success look like in my life?" See it clearly and vividly. When you can clearly articulate what you want in your life, you can then determine what you must change to ensure you can accomplish your goals. For example, when I was writing this book, my end goal was to have it completed in twelve weeks. (What a lofty goal!) However, since I was clear on what success would like for this project, I was able to adjust my schedule, my attitude, and my effort to achieve my goal.

Assess your belief system. Your outer world is a direct reflection of your inner world (thoughts, beliefs, feelings of importance, etc.). Your beliefs have a direct impact on how successful you will be in business and in life. When I'm coaching my clients, and we run into roadblocks dealing with money, attracting the right clients to work with, putting themselves out there in a bigger way in marketing and PR, or plateauing at a level of success in their business, we take a deep dive and look into the CEO's mindset. When you are executing the right strategy, you have systems in place, your team is rocking and rolling, and yet you still feel stuck or aren't moving like you want to, it's time to do a tune-up on your thoughts and belief system.

To change your outer world, you must first do the inner work to change how you think. One game-changer for me was learning about generational beliefs. We all have innate beliefs based on how we were raised, the environment we were raised in, and what we were exposed to. When I started self-reflecting and really looking at my beliefs, I learned a lot of them weren't good for me and weren't going to help me get to the next level. I realized that a lot of my beliefs about marriage were based on dysfunction. A lot of what I believed about money was based on lack, and a lot of what I believed about humility was based on fear. I started to hijack my own beliefs and change the stories I was telling myself. During this process, I developed the Belief Spectrum to help others start assessing their own beliefs. Take a look at the chart and simply follow the directions.

BELIEF SPECTRUM™

Review each belief and determine which word most accurately describes your current belief about yourself and/or the world. Select a number from 1 to 4 that describes the belief you have at least 90% of the time. Be honest. Don't select the belief you want to have. Select the true belief you currently have so you can start shifting your mindset.

1-Rarely 2-Sometimes 3-Often 4-Always

NEGATIVE BELIEF	POSITIVE BELIEF
FEAR ◀ 1 2 3 4 ▶	LOVE ◀ 1 2 3 4 ▶
SCARCITY ◀ 1 2 3 4 ▶	ABUNDANCE ◀ 1 2 3 4 ▶
SELFISH ◀ 1 2 3 4 ▶	GIVING ◀ 1 2 3 4 ▶
NEGATIVE THINKING ◀ 1 2 3 4 ▶	POSITIVE THINKING ◀ 1 2 3 4 ▶
BLAME ◀ 1 2 3 4 ▶	FORGIVENESS ◀ 1 2 3 4 ▶
GUILT ◀ 1 2 3 4 ▶	FREEDOM ◀ 1 2 3 4 ▶
SHAME ◀ 1 2 3 4 ▶	COURAGE ◀ 1 2 3 4 ▶

DOUBT ◄ 1 2 3 4 ►	TRUST ◄ 1 2 3 4 ►
TIRED ◄ 1 2 3 4 ►	HIGH-ENERGY ◄ 1 2 3 4 ►
UNHEALTHY ◄ 1 2 3 4 ►	HEALTHY ◄ 1 2 3 4 ►
SPIRITUALLY DISCONNECTED ◄ 1 2 3 4 ►	ALIGNED WITH SPIRIT ◄ 1 2 3 4 ►
INDIVIDUALLY DRIVEN ◄ 1 2 3 4 ►	GOD/PURPOSE DRIVEN ◄ 1 2 3 4 ►
UNWORTHY ◄ 1 2 3 4 ►	VALUABLE ◄ 1 2 3 4 ►
APPROVAL SEEKING ◄ 1 2 3 4 ►	SELF-ASSURED ◄ 1 2 3 4 ►
UNFULFILLED ◄ 1 2 3 4 ►	FULFILLED ◄ 1 2 3 4 ►
CRITICAL ◄ 1 2 3 4 ►	ACCEPTING ◄ 1 2 3 4 ►
UNATTRACTIVE ◄ 1 2 3 4 ►	BEAUTIFUL ◄ 1 2 3 4 ►
INSECURE ◄ 1 2 3 4 ►	CONFIDENT ◄ 1 2 3 4 ►
REJECTED ◄ 1 2 3 4 ►	CHERISHED ◄ 1 2 3 4 ►

ABANDONED ◀ 1 2 3 4 ▶	SECURE ◀ 1 2 3 4 ▶
UNAPPRECIATIVE ◀ 1 2 3 4 ▶	GRATEFUL ◀ 1 2 3 4 ▶
DECEITFUL ◀ 1 2 3 4 ▶	TRUTHFUL ◀ 1 2 3 4 ▶
SADNESS/PAIN ◀ 1 2 3 4 ▶	PLEASURE ◀ 1 2 3 4 ▶
CONFUSION ◀ 1 2 3 4 ▶	CLARITY ◀ 1 2 3 4 ▶
RESPOND IMPULSIVELY ◀ 1 2 3 4 ▶	MANAGE EMOTIONS ◀ 1 2 3 4 ▶
DAY DREAMER ◀ 1 2 3 4 ▶	ACTION TAKER ◀ 1 2 3 4 ▶
PEOPLE-PLEASER ◀ 1 2 3 4 ▶	GOD-PLEASER ◀ 1 2 3 4 ▶
SEE TRIALS AS ADVERSITY ◀ 1 2 3 4 ▶	SEE TRIALS AS LIFE LESSONS ◀ 1 2 3 4 ▶
ARROGANT ◀ 1 2 3 4 ▶	HUMBLE ◀ 1 2 3 4 ▶
FAKE ◀ 1 2 3 4 ▶	AUTHENTIC ◀ 1 2 3 4 ▶
BROKEN ◀ 1 2 3 4 ▶	WHOLE ◀ 1 2 3 4 ▶

WORRIED ◄ 1 2 3 4 ►	AT PEACE ◄ 1 2 3 4 ►
FAILURE ◄ 1 2 3 4 ►	SUCCESS ◄ 1 2 3 4 ►
INCONSISTENT ◄ 1 2 3 4 ►	COMMITTED ◄ 1 2 3 4 ►
EXISTING AND MAINTAINING ◄ 1 2 3 4 ►	LIVING WITH PASSION ◄ 1 2 3 4 ►
LIFE HAPPENING TO ME ◄ 1 2 3 4 ►	PURSUING MY PASSION ◄ 1 2 3 4 ►
ATTACHED TO OUTCOMES ◄ 1 2 3 4 ►	DETACHED FROM OUTCOMES ◄ 1 2 3 4 ►
NEGATIVE SELF-TALK ◄ 1 2 3 4 ►	POSITIVE AFFIRMATIONS ◄ 1 2 3 4 ►
STUCK IN PAST ◄ 1 2 3 4 ►	HEALED FROM PAST ◄ 1 2 3 4 ►
EXCUSES DRIVEN ◄ 1 2 3 4 ►	HOLD MYSELF ACCOUNTABLE ◄ 1 2 3 4 ►
CONSTANTLY FIGHTING LIFE ◄ 1 2 3 4 ►	GO WITH THE FLOW OF LIFE ◄ 1 2 3 4 ►
NEGLECT SELF-CARE ◄ 1 2 3 4 ►	DAILY SELF-CARE ◄ 1 2 3 4 ►

STAGNANT ◀ 1 2 3 4 ▶	CONTINUOUS LEARNER ◀ 1 2 3 4 ▶
DENIAL ◀ 1 2 3 4 ▶	SELF-AWARENESS ◀ 1 2 3 4 ▶
EXTERNALLY FOCUSED ◀ 1 2 3 4 ▶	INTERNALLY FOCUSED ◀ 1 2 3 4 ▶
MAKE ASSUMPTIONS ◀ 1 2 3 4 ▶	ASK QUESTIONS ◀ 1 2 3 4 ▶

Take a minute to look at your results from the Belief Spectrum™. Do you have more beliefs that are negative or positive? If you slant towards the negative-belief end of the spectrum, it's unlikely that you are experiencing the level of success you want to have in your life because your beliefs are blocking you. On the other hand, if you slant more towards the positive beliefs, you are well on your way to achieving success in both business and life. This exercise should serve as a wake-up call for which beliefs you need to work on changing.

Change your core beliefs. Here are seven steps to change them for good:

1. Identify the beliefs you need to change.
2. Identify the root cause.
3. Slow down.
4. Forgive yourself.
5. Check in with yourself.
6. Find an accountability partner.
7. Shift your mindset.

Step 1. Identify the beliefs you need to change. Maybe you constantly find yourself caught up in drama-filled relationships, you aren't able to grow your business, or you fall into endless cycles of overeating and guilt. Negative beliefs are often unconscious, making them challenging to address. However, we can retrain our minds to recognize negative beliefs by paying attention to our emotions. When you feel an emotion that you don't like, such as sadness, anxiety, anger, guilt, abandonment, frustration, or loneliness, take a minute to recognize it. Be honest with yourself about your feelings and don't suppress them.

I know this can be difficult, especially if you've been suppressing your emotions for a long time, because you may have become numb. After living in an emotionally abusive and dysfunctional relationship for over ten years, I became a pro at suppressing my feelings. When I was honest, and my ex didn't agree with my feelings or opinion, it would only lead to a disagreement or feelings of abandonment. However, once I started learning how to identify my feelings and process them, I could consciously decide what to do with them. At that point, my beliefs and thinking started to shift in a positive way and serve me by helping me achieve what I wanted in life.

Step 2. Identify the root cause. If you don't dig deep, real deep, (even if it hurts) to start identifying why you have a certain belief, you're likely to continue repeating the same mistakes. Therefore, it's essential to start analyzing your feelings and your thinking to get to the root cause. For instance, if you get angry when someone gives you constructive criticism or feedback on something that could greatly improve your business, there's something wrong. You're likely triggered by the criticism, which is a sign of something deeper. You may be dealing with a belief that you aren't good enough or not smart enough. Instead of continuing to respond negatively, pull back the layers to identify why you are getting angry. Once you do this, you can choose a different response. If you're not able to process these emotions on your own, get some help. I surely did, and it has changed the trajectory of my life and business.

Step 3. Slow down. Many patterns reoccur because you move too fast to see things for what they are. For example, one of your vendors makes an honest mistake; you go off and potentially damage your business relationship. You're moving at lightning speed and don't take time to realize that your core belief of perfectionism was triggered and you're projecting that on your vendor. On the personal side, your spouse says something that pisses you off, and you respond by hitting below the belt and saying something you can't take back. Your spouse's comments triggered insecurity and abandonment issues that you have yet to process. In both instances, you failed to take the time to pause, breathe, and assess the situation. The key is to dig a little bit deeper to see what's occurring right in front of you.

Step 4. Forgive yourself. Forgiveness clears out the residue of the past. Until you forgive yourself for what you did, did not do, or should have done, you will continue to repeat your patterns. When your mind is clear of guilt and shame, it focuses on what is here now instead of what was, and lets you take each moment as it comes.

Step 5. Check in with yourself. When you recognize that you're responding to a situation in an unproductive way, stop. Take a minute to breathe, assess the situation, and ask yourself two questions: 1) why am I responding like this, and 2) what triggered me? When you're able to take a minute to decide not to react or to choose your reaction, you start the process of identifying your belief behind your response. Every negative response is the result of a negative belief.

Step 6. Find an accountability partner. You may be familiar with the African proverb "It takes a village to raise a child," which it does, but it also takes a village to build a successful business, stay peacefully married for a long time, raise healthy children, and probably anything else that requires a substantial amount of work. One fundamental element of my success is having accountability partners, coaches, friends, and therapists who challenge me to think bigger and help me to recognize my blind spots. I always say a coach needs a coach. It's difficult to go at it alone when you want to achieve great things. When times get hard, which they will, you need a cheerleader or some re-enforcement to remind you of who you are and what you are capable of doing. Some people are blessed to have these wonderful people as friends, spouses, and family members. If that isn't the case for you, find someone to serve in this role.

Step 7. Shift your mindset. What story are you telling yourself? We all have stories going through our heads, and sometimes they're not good! Sometimes we tell ourselves that we can't do something because of x, y, and z. But if we just change the story, we'll stop holding ourselves back. Replace the stories that aren't serving you. Your perspective of what has and is happening to you in your life determines where you'll go. One story I told myself for a long time was that God was still working on and developing me, and until He was finished, I wasn't going to put myself out there in the marketplace as a business strategist. When I started looking at my story, I realized it was rooted in fear of failure, fear of being judged, and fear that I wasn't good enough to help other people. Another story I used to tell myself was that I couldn't tell people the truth, so I sugarcoated things. In actuality, when I examined that story, I found it was based on my fear of confrontation and my fear of disappointing people because I was a people pleaser. To change these stories, I had to redefine the meanings of several words that were huge obstacles for me.

Here are a few words I redefined to make it easier to shift my mindset.

WORD	NEW MEANING
NO	**N**ext **O**pportunity
FEAR	**F**ace **E**verything **A**nd **R**ise
FAIL	**F**irst **A**ttempt **I**n **L**earning
STUCK	**S**ome **T**imes **U**nique **C**larity **K**nocks
DOUBT	**D**efine **O**pportunity **U**ntil **B**reakthrough **T**ransforms
LACK	**L**earn **A**nd **C**ultivate **K**nowledge
ADVERSITY	**A**cknowledge **D**ifficulties, **V**alue **E**xperiences, **R**espond **S**martly, and **I**nnately **T**rust **Y**ourself
RISK	**R**ely on **I**nsight & **S**eek **K**nowledge
EGO	**E**dging **G**od **O**ut (phrase used by Wayne Dyer and Ken Blanchard)
CRITICISM	**C**almly **R**eact **I**nwardly **t**o **I**nformation, **C**hallenging **I**nsights, **S**hift your **M**indset

Your thoughts and self-talk can be empowering or disempowering, depending on which thoughts and self-talk you choose. So when trials and mishaps come into your life, tell yourself something positive about them and look for the lesson. There is no such thing as failure if you get the lesson. As John C. Maxwell says, fail forward.

Our mindset is the most powerful tool we have to create our success in business and life. Simply put, the way we think determines what we will ultimately have in life. If there are areas in your life that you would like to change, simply trace back to see how your mind is wired. Is your mind wired with positivity, the belief that anything is possible, faith, and abundance? Or is it wired with scarcity, fear, doubt, and lack? You will never achieve more than what your mind believes it can accomplish.

Take a minute to think about where you are in your life. Do you regularly set goals and accomplish them? Are you in loving relationships that celebrate you instead of simply tolerating you? Are you charging your clients premium rates and getting paid what you're worth? Are you living a happy, peaceful, and abundant life? If you answered yes to all of these questions, your mindset is probably set for success. If you answered no to any of these, it's probably time to adjust your mindset.

Life happens, and it throws you unexpected curveballs. You get disappointed in relationships, your career, business, family, and so many other areas. These experiences can leave you scarred and emotionally hurt. When this happens, it often has a negative impact on the way you think and how you act. You have to hit the reset button in your mind and retrain the way you think. The first step to resetting your mind is taking an honest assessment of what's currently going on in your life and deciding what you want to change.

How many days does it take to change your mindset? It depends on who you ask. Some experts say twenty-one days, others will say sixty days, and someone else might say ninety days. So indulge me for a moment, and I'll give you the rationale behind the twenty-one-day theory. Why is twenty-one such a magical number? It turns out that number came from the 1960 book *Psycho-Cybernetics*, by Maxwell Maltz, MD. In his book, Maltz, a plastic surgeon turned psychologist, claimed you could create or break any habit in just twenty-one days. He made this claim based on the fact that he observed that it usually takes plastic surgery patients twenty-one days to adjust to their new faces. Readers of Maltz's book must have rationalized that if it takes twenty-one days to change and heal from a physical surgery, then changing or forming a habit must take twenty-one days too. In theory, it makes sense, so let's dive a little deeper.

In my personal experience and my experience with many of my clients, we've found that it indeed takes a minimum of twenty-one days of *consistent* action to change or form a new habit. Yes, that means if you miss just one day, the twenty-one-day process starts all over again. If you have deep-seated negative beliefs, it may take you more than twenty-one days to shift your mindset because you first have to identify the wrong story and be conscious about telling yourself the new story. Below are daily mindset shifts you can make to ensure you consistently focus on retraining your mind.

21 Mindset Shifts to Succeed in Business and Life

Mindset shift #1. Look inward, instead of outward, and redefine what success means to you.

Mindset shift #2. Assess and challenge your current beliefs, release self-defeating beliefs, and affirm your life.

Mindset shift #3. Heal from your past, grieve the life you no longer have, and forgive yourself and others.

Mindset shift #4. Surrender, live in the now, follow your flow, detach from outcomes, and remain open.

Mindset shift #5. Use your personal story to serve you positively. You are not a victim; you are victorious.

Mindset shift #6. Hold yourself accountable. Success and happiness are relative, and you are in control of both.

Mindset shift #7. Pursue your purpose, live with passion, and serve the world with your gifts.

Mindset shift #8. Live a life of gratitude and giving; seek to serve first, and give before you ask.

Mindset shift #9. Choose healthy relationships that empower you, including the one with yourself.

Mindset shift #10. Make no assumptions or excuses; stop saying *but*, *try*, *can't*, and *someday*.

Mindset shift #11. Maintain a daily spiritual practice of meditation, mindfulness, and following your intuition.

Mindset shift #12. Build your confidence and self-love; self-care is non-negotiable.

Mindset shift #13. Focus on one thing first, master it, and then expand on it.

Mindset shift #14. Consistently choose to walk in love, trust, and courage, instead of fear, shame, and guilt.

Mindset shift #15. Develop self-awareness, evaluate your perceptions, and seek synergy instead of competition.

Mindset shift #16. Regulate your emotions and respond to people wisely instead of defensively.

Mindset shift #17. Live in your truth by being intentional with your thoughts, words, decisions, and actions.

Mindset shift #18. Always focus on the possibility instead of the problem. See the lesson in every experience.

Mindset shift #19. Create a clear vision, calculate the cost, make a plan, do the work, and then expect success.

Mindset shift #20. Manifest abundance in your life by raising your consciousness and energy level.

Mindset shift #21. Be a continuous learner, invest in your personal development, and never stop growing.

Establish priorities. It's easy, in the busyness of life, to respond to everything that comes up at the exact moment it arises. However, when you do, you are letting your schedule control you instead of you controlling your schedule. When you don't set priorities, you're not valuing your time, which is essential to experiencing success in your life. Your calendar (or schedule) is a reflection of your priorities. If you aren't able to get something done, it's not because you don't have enough time. It's because that thing isn't a priority for you. What is most important to you? Your list may include some or all of the following.

- Self-care (mind, body, spirit)
- Spouse
- Children
- Extended family
- Business
- Friends
- Volunteer work
- Hobbies
- Other priorities

Once you determine what your priorities are, rank them in order of importance. Make sure your daily actions align with your values and goals. If your top priority is self-care, then you shouldn't be focused on helping your extended family and friends before you take care of yourself. Nor should you be working on your business to the point of exhaustion. Instead, you should ensure that your mind, body, and spirit are healthy before you focus on work. Put first things first.

Set boundaries. Boundaries and structure, when properly implemented, give you more freedom and peace. Boundaries are guidelines or limits you create to define reasonable, safe, and acceptable ways for other people to treat you and how you will respond when someone steps outside those limits. It is so true that we teach people how to treat us, so if you aren't being treated how you want to be treated in a relationship, you have to assess the situation and determine what shifts you need to make. For instance, if you accepted a client project that was less than your regular fee, then you may be showing people you undervalue your services.

Now, there are instances when you will negotiate with a client and start with a much smaller fee to secure the business. The client recognizes this and understands you're making a short-term sacrifice to get your foot in the door. This is the "land first, then expand" concept. In essence, you provide a service for a lower fee, demonstrate your value and expertise, and then expand the business. Lowering your price in this circumstance is understandable, but if you're constantly underpricing your products and services, then you're teaching people that they can offer you anything and you will accept it. The same applies to personal relationships. If someone is disrespecting you, lying to you, or taking advantage of you, instead of celebrating you with honesty, compassion, and forgiveness, then somewhere along the way, you have taught them the wrong way to treat you.

The purpose of setting healthy boundaries is to protect you and to take better care of yourself. My husband says no a lot, and he says it with ease. It's often more difficult for women to say no. Some of us are people pleasers, or we feel the need to try to help and save everybody even at the detriment of our own wellbeing. In either case, being authentically you in every area of your life requires you to set healthy boundaries.

Boundaries are set to ensure you are mentally and emotionally strong. You may set boundaries that are rigid, loose, somewhere in between, or even non-existent. However, a complete lack of boundaries may indicate that you don't have a strong identity, you are codependent on someone else, or you are totally disregarding your needs, wants, and desires.

Why is it important to set healthy boundaries?

To practice self-love. To express your wants and needs. To remain in healthy, not codependent relationships.

Why do we fail to enforce or uphold our boundaries?

- Fear of rejection and abandonment
- Fear of confrontation
- Guilt
- Lack of understanding of healthy boundaries
- Safety concerns

It is very important to set healthy boundaries because they're essential to your productivity and success. Here are a few tips on how to set appropriate boundaries.

Step 1. Realize that a lack of boundaries = little self-esteem.

Step 2. Decide what your core values are.

Step 3. Develop boundaries based on your values.

Step 4. Decide the consequences ahead of time.

Step 5. Let your actions speak instead of your words.

Step 6. Say what you mean and mean what you say.

Step 7. Realize you can only change yourself and not others.

When you are clear about your boundaries in the beginning, you give people the option to choose whether or not they want to be in a business or personal relationship with you. I have learned that clear boundaries and clear expectations are crucial in any relationship. With my older son, at the beginning of the school year, we sit down and go over his boundaries and expectations for the year, including grades, behavior, attitude, chores, and extracurricular activities. We discuss the importance of honesty, hard work, perseverance, and self-care, and we explain what the boundaries and expectations are. We then discuss what the consequences will be if he does not adhere to those boundaries. If he goes outside of those boundaries, we let our actions speak instead of our words. Setting clear boundaries with our son has helped us have a more loving and authentic relationship because everyone involved understands their roles and expectations.

Take some time to determine in which areas of your life you need to establish or reestablish clear boundaries, and start that process today. Use the seven steps above as a guide and seek out additional resources for reinforcement if needed. One book I've gained some valuable insight from is *Boundaries*, by Dr. Henry Cloud and Dr. John Townsend.

Embrace Each Season

Understanding the season you're in can help remove anxiety, pressures, and fears that you place on yourself. Instead of racing through each season, especially the undesirable ones, seek to uncover what you are supposed to learn. There are three seasons that you'll go through in business and in life.

Sowing/Planting Season: This season is about putting a seed in the ground. It may involve researching, brainstorming, understanding your competition, putting in all of the heavy duty work to create a strategy, finding a mentor, or similar preparation.

Watering Season: This is the season when you begin to execute your strategies. You start networking, building relationships, providing prospective clients with demos and proposals, marketing yourself on social media, or accepting speaking engagements.

Harvesting Season: Your hard work has paid off. You're contracting with new clients; your business is expanding. You're hiring new people. Congratulations!

It's very important to understand that you will not receive a harvest for seeds that you have not sown. Even though my deadline for this book was five weeks, it was actually five years in the making. I'd been researching, interviewing business leaders, refining my coaching and consulting models, and drafting notes for a long time. So I may now be in the harvest season, but it has taken quite a bit of sowing and watering to get to this point.

Make sure you embrace each season in your life. If you're a new mom, enjoy the time bonding with your baby instead of rushing to get back to your business. If your business has hit the million-dollar mark, enjoy that and properly plan to scale up to five million dollars. If you are fully present in each season and learn the lessons you are supposed to learn, then you will be well equipped and prepared for your harvesting season.

Overnight success is actually ten years in the making. According to Malcolm Gladwell, as discussed in his best-selling book *Outliers*, it takes 10,000 hours (or approximately ten years) of deliberate practice to become an expert in your field. So instead of getting caught up in "Shiny Object Syndrome" by following what others are doing or banking on overnight success, embrace and respect each season you go through and you will truly be entitled to your harvest.

Recognize Your Purpose

According to *Webster's Dictionary*, purpose is defined as the reason for which something is done or created or for which something exists. Being an entrepreneur or small business owner can be all-consuming. It affects your mind, body, and spirit. Most successful entrepreneurs manage to infuse their passion and purpose into their business. The business may not be their complete passion, as with an artist who pursues her art full time, but there is enough of their passion in their business for them to feel they are serving the world with their gifts.

People often make discovering their purpose way more complicated than it needs to be. Discovering your purpose is a process, a journey. When you pay close attention, you will find clues that lead you to your purpose. There are seven key elements involved in discovering your purpose:

1. **P**inpoint your personality type
2. **U**nderstand your unique experiences.
3. **R**esonate with a cause.
4. **P**ursue your passions.
5. **O**ptimize your strengths.
6. **S**harpen your spiritual gifts.
7. **E**mpower yourself to change limiting beliefs.

Pinpoint your personality type. Understanding your personality type helps you to see and appreciate how you're wired. Are you more of an introvert or an extravert? Are you a leader or a team player? Are you more analytical or intuitive? Understanding your makeup will help you determine where you fit in the world. If you haven't already taken a personality test, the DiSC Assessment and Myers-Briggs Type Indicator are great places to start to investigate your personality type and glean insight into your desires and inclinations.

Understand your unique experiences. What life experiences and coincidences have shaped you? When did you turn your tests into triumphs? When was your pain turned into purpose? When did you overcome obstacles and fears and persevere? Look at the unique experiences in your life to identify patterns or hidden clues in your timeline of life-changing experiences. Consider how coincidences are often symbolic of greater meaning and purpose. Often, the challenges you want to forget about are the very things that hold the key to discovering your purpose.

Resonate with a cause. What cause do you feel drawn to serve? What injustice do you want to help eliminate? Who do you want to stand up for? What causes have you volunteered for or invested in over the long term? Your purpose will push you towards advocacy and helping others. Take a minute to think about those causes that resonate with you.

Pursue your passions. What do you do with excellence? What do you lose yourself in when you're doing it? What would you do for free just because it's a part of who you are? Look at the topics that you read about and study. What blogs do you like? What do you love to learn about, read about, or study? To jumpstart your process for identifying your passions, you can take a free Passion Test at https://thepassiontest.com.

Optimize your strengths. What are you naturally good at doing? What fills you with positive energy? What excites your inner child? Identifying your natural talents and skills will give you insight into your purpose. One assessment that can help you identify your strengths is the CliftonStrengths assessment. It measures recurring patterns of thoughts, feelings, and behaviors to help you understand your natural talents.

Sharpen your spiritual gifts. What natural, God-given gifts and abilities do you possess? These are things that other people might have to work at but which come easily for you. Natural talents are physical abilities to do special things. Some natural talents might be musical ability, carpentry, mechanical aptitude, and artistic skills. Spiritual gifts are spiritual abilities to do certain things. Natural talents are often the vehicle through which spiritual gifts can be used. Spiritual gifts can include administration, apostleship, discernment, evangelism, exhortation, faith, giving, healing, knowledge leadership, mercy, serving, teaching, and wisdom.

Empower yourself to change limiting beliefs. Eliminate limiting belief systems and choose new positive beliefs to overcome common excuses that can otherwise hold you back.

Apply the elements of P.U.R.P.O.S.E to your life to get a clearer vision of your purpose. Remember this is a process of discovery and not a one-time event.

Cultivate a Spiritual Practice

A spiritual practice is any regular and intentional activity that establishes, develops, and nourishes a personal relationship with your Higher Power (God, Spirit, Divine, Source, etc.) and through which you allow yourself to be transformed. A practice is a path you travel on your spiritual journey and can come in many shapes and forms, including prayer, affirmations, worship, going to church, meditation, aromatherapy, visualization, energy healing, and mindfulness, to name a few.

Benefits of a Daily Spiritual Practice

- Supports you in developing and strengthening your inner peace, intuition, and authentic identity
- Deepens and expands your awareness of your connection to your Source
- Interrupts the habitual flow of negative thoughts and emotions that often lead to unproductive reactions
- Increases your awareness of negative beliefs so you can choose beliefs that better serve you
- Supports you in discovering the roots of pain and suffering in your life so you can heal and live an abundant life.

Your spirit, like your mind and body, requires attention, dedication, and nourishment to grow. A daily spiritual practice is committed and focused time that you spend aligning your head, heart, and spirit. It's a process of using activities and tools that assist you in creating a sacred space and atmosphere to experience and increase your awareness of the Higher Power in your life.

If you are willing to invest the time and energy to develop a spiritual practice and to integrate those practice into your daily life, your understanding of who you are in life and in business will grow into an experience of greater freedom, peace, joy, abundance, and unconditional love. Without a consistent spiritual practice, your understanding of life and your awareness of your authentic self are likely to remain shallow.

Fundamentals of a Productive Spiritual Practice

Focus and the removal of distractions provide the foundation for a spiritual practice. One way to improve your focus is to listen to a guided meditation or inspired reading and follow this with journal writing or reflection. This level of your practice consistency in the face of any diversion, confusion, distraction, or perceived lack of progress.

Listen and receive. Focus within and notice the challenges or issues that come up. Suspend all judgments about them. As your practice deepens, the addition of prayer and silent or mantra meditation can help you clarify your desires and align your thoughts, beliefs, and actions with those desires. Through this practice, you'll learn how to follow the guidance you receive from your Higher Power to manifest your desires in your life.

Whatever practice you choose has to work for you. As busy business owners, spouses, and parents, managing our time can be quite challenging. Experiment with different practices to find what works best. Choose how often you'll engage in your spiritual practice and whether it will be in the morning, evening, or during the day. Choose a consistent time, and schedule your practice into your daily activities. Based on the season of life I'm in, I may get up fifteen minutes earlier to meditate, pray, and say affirmations to jump start my day. At night before bed, I'll spend fifteen meetings journaling, preparing my mind for what I want to accomplish the next day, and expressing my gratitude for three specific things.

Creating a sacred space in your home provides you with the comfort of knowing you have a designated safe space where you can go to receive spiritual encouragement and guidance. This should be a space free from distractions, interruptions, and noise. I've had several sacred spaces in my house for my spiritual practice, including a bedroom corner stocked with candles, motivational books, pillows, and other inspiring items. The space you choose is totally up to you and only needs to resonate with you. It could be in your closet, your bathroom, the basement, or wherever you feel most comfortable connecting with your Higher Power. Your intent and willingness to be open and receptive is more important than the actual space.

If you're new to a spiritual practice, it may be easiest to begin with five to ten minutes and progress to fifteen to thirty minutes.

The elements of your daily practice will also determine the amount of time you will need. Consider that five to ten minutes is better and more productive than no minutes. When I first started my spiritual practice, I created a business prayer challenge. For ninety days, I prayed for ten minutes every morning, and I invited other business owners to pray with me. The consistency and dedication of showing up every day, for ninety days, completely changed my business and my life. It gave me more clarity, a closer relationship with God, and a greater trust in my intuition about making the best decisions for my life.

Breathing, inspirational reading, prayer, affirmations, meditation, and silence can be basic elements of any spiritual practice. You can also include a Bible study, practice yoga, take a walk in nature, or do anything else that resonates with you and helps to spiritually ground and connect you. In determining the elements of your practice, choose what works for you and decide how you will combine the activities so they'll be meaningful for you.

Developing a consistent spiritual practice will help you get off the treadmill of life, stop being reactive to what life throws you, and start being proactive. It will help you to understand what you truly want in life and focus on a clear strategy of how to get it. It will give you insight into your health, relationships, business, children, and other areas of your life. Having a spiritual practice has truly been a game-changer in my life and the lives of my clients because it allows us to go confidently and boldly into the things we know God has destined for us. Regardless of what challenges or hiccups arise, we have the tools to persevere and live an abundant and peaceful life.

Take Care of Your Mind and Body

To round out your spiritual practice, it's important to also focus on the health of your mind and body. This is a multifaceted, ongoing process. To start, it's vital to limit the stress in your life. Forty-three percent of all adults suffer adverse health effects from excessive stress.[1]

Stress can play a part in problems such as headaches, high blood pressure, heart problems, diabetes, skin conditions, asthma, arthritis, depression, and anxiety. Stress affects us all.

You may notice symptoms of stress when managing your finances, during busy times at work, when coping with a challenging relationship, or when disciplining your kids. A little stress is normal; however, too much stress can wear you down and make you sick, both mentally and physically. Our bodies are designed to handle small doses of stress, but we are not equipped to handle long-term, chronic stress without negative consequences. Take some time to look at those areas in your life that are causing you stress, and develop a plan to eliminate or minimize it.

Here are a few simple ways to reduce stress:

1. Minimize caffeine, alcohol, and nicotine.
2. Increase your physical activity.
3. Get more sleep.
4. Try relaxation techniques.
5. Talk to a trusted friend or mental health professional.
6. Journal.
7. Problem solve.
8. Manage your time and take care of priorities first.
9. Say no to others so you can say yes to yourself.
10. If you are sick, rest.
11. Get sufficient sleep.

Sleep is a great way to reduce stress, but it's often the first form of self-care to go for busy business owners. Make sure you aren't burning the candle at both ends, and get the rest you require. Most adults need seven to eight hours of good quality sleep on a regular schedule each night. If you aren't getting the required sleep, make changes to your routine. Getting enough sleep isn't only about total hours. It's also about the quality of sleep. This means ensuring you are on a regular schedule so you feel rested when you wake up.

If you often have trouble sleeping or if you often still feel tired after sleeping, speak to your doctor. If you have children, they're growing and developing and need even more sleep than you. Here are the recommended guidelines:

- Teens need eight to ten hours of sleep each night.
- School-aged children need nine to twelve hours of sleep each night.
- Preschoolers need to sleep between ten and thirteen hours a day (including naps).
- Toddlers need to sleep between eleven and fourteen hours a day (including naps).
- Babies need to sleep between twelve and sixteen hours a day (including naps).

Here are just a few of the many benefits of getting enough sleep:

- More easily maintain a healthy weight.
- Strengthen your immune system and get sick less.
- Reduce stress and improve your mood.
- Focus better and have more clarity in your business and life.
- Lower your risk for serious health problems, like diabetes and heart disease.
- Improve relationships through more stable moods and increased patience.

Just like it's important to make time for sleep, it's just as important to make time for exercise. Regular physical activity boosts your health in many ways. Most of us know staying active is one of the best ways to keep our bodies healthy, but did you know it can also improve your overall wellbeing and quality of life? Regular physical activity improves your stamina, endurance, and energy, so it pays to incorporate physical activity in your busy schedule. My workout routine varies based on my schedule. Sometimes I opt to go to the gym to do twenty to thirty minutes of cardio, weight training, sit-ups, and stretching. Other times I'll do fifteen to twenty minutes of yoga and stretching, and some days my exercise comes from running after my kids, taking the stairs, or walking a little extra distance because I didn't park close to the grocery store door. I've found that whatever routine I choose, doing at least fifteen to twenty minutes of physical activity every day increases my energy and overall health.

Proper nutrition and supplementation will also help you maintain your physical and mental health. Most of us aren't eating our optimal daily intake of fruits, vegetables, and herbs (I'm talking about the non-mind-altering kind of herbs). It's important to eat a variety of fruits and vegetables, but supplements and herbs can provide additional nutrients when your diet is lacking or when certain health conditions cause you to develop an insufficiency or deficiency.

Last year, I went to an integrative and functional gynecologist for the first time. The core philosophy of integrative and functional medicine is a holistic, personalized approach to health and healing. This approach focuses on physical, emotional, mental, social, spiritual, and environmental influences that affect your health. Through a series of blood tests, the doctor provided me with a clear picture of my health. It was amazing that a thirteen-page report could tell me which areas of my health were at optimal levels and in which areas I had intermediate or high risks of developing medical problems.

In my big "aha" moment, I realized I have to put the same amount of effort and time into improving and maintaining my health as I put into growing my business. Today, my daily routine of supplements includes a multivitamin, DHA/EPA (Omega-3s), CoQ10, and probiotics. It's important for you to talk with your health care professional to ensure you're getting the right daily dose of nutrients. It's also essential to stay current with your annual physical exams.

There's one last element many of us overlook when it comes to maintaining our physical and mental health. That element is detoxification. I know. I know. You're in meetings all day and have to grab something quick or on the go, and most drive-thru restaurants don't have the healthiest options. Too often, small business owners find themselves in a daily rat race that results in bad food choices. However, to maintain the stamina required to grow a successful business, we have to evolve our thoughts about what we put into our bodies. Every year after the holidays I do a detox, a process during which I abstain from toxic or unhealthy substances for a period of time. It helps to get rid of toxins in the body and develop the habits that keep me on track for a healthier life.

There are several benefits to a detox, including:

- Increased energy
- Weight loss and weight management
- Improved organ function
- Strengthened immune system
- Stress management
- Reset food preferences for reduced cravings
- Elimination of toxins found in foods, beverages, and beauty and hygiene products

Detox cleanses are incredibly trendy these days, and there are endless programs to choose from, depending on your needs and preferences. I've tried several options in the past; some went well, and others I quit mid-way. When I did an all-juice fast, I stopped on day two. When I did a twenty-one-day fast, for which I had to take about seven pills a day, I stopped on day eight. These experiences taught me that our relationship with food comes from our mindset, what we believe about food. I quit early the first few times because there was no "why" behind what I was doing. I had to dig deep and determine why I wanted to live a healthy lifestyle.

After doing some deep soul searching, I realized I wanted to be healthy to run behind my two active boys, to have more energy to run my business, to age gracefully, to fulfill my purpose—heck, to have a healthy and very active sex life with my husband. The more I understood my why, the easier it was for me to put down the macaroni and cheese, the strawberry shortcake, and those yummy, sweet Hawaiian rolls. My why helped me to have the discipline I needed to meal plan and prepare my meals ahead of time and to remain dedicated to my detox program.

I finally found my groove when I decided to do a food-based cleanse and cut out processed foods, refined sugar, and bread, and eat mostly healthy organic fruits and vegetables. I'm a pescatarian, so the only meats I eat are wild-caught salmon and tuna. As I learn more about clean eating and living I work to incorporate that new knowledge into my daily lifestyle. I've also started buying organic, natural, and non-GMO personal hygiene and home care products. I've been on this journey over the last eight to ten years, and I continue to learn new things every day.

Being successful in business requires mastery of the tangible things, such as marketing and sales, but also the intangible things that people don't often think about, like health, mental clarity, energy, and longevity. Take some time to research and learn about detoxing from harmful foods and substances to improve the way you're showing up in your life and business. Be sure to consult a health professional before starting any detox program.

Execute in Spite of Fear

Fear is a natural part of life, especially when you're a business owner. You take calculated and sometimes not so calculated risks to get your business off the ground and grow it over time. My journey of entrepreneurship has been filled with doing things afraid. When I was younger, I often heard people say fear and faith can't reside in the same space. As I have gotten older, I've learned that doing anything new comes with some fear because I have never experienced the situation before. That's normal. I've learned that fear and nervousness are closely related to excitement, and I can channel them to work on my behalf. Instead of getting stuck in fear, I turn it around to **F**ace **E**verything **a**nd **R**ise.

Fear occurs as a response to something perceived as threatening, scary, dangerous, or harmful. Fear of danger, failure, rejection, judgment, loss of money, and loss of a relationship are common. However, failure is not fatal; it's only feedback. If you are going to succeed, you're going to have to fail. You won't get everything right, so you have to step outside your comfort zone and know you are strong enough to handle whatever results you get, positive or negative.

Typically, we have one of these three reactions to fear:

1. **Fight.** You look at the situation aggressively and fight to control the outcome.
2. **Flight.** You avoid facing the situation altogether and physically or figuratively run away.
3. **Freeze.** You find yourself paralyzed in the situation and unable to take any action.

In some cases, healthy fear can motivate you if it propels you to have a sense of urgency to accomplish your goals. For instance, you work to launch your business because you fear being the last to market. If you have a healthy relationship with fear, this can be positive. However, if you have a negative relationship with fear, such as fear of success, fear of failure, fear of missing out, or the fear of rejection, that can paralyze you and you'll never get your launch off the ground.

Fear often comes from not having enough information. If you ask yourself, "What's the worst that could happen?" and visualize the situation all the way through the potential end results, you can eliminate or reduce fear. Gather as much information as possible, do the research, play out the scenarios, and move beyond the fear. This decision-making process works equally well in business and personal matters, and it's a skill you can learn. (I recently started teaching my eleven-year-old son how to use critical thinking to make decisions. I walk him through this process on a regular basis.) To help you with this process, here are six steps to effective decision-making.

Six Steps to Effective Decision-Making

Decision-making is a vital part of small business ownership. The results you're experiencing in your business and life are in direct response to the decisions and choices you've made, good or bad, conscious or unconscious. Therefore, it is very important for you to have a step-by-step process for quickly making sound business decisions. As small business owners, we wear many hats, and we often fail to take the time to weigh the pros and cons and assess the potential risks of all of our decisions.

I admit there have been many times when I've made "fly by the seat of my pants" decisions in my business, only to regret them later. When I consistently use this six-step process to make small or big decisions, I'm happier with the results I create. Many times we get stuck in researching, looking for expert advice, or just being indecisive. You can use this six-step process for making any important business decisions, ranging from fine-tuning your business operations to expanding your marketing, hiring a vendor, and every other aspect of your business.

Step 1. Define the decision to be made.

Step 2. Identify the desired outcome.

Step 3. Research to identify two to four potential solutions.

Step 4. Review the pros and cons of each solution and assess potential risks.

Step 5. Choose a solution and take action.

Step 6. Review the results and determine if adjustments need to be made.

The Rules of Life

To win in any sport, in business, or in life, you must first know the rules. On my journey, I've established some basic rules for how I play the game of life in my business and personal life. These rules guide me in making decisions, setting goals, and pursuing my dreams. They have been paramount in helping me set boundaries; find harmony in my marriage, family, and business; and learn how to be authentically me.

These eight rules will help you on your path to creating success in your life and in your business at the same time.

1. No one is in charge of your happiness, but you.
2. What others think of you is none of your business.
3. Don't compare your life or business with others; live authentically.
4. Make peace with your past so it doesn't hinder your present or future; forgive.

5. You are free to choose whatever action you want to take, but you are *not* free from the consequences.
6. If you don't go after what you want, you will never get it.
7. If you do not ask, the answer will always be no.
8. You have to want to succeed more than you fear disappointing others or failing.

Your past, current, and future decisions will determine your success. It's crucial that you get clarity about what you really want in your life and business and make calculated decisions that will yield those results. Take some time to evaluate areas in your life in which you need to make some adjustments, whether it's your self-care routine, family relationships, or business practices.

As you embark on this intense journey of building and growing your business, you want to make sure your foundation is strong and able to withstand the ups and downs. Don't let life happen to you. Take control and ensure you happen to life instead. Every day, focus on living a F.I.E.R.C.E. life, full of love and gratitude.

F.I.E.R.C.E. stands for:

Forgive yourself and others.

Intentional living is a daily choice.

Embrace each season.

Recognize your purpose.

Cultivate a spiritual practice.

Execute in spite of fear.

From the Desk of the Decision-Maker

Stephanie L. Lee, MA, ELMCA

Supplier Diversity Program Analyst | Office of Diversity and Inclusion, MARTA

BASED ON MY YEARS of meeting with small business owners, the one thing I would recommend is that you never lead the conversation with "How can I get a contract?" That is a huge turn-off. As an advocate of small businesses, my passion is identifying opportunities that will show the greatness of your work. You make it easier for me to advocate on your behalf when you show me the value that your business offers to MARTA. Do your homework to ensure that your product or service directly aligns with our business needs. Additionally, love what you do, and don't just chase the money. As Oprah Winfrey says, "What I know is that, if you do work that you love, and the work fulfills you, the rest will come." I highly believe that and want that so much for small businesses.

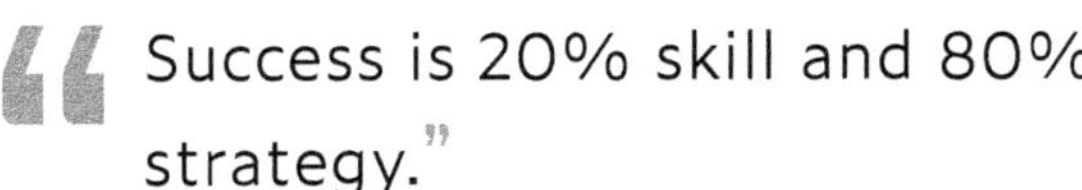

"Success is 20% skill and 80% strategy."

— JIM ROHN

CHAPTER TWO

Business Strategy

S 01

Sustainable Business Principles

- Core values
- Purpose and mission
- Vision
- Business culture
- Goal setting

C 02

Concise SWOT Analysis

- Strengths
- Weaknesses
- Opportunities
- Threats

A 03

Accelerated Growth Strategy

- Market penetration and expansion
- Product or service expansion
- Diversification or acquisition
- Business financing

L 04

Leveraged Value Proposition

- Products and services
- Target audience, pain points, benefits
- Unique differentiation
- Proprietary methodology

E 05

Executable Action Plan

- Strategic objective
- Action items with deadlines
- Financial resources and risks
- Performance measurement

The Business S.C.A.L.E. Formula

THROUGHOUT MY MORE THAN twenty-five years of business ownership in various industries, including technology, construction, business consulting, online retail, and entertainment, I've learned firsthand that a business without a sound strategy can easily fail. About twenty years ago, I had to file business bankruptcy because I had no strategy. In the early years, my business strategy was to fly by the seat of my pants, put out fires, and respond reactively. Today, I can see so vividly how taking on projects that weren't a good fit for my expertise, charging below what I was worth just to get the business, and running up my credit cards in hopes of landing a big client were not sound business decisions. Since that time, I have dedicated myself to learning as much as possible about business strategy and all the components required to scale a successful business. I wrote *The CEO Life* to share with you everything I wish I'd known when I first started my business and when I was growing my business in the early years.

It has been my experience that many business owners are amazing at their craft or providing a quality service or product but not so great with the fundamentals of running a business. Let me give you an example. I used to do a lot of consulting for medical practices from obstetrics and gynecology to chiropractic care and family practice. One thing all the doctors had in common, whether they had been in business two years or twenty years, was that they were experts as medical professionals because they had gone to medical school, but they weren't good at running a business. They had spent so many years honing their craft as a doctor that they hadn't put any energy into learning how to grow a business. Jim Rohn said, "Success is twenty percent skill and eighty percent strategy." This one line says it all, and it's one of my favorite quotes. You can be skilled at doing something, but if you don't have the right strategy, you'll have a hard time building a business with that skill. This is why I created the Business S.C.A.L.E. Formula to provide an easy framework of all the required components to smartly scale your business:

Sustainable Business Principles

Concise SWOT Analysis

Accelerated Growth Strategy & Financing

Leveraged Proprietary Methodology

Executable Action Plan

Before we break down each component let's take a look at what the statistics say.

The Statistics

The U.S. Small Business Administration (SBA) defines a small business as one that has fewer than five hundred employees. According to the latest U.S. Small Business Administration data, there are 30.2 million small businesses in the United States.[2] Undoubtedly, with millions of businesses in the country, some are bound to fail, but the data on business failure rates can be contradictory and confusing. A recent article at www.fitsmallbusiness.com highlighted some important statistics gathered from various sources:[3]

According to the article, 80% of entrepreneurs who start a business fail within the first eighteen months. (Forbes) Additionally, 50% of small businesses fail after five years. (Small Business Trends) Finally, 66% of small businesses will fail within ten years. (Tutsplus) The rates of failure are fairly consistent even during economic downturns.

Those statistics apply to all small businesses, but I also want to take a closer look at success rates for women in business.

The following stats are from the American Express OPEN report *The State of Women-Owned Businesses*:[4]

Women in Small Businesses:

- More than 11.6 million firms are owned by women.
- These firms employ nearly 9 million people.
- They generate$1.7 trillion in sales each year.

Businesses Owned by Women of Color:

- 5.4 million firms in the U.S. are majority-owned by women of color.
- These firms employ 2.1 million people.
- They generate $361 billion in annual revenues.

Million-Dollar Businesses:

- One in five firms with revenue of $1 million or more is woman-owned.
- 4.2% of all women-owned firms have annual revenues of $1 million or more.
- Women-owned firms (51% or more) account for 39% of all privately held firms and contribute 8% of employment and 4.2% of revenues.

With such promising statistics for women in small business, why is the ten-year survival rate of businesses only 34%? Let's take a closer look.

Why Businesses Fail

Businesses fail for a variety of reasons. According to Investopedia, the most common reasons why small businesses fail include the following:

- Lack of sufficient capital
- Poor management
- Inadequate business planning
- Overspending on marketing
- Cash flow problems

A CB Insights analysis of 101 startups gathered the reasons why the businesses surveyed failed. According to the business founders, here are the top reasons they closed their doors:[5]

- **42%** of small businesses failed because there was no market need for their services or products.
- **29%** failed because they ran out of cash.
- **23%** failed because they didn't have the right team running the business.
- **19%** were outcompeted.
- **18%** failed because of pricing and cost issues.
- **17%** failed because of a poor product offering.
- **17%** failed because they lacked a business model.
- **14%** failed because of poor marketing.
- **14%** failed because they ignored their customers.

Simply put, small businesses fail because they fail to consistently implement and modify sound business strategies. They fail to meet the changing demands of their clients and the business environment.

According to the *Harvard Business Review*, only 8% of leaders excel at both strategy and execution.[6] Often, small business owners have a vision but don't have a strategy to make it a reality. A strategy is a clear direction of where your business is going and the steps necessary to achieve your goals. Strategy requires an understanding of your business's core competencies and the value proposition that sets you apart from your competition.

A sound business strategy can help you accomplish the following:

- Be clear about your business priorities so you and your team can focus your time, energy, and resources. (F.O.C.U.S. means to **F**ollow **O**ne **C**ourse **U**ntil **S**uccessful.)
- Strengthen operations by ensuring every action taken is aligned with your business strategy.
- Ensure your team members are working toward a common goal
- Establish accountability for intended outcomes and desired results.
- Assess and measure results and adjust the businesses direction when necessary.

Ask yourself these five questions to establish the foundation for your business strategy.

1. **Who are you?** What are your guiding principles or the core values by which your company operates?
2. **Why do you do what you do?** What are your purpose, mission, culture, and value proposition?
3. **Who do you want to be?** What's your ten-year vision for your business? Your twenty-year vision?

4. **Where do you want to go?** What are your strategic objectives?
5. **How will you get there?** What is your action plan with tactical strategies?

Sustainable Business Principles

There are five essential components of what I call Sustainable Business Principles:

1. Core Values
2. Purpose and Mission
3. Vision
4. Business Culture
5. Goal Setting

Core Values: What You Stand For

A core value defines what you stand for or believe. It communicates your principles, your mission, and your vision. Core values are the guiding principles by which your business operates. They support the vision, shape the culture, and reflect what your business represents. They are the essence of the business's identity. Core values help you in the decision-making process, and getting clear on your core values helps you to communicate your value to prospective clients with greater clarity.

Disney's core values are creativity, dreams, imagination, and wholesome fun. Sony's core values are to be a pioneer, not a follower, and to do the impossible. These values dictate projects the companies take on, who they hire, who they partner with, and more. Core values will guide the decisions you make in your business and keep you on course to achieve your goals. They are the foundation for ensuring your mission and your vision are executed in every area of your business, including marketing, sales, operations, and customer service.

Purpose and Mission: Why You Do What You Do

Your purpose and mission explain the fundamental reasons you are in business. Many prospective clients are looking for businesses that provide much more than just products and services. They want to connect with a business serving a higher purpose that they resonate with or giving back in some way. Yes, they want quality products and services, but many people also have a deep desire for social change. For example, TOMS, founded by Blake Mycoskie, is more than just a fashion business. The company also invests in social change. The company's tagline is "One for One." Initially, for every pair of shoes purchased, the company donated a new pair of shoes to a child in need. The company believes in supporting sustainable and responsible programs for communities in need and has expanded beyond its "one for one" shoe program.

TOMS has tapped into their prospective clients' deep desire for purpose. When a client has a choice between TOMS shoes and another shoe company that provides the same quality of product and has comparable pricing, who do you think they will choose? Since TOMS provides a platform for social change, the company doesn't have to compete solely on price and can offer a higher-priced product with high quality and great value.

Disney's purpose is to make people happy (not to build theme parks and make cartoons). Mary Kay Cosmetics aims is to give unlimited opportunity to women. Nike's purpose is for customers to experience the emotion of competition, winning, and crushing opportunities. Walmart's purpose is to give ordinary people the chance to buy the same things as people with greater financial means. While you may never see the purpose behind these companies in ad copy or painted on signs hanging in their stores, it's always there, in every decision they make.

Your Vision Is Bigger Than You

A vision is a vivid mental image of what you want your business to be in the future, based on your goals and aspirations. Having a vision will give your business a clear focus and prevent you from doing things that get in the way of achieving your goals.

Many years ago, Nike's goal was to crush Adidas. The company accomplished this goal in 1960. In 1990, Walmart said it wanted to become a $125 billion company by the year 2000. As we both know, they accomplished that. A vision keeps you on track and reminds you every day of what you are aspiring to accomplish.

When developing your vision, you always want to start with the end in mind. My big ten-year vision is to be the leading industry expert for women small business owners. I envision *The CEO Life* book and online business learning academy as the go-to resources for small business owners who want to succeed in both their business and personal life. This vision guides all of my business decisions and helps me to only work on projects that will ultimately lead me to the goal. My vision prevents me from becoming distracted or bogged down by doing a bunch of busy work that's leading me nowhere.

Take a few minutes to think about and write down what your vision is for your business.

Business Culture: What You Believe In

Culture is the personality of your business. It defines the environment in which employees, clients, and vendors interact. It's the energy people feel when they walk into your office. It's the way your team members interact with one another. It's how you celebrate wins and handle defeats and whether you maintain positive morale or not. Your business culture consists of a variety of elements, including work environment, company mission, values, ethics, expectations, and goals.

I know you may be thinking, "I run a small business, and I don't need to focus on building morale. Sure if I were Amazon or

Google, then that would be on my radar, but since I'm not, I will continue to focus on increasing sales because what I need most right now is revenue." That would be a huge mistake. Remember success and victory come from focusing on the details. Establishing a great business culture will help you attract the best employees, charge premium rates or negotiate lower rates with better vendors, and establish great strategic partnerships. People love working with people they like, and they love being in environments that are positive, fun, uplifting, and productive.

Developing a strong culture requires being intentional about how your business operates. Establish your business's core values and define what you aspire to be. Lead by example and communicate your core values and mission by the way you operate with integrity, honesty, and a stellar work ethic. If one of your core values is innovation, you should constantly be innovating. If one of your core values is transparency, you should lead with transparency. Leading by example sets the tone for your employees and communicates to the team what you want to foster in your business.

Ensure alignment within your business culture by hiring like-minded people who support the business goal and vision. You can't teach or force this. People either innately and genuinely support your mission and vision or they don't. Don't just hire employees for their skillsets. Hire people who get your vision and can run with it. Continually reinforce your desired culture by constantly communicating your mission and vision. Make a conscious effort to communicate it in everything you do, including meetings, email, training, annual reports, interviews, performance appraisals, and other activities.

A well-developed business culture encourages dramatic, sustained increases in productivity and performance. This is no surprise given that psychologists estimate that the average employee contributes only 20% of their potential, according to the website Company Culture.[7] A culture that deeply engages people is understandably much more productive. Businesses with a strong, productive culture see many benefits including:

- Improved financial performance
- High employee morale
- Motivated employees
- Great customer service
- Engaged employees
- Strong leadership
- Responsiveness to change
- Responsibility
- Better teamwork
- Employee retention

To make it easier to understand the type of business culture you currently have or would like to have, look at the four different types of business culture: chaotic, reactive, proactive, and optimized. Which one most closely describes your current culture?

- **Chaotic:** The culture develops organically. You, as a leader, are unaware of how your culture impacts the day-to-day business operations.
- **Reactive:** You and your team are constantly fighting fires. The culture is misaligned to your business goals.
- **Proactive:** The culture is focused on achieving business goals and has some strong positive cultural traits that support business strategies.
- **Optimized:** The culture is aligned with your vision, mission, and business goals. The culture is well-defined, ingrained in your team members, and sustainable. Your

team identifies with the culture as "the way we work" or "the way we do business here." Your team is easily able to adapt to changing business needs and strives to enhance the employee experience and the customer experience.

Take some time to think about your current business culture and determine what's working and what is not. What shifts do you need to make to ensure your team is engaged, productive, and committed?

The Value of Goal Setting

There is power in setting goals for your business because it focuses your attention on achieving desirable outcomes. Without establishing goals and objectives, doing business is like getting in a car and driving with no destination and no navigation system.

There is a difference between business goals and objectives. Goals are accomplishments a business hopes to achieve. Objectives are the exact steps a business must take to reach a goal. They are both measurable and quantifiable. Setting goals and objectives for a small business is beneficial because they provide direction at all stages of planning, operating, building, and growing a business.

Benefits of goal setting include the following:

- **Develop clear and focused intentions.** Goal setting enables you and your team to work collaboratively to make deliberate decisions.
- **Create a sense of purpose.** Goals give meaning and aspiration to your team, which helps to boost productivity.
- **Overcome procrastination.** Establishing goals at the beginning of a project helps team members know what actions to take.

- **Foster better time management.** Setting goals enables you and your team to manage your time more effectively by understanding the best use of your time.
- **Drive motivation.** Seeing your business goals ahead of you will inspire you and your team; they give you a sense of urgency and a push in the right direction.
- **Drive accountability.** Accountability is what separates the super-successful businesses from the mediocre. When you have goals written down, you can hold yourself and your team accountable.
- **Measure progress.** Regular assessment of written goals helps you measure the progress of your business.

Growing a business requires setting short and long-term goals. Short-term planning includes the present and near future, normally a period of about twelve months. Long-term planning looks beyond twelve months.

S.M.A.R.T. Goals

Developing business goals is a critical step to achieving business success. The S.M.A.R.T. acronym was first introduced in the November 1981 issue of *Management Review* in an article titled "There's a S.M.A.R.T. Way to Write Management Goals and Objectives," by George Doran, Arthur Miller, and James Cunningham.[8] A S.M.A.R.T. goal is specific, measurable, achievable, results-focused, and time-bound. Below is a definition of each of the S.M.A.R.T. goal criteria.

Specific	What do you want to accomplish?
Measurable	How will you know when you have achieved the goal?
Achievable	Is this goal realistic? Do you have the necessary knowledge, skills, abilities, and resources to accomplish the goal?
Results-focused	What is your "why" for accomplishing this goal?
Time-bound	When will you achieve the goal?

Concise SWOT Analysis

Many small business owners have heard of a SWOT analysis but may not be sure of its purpose. A SWOT analysis is a simple but useful framework for analyzing your business's strengths, weaknesses, opportunities, and threats. It helps you focus on your strengths, make up for or reduce weaknesses, leverage opportunities, and minimize threats. Are your actions strategic, or are you being reactive based on your bank account, what the competition is doing, or random happenings in the marketplace? A SWOT analysis can help you decide.

Strengths

Strengths are the qualities that make your business unique and competitive. They can be tangible or intangible. Strengths of a business can range from committed employees, manufacturing resources, and strategic partners to intellectual property, huge financial reserves, proprietary systems, experience, or a lack of debt. Understanding your strengths provides insight into your competitive edge in the marketplace. It helps you understand why a prospective client would choose your business over the competition.

Weaknesses

Weaknesses hinder your business productivity. They prevent you from accomplishing your mission and reaching your fullest potential. Fortunately, weaknesses are controllable if you identify them and plan to eliminate or strengthen them. Examples of common weaknesses include incompetent employees, lack of funds, over-dependence on a few clients, and limited production or manufacturing capabilities.

There are two approaches to dealing with weaknesses. You can either seek to improve them, if those weaknesses prevent you from achieving your business goals, or you can accept that the weaknesses are simply a part of your business and focus on your strengths.

Opportunities

Opportunities are areas in which your business can improve and grow. Existing opportunities might be the use of new technology, the failure of a competitor, or taking advantage of the business's existing, untapped resources. Reviewing market opportunities will help you take advantage of emerging markets or changes in the marketplace that would be a fit for the products and services you offer.

Threats

Analyzing threats to your business is not a fun part of a SWOT analysis, but it helps your business protect itself from external threats. The environment, regulations, technology, and trends are among possible factors that can threaten the viability and ongoing success of your business. By assessing these risks and challenges, you can better prepare and decide how to respond strategically.

On the next page is a breakdown of a SWOT analysis.

STRENGTHS (internal) *Maintain and build; leverage* • What we do well • Our advantages • Our assets • Our resources • Our capabilities	**WEAKNESSES (internal)** *Eliminate or strengthen* • Lack of competitive strength • Employees • Financials • Vulnerabilities • Sustainability
OPPORTUNITIES (external) *Prioritize and optimize* • Known trends • Environmental changes • New products • New technologies	**THREATS (external)** *Counter or minimize* • External roadblocks • Marketplace changes • Obstacles

Take some time to analyze your strengths, weaknesses, opportunities, and threats to create a strong foundation for your business strategy.

Accelerated Growth Strategy

Every business will have different goals, but it's critical that you have a well-thought-out strategy to grow your business. A lot of small businesses have a "fly by the seat of your pants" strategy for increasing sales and profits, but there are specific growth strategies you can implement. The method you choose is largely contingent upon your business's financial situation, the competition, and even government regulation.

If you want to grow like the big boys, you have to plan like the big boys. Often a growth strategy is discussed as a part of strategic planning. I included it as part of the marketing section of *The CEO Life* because a lot of small businesses plan marketing efforts without any considering how they will grow their business. So before you start spending money on social media advertising or attending industry trade shows, let's spend some time understanding which growth strategy is the best fit for your business. Some common growth strategies in business include:

- Market penetration
- Market expansion
- Product or service expansion
- Diversification
- Acquisition

Market penetration. Penetrating the market means marketing existing products and services to more of your current target audience. One of the best ways to grow this way is to expand your reach and market to a larger audience. Let's look at Under Armour. Many years back it seemed like Under Armour came out of nowhere. As an Atlanta native, I first heard of Under Armour when the company signed Cam Newton, quarterback for the Carolina Panthers, to a multiyear deal. Just as Cam laser-focused on the game of football, Under Armour laser-focused on providing performance apparel. So much so that, in recent years, it has surpassed Adidas to become the number-two athletic apparel provider in the U.S. How did Armour achieve this? They tenaciously focused on selling athletic clothing, footwear, and accessories. As a result, they were able to garner a leadership position in the fitness apparel market with this market penetration strategy. Simply put they understand their target audience, developed a value proposition that resonates with them, and consistently connects with their audience through their marketing and promotion efforts.

Market expansion. A market-expansion growth strategy involves selling your current products in a new market. For example, a catering company that normally targets high-end corporate events starts targeting weddings and other private events. An office products company that sells standard office stationery, like sticky notes, starts selling promotional items that businesses can give to clients. An office furniture store that normally sells high-end, ergonomic office chairs to corporations starts selling those chairs to entrepreneurs with a home-based business. In short, market expansion requires expanding your product and service offerings into new markets.

Product or service expansion. A business may also expand its product line or service offerings to add new features to increase its sales and profits. For example, you own a chiropractic business that offers, of course, chiropractor care. You expand that business to offer value-added specialty services, including massage, acupuncture, or other spa services. When small businesses employ a product-expansion or service-expansion strategy, they continue selling within the existing market. A product expansion growth strategy often works well when technology starts to change. A small business may also be forced to add new products as older ones become outmoded.

Diversification strategies. With diversification, a small business sells new products to new markets. Go down memory lane with me for a second. Do you remember Blockbuster or Kodak? Both of these companies had an opportunity to enter new markets with new products as technology quickly changed the way we watched movies and took pictures. Since they continued doing business as usual and failed to respond to industry trends and changes they lost their place as industry leaders. Diversifying your business can be very risky since you are entering new territory. Small business owners need to plan carefully when using a diversification growth strategy. Marketing research is essential to determining the probability that consumers in the new market will like the new products.

Acquisition strategies. Growth strategies in business can also include acquisition. In an acquisition, one business purchases another business to expand its operations. For example, you own an accounting firm and purchase a business consulting firm that focuses on strategy. This expands the services you can offer your clients. Or you may have a tax business located in Atlanta and acquire tax businesses in Chicago and New York so you can service national clients.A small business may use this type of strategy to expand its product line or service offerings or to enter new markets.

Regardless of the size of your business, whether you are a one-man or one-woman operation or a multimillion-dollar company, take time to map out your growth strategy for the next three to five years. Revisit this strategy often, and apply performance measurements to ensure you are on track.

Financing Your Business Expansion

You've seen the many ways you can grow your business, but what do you do if you need help financing your growth? Many small businesses fail not because of talent and skill but because of an inability to finance the business due to limited working capital. Most businesses will go through three periods of growth:

- Loss
- Break-Even
- Profit

When you develop your growth strategy and determine financing methods for your business, it's important to plan through the lens of a three-year to five-year strategy. The loss phase is a period when your business is not making enough money to sustain itself. You're investing personal capital or have borrowed funds through a loan, line of credit, equity investment, or another source of funding. You reach a break-even point when your annual revenue matches your expenses. You are no longer losing money, but you are yet to become profitable. Finally, during the profit stage, your revenue exceeds your income. What a glorious day!

You will hear people talk about their annual revenue but their profitability is a more important number to watch. If your business is making $50 million in revenue but reports a loss every year, then you still have work to do because you are striving for profitability. Make sure your strategic financing plan takes into considerations lean times in your business or industry.

How long does it typically take for a business to become profitable? That, of course, is a million-dollar question, and there's no hard-and-fast rule for any company because every business is different. According to the SEC filings, it took Google less than three years to become profitable.[9] As of the date of this book's publication Uber, which was founded ten years ago, is still not profitable. From my experience, the first one to three years are crucial for a business because you should reinvest in the business to build a solid infastructure and hire the right people for your team. Let's delve into the nitty-gritty of financing.

Business financing is capital necessary to start, run, and grow your small business. Here are some small business financing options:

- Short-term loans
- Term loans
- SBA loans
- Business lines of credit
- Business credit cards

- Equipment financing
- Invoice financing
- Merchant cash advances
- Angel investors
- Venture capital
- Family and friends
- Crowdfunding
- 401(k) financing
- Small business grants

Working Capital and Business Credit

Working capital is essential to scaling your business. As your business continues to grow, the amount of working capital required will change. You must have a financing plan in place to sustain your business growth through a business line of credit, business loan, infusion of capital from the owners, or other financing.

One important component of qualifying for business financing is ensuring you have established business credit. Your business credit should be separate from your personal credit. At a minimum, you should have established business accounts and business credit cards. According to Fundera, "A business credit score is a way for lenders to predict how likely you are to repay debt. The business credit score ranges from zero to 100 and, as with personal credit scores, the higher your number, the more likely you'll qualify for affordable financing. The three business credit reporting agencies are Dun & Bradstreet (D&B), Equifax, and Experian."[10]

It's important to pay your bills on time or early, establish new business credit accounts, and set-up a D&B account. The D&B account houses your business credit information and you should monitor the information being reported on a quarterly or annual basis. For more information visit www.dnb.com.

Let's look at the 5 C's of credit to ensure your business qualifies for business financing should you need it for expansion efforts.

The 5 Cs of Credit

Understanding the five Cs of credit is the key to getting funding from banks and other financial institutions. The five Cs of credit make up a framework used by many traditional lenders to evaluate potential borrowers.

The five Cs of credit are:

1. Character
2. Capacity or cash flow
3. Capital
4. Conditions
5. Collateral.

Character: a lender's perspective of a borrower's general trustworthiness, credibility, and personality. Banks want to loan to people they believe will pay their bills on time. Your character, in terms of business financing, is assessed from credentials, references, reputation, and interaction with lenders. It's important that you work to build a relationship with your banks, vendors, and creditors to help establish great business financial character.

Capacity or cash flow: your ability to repay the loan. A business must generate adequate cash flow to ensure they are able to repay the loan. A potential lender will review your cash flow statements and your credit story to determine your repayment history and make an assumption on your ability to repay the loan.

Capital: the amount of money a business owner or other management team members have invested in the business. Lenders are more likely to lend to business owners who have already invested their own money into the company. The lender does not want to assume 100% of the risk. They want business owners to have some skin in the game. Make sure you put some of your own resources into your business.

Conditions: how the business will use the loan and how that business could be affected by economic or industry factors. Lenders prefer to lend to businesses operating under favorable conditions, like a business that's profitable and needs additional capital for further expansion. They want to identify potential risks—a business with extreme debt or high attrition or in an industry with regulatory changes on the horizon—and protect themselves. Lenders assess conditions by reviewing the competitive landscape, supplier and customer relationships, and industry-specific issues to identify and mitigate risks.

Collateral: assets pledged as security. Collateral serves as a backup source of repayment if the borrower cannot repay a loan as agreed. A potential lender looks at assets such as business equipment, real estate, inventory, accounts receivable, the borrowers home or other personal assets (stocks, bonds, etc.) that a borrower can use as collateral.

It's very important to focus on building or rebuilding your business credit. What happens if you invest a significant amount of your savings and run up your credit cards just to keep your business afloat? You have some negative marks on your credit and don't qualify for a business loan or traditional financing options. Is your business doomed? Fortunately, the answer is no. There are creative financing options available that allow you to build or rebuild your business credit in a short amount of time (normally within sixty to ninety days). One such program is the NOWaccount.

The NOWaccount is a business-to-business payment system co-founded by Lara Hodgson. It enables you to invoice your customer as normal and receive advanced funding prior to your customer paying the invoice. According to NOWaccount, this is the process for utilizing their payment system[11]:

1. Deliver your goods or services to your customer.
2. Send your invoice to your customer and upload it to the NOWaccount app or via QuickBooks Online.
3. You receive payment in less than 5 days from NOWaccount for the amount of your invoice minus a nominal flat fee.
4. Your customer remits payment to NOWaccount via a lock box or account.

The amazing thing about this program is your business is guaranteed payment—even if your customer defaults and doesn't pay the invoice. NOWaccount. is not a loan nor is it factoring. It is a creative financing vehicle that enables your business to go after larger contracts and receive funding immediately. This program works in conjunction with other business financing options.

Small businesses often struggle with inconsistent cash flow and limited working capital. Since most payment cycles for corporate, government, and large business-to-business customers are net 30, 60, or 90 days, you must have the cash flow to self-fund these projects. Trying to self-fund five or six new projects can send you straight out of business. An alternative to self-financing is the NOWaccount®. The program works for most business-to-business customers, corporations, and government agencies. For more information please visit www.nowcorp.com.

Several of my clients utilize the NOWaccount. One client was asked to bid on a $2.5 million project, over a 12-month period, by a fortune 100 corporation. Her company could absolutely perform the work. Her team had the skillset, knowledge, and experience to execute the project flawlessly. The only problem was that she couldn't self-fund the project. She already had business loans and a line of credit, so she didn't qualify for additional financing in those areas. Instead, she looked to the NOWaccount. The company was approved for the program and, as a result, was able to bid on the contract and won. Without the financing in place, this would have been a lost opportunity. The moral of this story is to take the time to ensure you have a solid financial infrastructure.

It's exciting to talk about the growth strategies you'll use to grow your business. It's equally as important to understand how you will finance your growth and ensure you have the working capital to sustain your business. Many small business owners don't pay enough attention to paying all bills on time, maintaining good credit, and keeping an appropriate amount of money in the business for working capital. Don't make those mistakes; use this information to keep your business credit ready and properly position yourself to be prepared to secure financing to grow your business.

That's enough about financing. Let's jump into the really good stuff and learn more about how you can utilize your value proposition to become an industry leader.

Leveraged Value Proposition

A value proposition is a promise of the value you will deliver to your client. It's the primary reason a prospect will buy from you. A value proposition is a positioning statement that explains what benefit you provide for your client and how you do it uniquely well. It describes your target buyer, the pain points you solve for them, and why you're distinctly better than the alternatives.

A clear and compelling value proposition includes the following:

- **Product:** Clearly state the product or service you're providing.
- **Target buyer:** Identify your target buyer for this product or service.
- **Benefits:** Describe how your product or service solves customers' problems, addresses their pain points, or helps them achieve their goals. Simply put, what is the end benefit of using your product or service?
- **Unique differentiation:** Define why your target buyer should buy from you and not from the competition. How are you different?

OptinMonster did a great job of showcasing thirty-two of the best value propositions and benefits. Here are four examples to get your wheels turning before you work on developing or revising your own.[12]

Company	Value Proposition	Benefits
Lyft	Rides in minutes	**Product:** On-demand car service **Target buyer:** People who need a simple method for getting from "point A" to "point B" **Primary benefit:** Immediate response **What makes it unique?** Lyft focuses on providing local service without any delays.

Stripe	Web and mobile payments, built for developers	**Product:** A set of tools that empower businesses to accept and manage online payments **Target buyer:** Developers and business owners **Primary benefit:** Simple and streamlined payments **What makes it unique?** Simplicity
Uber	Get there: Your day belongs to you.	**Product:** Low-cost taxi service **Target buyer:** People who need low-cost, on-demand transportation **Primary benefit:** Eliminates the frustrations of travel **What makes it unique?** The proposition focuses on the needs of the customer by using the word "you."

Proprietary Methodology

Once you've clearly defined your products or services, target audience, primary benefits, and unique differentiation, it's important to document your proprietary methodology or system for your way of doing business. Delta Air Lines, one of my clients, has two booklets that every employee and strategic partner (vendors) must read. One is *The Way We Fly* and the other is *The Rules of the Road.* Both of these booklets document the "Delta Difference" and the "Delta Experience." It includes their core values, what the company believes, how they are different from their competitors, and other unique information. This ensures that anyone who works for or with Delta understands how they do business.

You might be thinking, "Well, that's Delta Air Lines. Of course, they should have that." Wait one second. A documented methodology is a must for any size business wanting to scale. Just yesterday I had a strategic planning session with one of my clients who owns a construction company with a niche focus on technology integration. For six hours, we worked on their sustainable principles, performed a SWOT analysis, defined their growth strategy, and developed their proprietary methodology. We documented every process in their business from client engagement all the way to project close-out and value-added customer service. We researched competitors, looked at industry trends and forecasts, identified gaps in their processes, and documented areas for improvement. Imagine three whiteboards full of information and flip chart pages posted all around the conference room walls. From the outside looking in, it was organized chaos, but ultimately, this visual representation of their processes helped us to identify their niche in the market and fine-tune their value proposition.

You will find my proprietary methodologies throughout the book. The Business S.C.A.L.E. Formula is comprised of the exact steps I take my clients through during the strategic planning process. It has taken me years of fine-tuning to nail this process. As the industry changes and my knowledge increases, I continue to learn and grow to ensure our business is cutting-edge and implementing consulting industry best practices.

Here are the steps to creating your proprietary methodology.

1. Document all of your business processes from client engagement to execution and support.
2. Identify gaps in your processes and implement corrective actions.

3. Research competitors to get a birds-eye view of their process to see how you compare.
4. Analyze industry trends and forecasts to see if you can incorporate any of these in your business processes to help niche your business or give you a competitive edge.
5. Compile all your information and create a concise graphic illustrating your documented processes.
6. Train your team on your process and share it with your clients.
7. Refine your business processes as needed.

A well-thought-out proprietary methodology is a true game-changer for your business. (I use the word "game-changer" when something is an essential element or strategy for your business, so please pay attention.) As an example, I'm a business consultant just like a ton of other businesses out there, but what makes me different are the proprietary methodologies I use to teach, coach, and consult with small businesses. The way I utilize my knowledge and my experience gives me a competitive advantage. You can work with another business consultant or coach, but they won't teach you the Business S.C.A.L.E. Formula because that is my proprietary methodology. Make your methodology concise and easy to understand so it's easy for your clients to raise their hand and say that they want to work with you because you've established yourself as an industry expert.

Knowing your unique value proposition is necessary so you can clearly articulate why a prospective client should choose you. Take some time to brainstorm and create your unique value proposition, also known as a unique selling proposition (USP). I use the word "value" because you're offering value to your clients instead of just selling them a product or service.

Executable Action Plan

A business strategy is a blueprint that gives you specific instructions on how to achieve your goals. It enables you to see the big picture of your business to ensure you and your team are working on tasks in direct alignment with the vision and goals of your business.

Creating your business strategy helps you to:

- Set priorities.
- Focus energy and resources.
- Strengthen operations.
- Align team members.
- Create agreement around outcomes.
- Increase your ability to adapt to external changes.

Your business strategy includes five components:

1. Strategic objective/outcome
2. Action items with deadlines and responsibilities
3. Financial resources
4. Risk management
5. Quantitative or qualitative measures of performance

Strategic objectives or outcomes are long-term business goals that help to translate your mission statement from a broad vision into more specific plans and projects. They establish benchmarks for success and are designed to be measurable and specific to guide decision-making. Strategic objectives are usually developed as a part of a two-year to five-year plan. This strategic plan identifies key strengths, weaknesses, and potential risks and establishes specific actions that will allow the business to achieve its mission and goals.

Many small business owners think strategic objectives are just for large corporations. That's not true. Every year, you should have at least three to five big strategic objectives you're working on, including financial, customer, and operational objectives.

Action items with deadlines and responsible party. Action items are specific tasks that must be accomplished by a specific date. Each task should be assigned to a person responsible for completing it and measurements should be put in place to hold them accountable.

Financial resources. List the financial resources required to achieve your strategic objective or expected outcome.

Risk management. A risk is as an event or circumstance that has the potential to negatively impact your business. Types of risk vary from business to business. You must assess the risks of each strategic objective. The wrong types of risk may be harmful to your business.

The most common business risks are:

- Strategic: decisions concerning your business objectives
- Operational: your operational and administrative procedures
- Financial: financial systems and structure of your business
- Compliance: complying with laws, regulations, standards, and codes of practice
- Environmental: external events the business has little control over, such as economic conditions and legislation that negatively impact the business
- Reputational: the character or brand of the business

Other risks can include health and safety, equipment, security, technology, stakeholder management, and service delivery. Risk is an inherent part of being in business. It can be managed, and adverse outcomes can be mitigated through proper risk analysis. Attempting to completely eliminate risk from your business is unrealistic. Risk management is not limited to purchasing standard insurance protection, but mitigating business risks doesn't have to be a complex process.

Complete these four steps to develop an initial risk-management plan for each strategic objective:

Step 1. Identify risks.

Step 2. Determine your company's vulnerability for each risk.

Step 3. Prepare a contingency plan.

Step 4. Monitor and adapt as needed.

Establishing a strategic objective is not enough. You have to put performance measures in place to determine if your objective was met.

A quantitative or qualitative performance measurement is used to determine if you have achieved your desired outcomes. Quantitative analysis is information about quantities or numbers. For instance, the business achieved a 25% growth in revenue, increased customer satisfaction by 10%, decreased employee attrition by 5%, or decreased expenses by 15%. You can measure this information with numbers. Qualitative data, on the other hand, is information about qualities. Examples of qualitative analysis can be the taste of the product, the look of the packaging, the company's competitive advantage, or employee morale. These qualities are not measured by hard numbers but are just as important as quantitative factors.

As a small business owner, being nimble and quick to change is critical to your ability to grow your business. You'll increase your chances of success with a sound business strategy that enables you to measure results. I love this quote from Peter Drucker, author of *Managing Oneself.* "If you can't measure it, you can't manage it." This means you must have a plan to refer to so you can determine whether or not you are on the right track. If you have no plan, you will be wandering around and constantly playing catch-up in your business. Growing your business requires a concentrated focus on specific goals to ensure you get results.

Often, small business owners are so busy working *in* their business that they aren't able to work *on* their business. Have you ever thought, "If it's going to be done right, I'll have to do it myself"? That's the quickest way to ensure your business stagnates. A great empire can't be built by one person; a solid business is built by a team of people working within their areas of expertise.

When you have a strategy that outlines your goals and objectives, action steps, risks, and measurement criteria, it's easy to delegate because you have a road map. Strategic plans are not just for large corporations. They're for any business that wants to succeed. Whether you are a start-up, running the business by yourself, or a multimillion-dollar corporation, take some time to map out the direction for your business, follow the plan, and revise as needed.

My business began to grow consistently when I made it my routine, every December, to take the entire month to focus on strategy. During this time, I performed a SWOT analysis with my team and prepared a strategic plan. We broke the upcoming year into quarters and decided which three goals we would tackle each quarter. (We chose just three goals to ensure we didn't overwhelm ourselves or spread our efforts to thin.) Our top three goals for the first quarter of this year were to: 1) complete this book, 2) build a strong social media following with high engagement, and 3) implement a new CRM (customer relationship management) system to automate our marketing.

For the first quarter, my team and I focused on those three goals. I made sure the projects and new clients I took on would not interfere with achieving those goals. I was tempted many times to get distracted and focus on other marketing or sales activities, but I referred back to my strategy to keep me focused. My team was on board with the strategy, and we relied heavily on our action steps to ensure we remained on task. We consistently checked in and evaluated our progress. In the past, when I was less focused and didn't have a strategy, it would have taken us much longer to achieve our desired results—if we achieved them at all.

Remember that whatever you focus on will expand. If you're not focused on your objectives, chaos and confusion (putting out fires) will continue to expand. Regardless of the size of your business and whether you are in the start-up, sustaining, or scale-up phase, you can take the information in this book and go step by step to create your strategic plan.

Use the Business S.C.A.L.E. Formula

Sustainable Business Principles

Concise SWOT Analysis

Accelerated Growth Strategy & Financing

Leveraged Proprietary Methodology

Executable Action Plan

If this process seems a bit overwhelming, my team and I will be happy to consult with your business. Or join me in *The CEO Life* online business academy, where we'll walk through creating your strategic plan together. Either way, make it your routine to create or revise your strategic plan every year. It will set you on track to intentionally build the business you desire.

From the Desk of the Decision-Maker

Sandra Duckworth

Program Manager, Supplier Diversity Supply Chain Management, Delta Air Lines

BECOMING A CORPORATE-READY supplier involves intention, research, a well-thought-out strategy, and a diverse team that consistently executes on time and within budget. To ensure your small business is corporate ready, you must do three key things: 1) know your customer's needs, 2) don't extend yourself beyond your capabilities, and 3) stand behind your brand.

"Your personal brand is what other people say about you when you're not in the room."

— Jeff Bezos

CHAPTER THREE

Branding

THE BRAND STRATEGY MAP

01	**Branding Mistakes** ▶ Brand isn't clear and concise ▶ Brand isn't compelling and convincing ▶ Brand doesn't emotionally connect with target audience
02	**Discover** ▶ Purpose (your why) ▶ Personal story ▶ Brand personality ▶ Mission
03	**Define** ▶ Target audience ▶ Competitive analysis ▶ Products and services ▶ Pricing
04	**Develop** ▶ Naming ▶ Promise ▶ Positioning and tagline ▶ Brand story and messaging
05	**Design** ▶ Brand identity ▶ Brand image ▶ Brand design ▶ Brand audit

The Brand Strategy Map

BUILD IT, AND THEY WILL COME? Not necessarily. It's a crowded marketplace, and your prospective clients have a very short attention span and lots of options. No matter how great your product or service is, there's probably someone else offering a similar product or service. What's the solution? Brand your product or service. The concept of branding has been around for a while, but it has never been more important than it is now.

Regardless of the industry you're in, you need a strong, authentic brand. Before you go out and hire an expensive branding agency to craft a brand for you, let me give you an example. I loved so many of Whitney Houston's songs, including "I Will Always Love You," "I Have Nothing," "One Moment in Time," I'm Every Woman," and the list goes on and on. Whitney had an amazing voice and was extremely talented. Years ago, an article in *Rolling Stone* attempted to explain where Whitney Houston's life got off track. The author of the article said Whitney's team crafted a brand for her that wasn't authentic to who she was. They gave her a very refined look and image, but she was really just a down-home, round-the-way girl. The author theorized that this misalignment was one of the reasons why Whitney Houston turned to drugs. She felt conflicted and grew weary of keeping up this façade.

However true that theory may or may not be in the case of the pop star, it's a reminder that your brand should be authentic to who you are, not based on some persona created to make you or your business look good. If you don't have a strong brand, growing your business will be an uphill battle. You will constantly be fighting against the competition instead of establishing yourself as the leading authority in your industry.

Your brand isn't just a recognizable name and logo that distinguish you in a crowded market. It's your promise to your clients and prospective clients and the perception that they have of you and your business. Think about the Walmart brand compared to the Whole Foods brand. When you hear the name Walmart, you think of an image totally different from the Whole Foods image. Think about Mercedes-Benz and Ford. What are the first thoughts that come to your mind for each brand? Those thoughts are the brand perceptions you've formed in your mind. Your brand tells a prospective client what to expect from your product or service; it differentiates you from your competition. Your brand is derived from who you are, who you want to be, and who people perceive you to be. You need a strong brand regardless of the size of your business.

People have personal brands too. You have your personal style, a distinctive way of communicating, your energy, and a unique way of interacting with others. Your personal brand is what people say about all of those things when you're not in the room. If you consistently show up late and unprepared, that becomes part of your brand. If you show up early, are always prepared, and dress to match the occasion, that all becomes a part of your brand. You must be intentional about developing and cultivating both your personal and business brands.

You can't build a brand without being consistent and maintaining that consistency as you extend your brand to every part of your business. It all starts with establishing what that consistency is going to *look like* and what *feeling* you want it to evoke. This includes, but is not limited to, your business name, products, services, logos, colors, fonts, messaging, packaging, visual imaging. It also includes customer service and every interaction you have with your client or prospective client, which is called the client experience.

Are you the innovator in your industry or the experienced and reliable service provider? Is your product the high-cost, high-quality option or the low-cost, high-value option? You can't be both, and you can't be all things to all people. Your brand should be authentic to who you are and a match to the wants and needs of your target audience.

Defining your brand is like a journey of business self-discovery. It can be difficult, time-consuming, and uncomfortable. It requires, at the very least, that you answer six basic questions:

1. What is your business mission?
2. What are the benefits and features of your products or services?
3. What qualities do you want your clients and prospective clients to associate with your business?
4. What should your brand imaging look like?
5. How will that image make people feel?
6. Will it resonate with your target audience?

Perform a little research to find out what your current clients already think of your brand. This will help you understand whether or not your brand aligns with your business strategy.

5 Branding Mistakes

There are five branding mistakes that small business owners commonly make.

Mistake #1. Your brand strategy isn't clear. Clarity is a huge challenge for a lot of small business owners. Your strategy has to be clear and very easy for your clients and prospective clients to understand.

Sometimes, you're so close to your passion and ideas that it's hard to be objective. You think your brand is clear because you have it in your heart, but other people don't get it. You need to make it easy for people to understand who you are and what your business offers. You should be able to explain who you are, how you add value, the problem you solve, and the benefits people receive from working with you in a few sentences. If you aren't able to do that, then your brand message isn't clear.

Mistake #2. Your brand isn't concise. Your brand message needs to be concise because people retain very little of what you say. As a trainer and teacher at heart, I sometimes find it difficult to keep it short, whether I'm speaking or writing. I was trained to explain, explain, explain, explain, and then explain some more. However, that doesn't work when it comes to branding. Instead, always remember to keep it short and sweet (K.I.S.S.).

To keep your brand concise, focus on your client, not on you or the business. What problem do you solve for your clients? What are the benefits they'll experience from working with you? What value can you add to their business or personal life? Value should be integrated into all aspects of your brand message, not just sprinkled on top.

Mistake #3. Your brand isn't compelling. You don't want boring, copy-cat messaging. What makes your brand message compelling is *you*: your personality, passion, energy, approach, personal story, humor, and your "why." These things not only create awareness but emotional connection and visibility. If your message is compelling, the person who hears it naturally wants to tell everybody about you. This creates energy and momentum that helps your brand grow and makes people gravitate to you. When people feel like they can relate to you, it helps you build a loyal tribe. Remember that people move with memorable movements. Be memorable.

Mistake #4. Your brand isn't convincing. Your brand must be convincing. You have to show that what you offer has real value. Your value comes from providing real solutions and benefits with real substance, not just pretty marketing with a bunch of fluff. Regardless of what industry you're in, your value should provide a transformation or powerful service to your clients. You're not trying to convince them of your value, rather you are making clear the value you offer. There's a real big difference here! Your brand also has to be authentic; it has to be you. That authenticity will only make your brand more convincing.

Mistake #5. Your brand does not connect with your target audience. You must establish a genuine connection with your target audience so they know you care about them. Your audience doesn't care about the product or service you offer until they know you care about them. This connection will help to establish a foundation of trust. Your voice, experience, and personality will only attract your target audience to you if you clearly present your brand. Remember the bottom line is to keep in mind that *you* are the brand. Think of how closely Steve Jobs was tied to Apple, Bill Gates with Microsoft, Mark Zuckerberg with Facebook, or Dave Thomas with Wendy's. Whether you run a start-up or established business, your personal brand is the foundation for your business brand.

Let's just take a quick pause for an authentic moment. Over the course of my years of business ownership, I have committed all of these branding mistakes at one time or another. My brand colors were hot pink and green when I was working in a male-dominated industry. (Don't judge me!) I once had a tagline that was about four sentences, and I spent some time shoving my services down my prospects' throats because I didn't know what would connect with them.

Take it from me. Spending some much-needed introspective time on defining your brand will yield dividends for your business growth. Your brand imaging and messaging should be able to withstand your growth, industry trends, product expansion, and business evolution for at least three to five years. You'll make minor tweaks here and there, but a brand overhaul is not only costly in terms of finances but also in terms of brand recognition and value. As you prepare to build your brand be strategic, creative, and concise.

Building Your Brand

Successful brands are built on values, mission, beliefs, and capabilities. Your brand is the sum of all the perceptions, feelings, associations, and attitudes that clients and prospective clients form about your brand. Your brand is, in essence, a promise of a specific set of features, benefits, and services you'll deliver. There are four phases in the brand-building process. I refer to these phases as **the Brand Strategy Map**:

1. **Discover**: You are the brand.
2. **Define**: Clarify your brand to avoid a split personality.
3. **Develop**: Your message is heard before you are seen.
4. **Design**: An image is worth a thousand words.

These phases should be followed in order to build a solid foundation for your brand.

From the Desk of the Decision-Maker

SALLY WILSON

SUPPLIER DIVERSITY MANAGER | STRATEGIC SOURCING & PROCUREMENT, AFLAC

TO BE CORPORATE READY, know who you're approaching. Too often, I am asked where we're located and what we do, and I'm tasked to tell a small business how they can fit into our business model. Do your research before approaching supplier diversity professionals. I am attracted to small businesses that know how they can help our company grow, improve our operational efficiencies, provide cost savings, and contribute to our social responsibility.

Discover: You Are the Brand

A powerful brand is built on psychology and emotion, not on logic. The key to building a sustainable brand is to link the heart of your prospective client with the soul of your brand. A well-thought-out brand enables you to connect with your clients and prospective clients at the deepest level. During the "discover" phase, you will focus on four key elements:

1. Brand purpose
2. Personal story
3. Brand personality
4. Mission

Brand Purpose (Your Why)

Simon Sinek, author of *Start with Why*, explains that the reason the most powerful brands in the world, like Apple, Starbucks, and Nike, succeed is not because of what they do or how they do it. It's because of *why* they do what they do. Your brand purpose explains why you choose to do what you do, why your business exists, and why it matters. It's important for you to understand why you do what you do. Your "why" will sustain you during the building stage of your business. You have to be in business for more than just monetary gain, so define your brand purpose and keep it in mind as you build your brand.

Personal Story

Your personal story may create your why. That story encompasses the experiences in your life that led you to do what you do in business. It creates an emotional connection with your target audience because it shows that you know exactly what they've gone through, you feel their pain, and you can help them solve their problem. Part of your personal story will create your brand purpose.

You'll decide how much or how little of your personal story to incorporate into your brand purpose. For instance, my brand purpose is to provide step-by-step business strategies for small business owners who want to have success in business and life. My personal story is that I filed business bankruptcy and experienced a slew of business failures because I didn't have the right business strategies in place. When I learned that success leaves clues and there's a roadmap to success, I wanted to share my new knowledge with other small businesses to shorten their learning curve.

Brand Personality

Your brand personality is the way your brand behaves, speaks, and engages with the outside world. It's the more emotional and relatable side of your brand. Make sure your authentic personality shines through when you deliver your total brand experience. A brand personality is a set of human characteristics attributed to a brand name. According to Jennifer Aaker, creator of Five Dimensions of Brand Personality, there are five main brand personalities: sincerity, excitement, competence, sophistication, and ruggedness.[13]

Luxury brands, such as Gucci, Ritz-Carlton, and Mercedes-Benz, embrace sophistication. Brands like Dove, a beauty products company, work to demonstrate sincerity. It is extremely important for a business to accurately define its brand personality so it resonates with the correct prospective client. Brand personality defines the brand's attitude in the marketplace. It's also the key factor of any successful marketing campaign. To choose your brand's personality, look at the chart below to consider the five personality types, and select the one that resonates with you the most.[14]

BRAND PERSONALITY				
Sincerity	**Excitement**	**Competence**	**Sophistication**	**Ruggedness**
Down-to-earth Honest Carefree Spirited Youthful	Kind Thoughtful Family Values Imaginative	Reliable Intelligent Successful Influential Leadership	Elegant Prestigious Glamorous Charming Feminine	Outdoorsy Tough Rough Masculine Athletic

Brand Mission

In the business strategy section of this book, you spent some time writing out your mission and vision for your business. If you didn't complete the exercises in that section, stop, go back, and complete them. Once you're done, it's time to incorporate your mission into your branding. Your brand mission, in essence, is a clear expression of what your company is most passionate about. Before you can build a brand your target audience trusts, you need to know what value your business provides. Your mission statement defines the business's purpose for existing. It informs every aspect of your brand-building strategies.

Define: Clarify Your Brand to Avoid a Split Personality

Have you gotten caught up in the copy-cat syndrome? Are you trying to replicate another company's brand and make it appear as if it's your own? If so, your brand might have a split personality. This simply means the way in which your business is representing itself is inconsistent with who you are, your mission, and your core values.

Take the necessary time to do a deep internal examination to identify what your brand truly is and what resonates with your target audience. When your service or product looks like someone else, you'll always find it difficult to connect with their target audience. Meanwhile, if you're replicating the work and efforts of others, you miss a prime opportunity to build your own unique brand. Don't reinvent the wheel; personalize it. Branding is the visual and social identity of your business and it's okay if it changes as your business grows.

During the "define" phase, you'll focus on four key areas:

1. Target audience
2. Competitive analysis
3. Products and service offerings
4. Pricing

Target Audience

Having a well-defined target audience, also referred to as a target market, helps you to determine where to focus your marketing efforts. You might be asking yourself how your business can compete with larger companies that have more capital and a larger staff. The answer: you compete by taking time to understand who your niche audience is and marketing specifically to them. Targeting a niche market doesn't mean you exclude anybody. It means you focus your brand efforts and marketing dollars more efficiently. Focusing on too many audiences is like dating multiple people at one time; one of them is bound to feel left out.

Demographics

First, figure out who needs your product or service *and* is most likely to buy it. Think about specific demographics to target, including the following:

- Age
- Location
- Gender
- Income level
- Education level
- Marital or family status
- Occupation
- Ethnic background

Psychographics

Next, consider the psychographics of your target audience. The psychographics are the psychological traits of a person, including the following:

- Personality
- Attitudes
- Values
- Concerns
- Interests/hobbies
- Lifestyles
- Behaviors
- Likes/Dislikes

Goals, Challenges, and Objections

Finally, consider the goals, challenges, and objections of your target audience. Goals are what your target audience wants to achieve in the short term or long term. Do your clients want more money, to save time, avoid effort, improve their health, have better relationships, increase confidence, or build higher self-esteem? What are the perceived challenges your clients face in achieving their goals? This could include challenges like limited finances, lack of time, inadequate resources, not enough knowledge, overcrowded market, incompetent employees, family obligations, or a lack of contacts. (Notice I refer to "perceived" challenges. Typically, challenges are simply a matter of not having the right strategy and action plan.)

Objections, on the other hand, are reasons why your client wouldn't purchase your product or service. Common objections are: it's too costly, they don't have the time to implement it, they're considering purchasing from a competitor, or it doesn't provide the right solution.

Consider the following questions:

- What are the primary and secondary goals of your target audience in life and/or business?
- How can your product or service help them achieve their goal(s) or solve their problem(s)?
- What are their primary and secondary challenges in their life or business?
- How can your product or service help them overcome their challenge(s)?
- What objections would your target audience have to buying your product or service?

Evaluate your target audience

Don't narrow your target audience to the point of not having anyone left in it. You want to make sure your audience is viable so you can carve out a niche for your business. Remember you can have more than one niche market. Later, we'll address developing a different marketing message for each niche. If you can reach multiple niches effectively with the same message, then you've broken down your market too far and need to modify your target audience. Also, if you find there are only one hundred people who fit all of your criteria, you should reevaluate your target audience and expand it to ensure you have enough people in it. The trick is to find that perfect balance. Once you've narrowed down your target audience, it's time to evaluate that audience to see if they will actually buy your product and service.

Consider these questions:

- Are there enough people who fit your criteria?
- Will your target audience benefit from your product/service?
- Will they see a need for your product/service?
- Do you understand what drives your target audience to make decisions?
- Can they afford your product/service?
- Can you reach them with your message?
- Are they easily accessible?

You may be asking yourself, "How do I find all this information?" Great question. Search online for research other people have done on your target audience. Then search through magazines, online articles, blog posts, social media groups, and forums, and survey your customers, or interview potential customers. You can also utilize online data resources, including:

- **Quantcast:** provides free audience insights for over one hundred million web and mobile destinations
- **Alexa:** transforms raw data into meaningful insights that will help you find your competitive advantage

- **Google Trends:** uncovers where your target customers are predominantly located

I know niching your audience can be pretty scary because you might feel like your products or services will work for everyone. Well, let me tell you from personal experience that "everyone" is not going to buy from you. You have to take a real honest look at which type of clients bring you immense joy to work with and allow you to flow in your "sweet spot," which means operating in your gifts and talents. For me, those clients are women business owners who struggle with running a successful business and maintaining a happy personal life. I went back and forth for at least five years, trying to decide if I would niche down my target audience. Let me tell you the magical thing that happened when I finally did. My business grew, my brand became clear, and I still attracted clients who weren't in my target audience.

Buyer Persona

Once you've defined and evaluated your target audience, it's time to create individual buyer personas. A buyer persona is a fictional representation of your target audience, used as a guide when creating content, developing products or services, and acquiring clients. Each target audience you have needs a separate buyer persona. To emotionally connect with prospective clients, you need to know how they think and behave, and you need to speak their language. This helps you to realize that they're real people with real challenges they need you to help them solve.

There is no right or wrong way to create a buyer persona. You just want it to provide you with the necessary information to effectively market to your target audience. There are tons of examples online. For ideas, do some research to find one that resonates with you most. Here's a sample buyer persona.

Maverick Michelle

- **Age:** 35
- **Title:** Marketing Manager
- **Decision-maker:** Yes
- **Industry:** Software and Technology
- **Salary:** $95,000/year
- **Education:** B.S. in Marketing
- **Goals:** Deliver qualified leads to sales team to grow customer base and achieve revenue goals.
- **Challenges:** Needs to improve conversion rates on website with more relevant content.
- **How we help:** Connect her with savvy writers to create value-based content.
- **Messaging strategy:** Focus on how to increase engagement for Michelle by providing subject matter experts to write engaging and emotionally appealing B2B content.

Competitive Research

You should never imitate exactly what the big brands are doing in your industry. However, you should be aware of what they do well and what they can improve on. The goal is to differentiate your business from the competition. You want to convince a prospective client to purchase from you over your competitor. Research your main competitors and study how they have effectively built their brand name and where they fall short. One of the easiest ways to track all of your data is to create a brand-competitor research spreadsheet. You want to include the following in your research:

- Competitor name
- Message (brand messaging)
- Visual imaging (website, samples of blog posts, memes, etc.)
- Product/service offerings and benefits
- Reviews (client testimonials, product reviews, etc.)
- Social media mentions
- Marketing efforts (ads, email marketing campaigns, trade shows, etc.)

Choose two to four competitors for your comparison chart. You might want to take a look at other local businesses or even aim to benchmark against name brands. While performing your research, consider the following questions:

- Is the competitor consistent with messaging and visual identity across channels?
- What is the quality of the competitor's products or services?
- What benefits do they offer, or what problem do they solve for their clients?
- Does the competitor have customer reviews or social mentions you can read?
- In what ways does the competitor market their business, both online and offline?

Defining your target audience is essential to brand development. A lot of small businesses make the mistake of assuming "everybody" is their target audience, and it costs them in terms of developing brand loyalty and increasing bottom line revenues. Remember that defining your audience won't stop other people from buying from you. Instead, you'll focus most of your efforts on a group that represents your "ideal client." You can have a primary and secondary target market and tailor your product or service to your clients' needs.

Product and Service Offerings

Understanding your core product and service offerings is crucial to your brand. To stand out in a crowded marketplace, you must provide a superb product or service, excellent quality, consistent customer service, and value that your client can't get anywhere else. During the research phase of defining your brand, you identified the biggest needs of your clients and the results they want to achieve from your product or service. Take a serious look at your product and service offerings, and determine what you need to tweak to become more competitive. You want to choose your "core" competencies to offer as a product or service. You don't want your business to appear to be a Jack of all trades, so determine the areas you excel in and offer those to your clients in the form of products or services. Additionally, you should have a systemized way to offer your products and services to your clients so you don't have to reinvent the wheel every time you work with a new client.

Pricing

A lot of experts discuss pricing under the umbrella of marketing, but I've found pricing to be an important part of the branding discussion. The way you price your products and services says a lot about your brand. Your pricing must be consistent with your brand. You can't brand yourself as a premium product or service provider and price those products and services at 50% less than your competitors. Nor can you brand yourself as the low-cost, value-added provider and set your prices 50% higher than your competitors. Accurately defining your price takes research and a little bit of elbow grease.

The price you charge for your products or services is one of the most important business decisions you'll make. Ask clients to pay too much, and they might stop buying. Ask clients to pay too little, and you diminish your brand value, lessen your profit margin, and run the risk of clients assuming your product or service is of poor quality. Your optimal price involves several factors that will maximize your profit margins, ensure you remain competitive, and attract your ideal clients.

You have some flexibility in how you set your prices because there's no exact formula-based approach that applies equally to all businesses. Pricing services is a little more difficult than pricing products because you can easily identify the cost of making a physical product. However, pricing a service is a bit more subjective because you have to place a value on your and your team's expertise and time.

Let's look at five common pricing strategies:

1. Cost-plus pricing
2. Competitive pricing
3. Value-based pricing
4. Price skimming
5. Penetration pricing

Cost-plus pricing. With this method of pricing, you first determine the cost of making a product or providing a service, and then, you add on your profit. To determine your costs, you need to figure out direct costs and indirect costs. Direct costs include labor, materials, commissions, manufacturing supplies, and the like. Indirect costs, frequently referred to as overhead and general operating expenses, include rent, utilities, officers' salaries, insurance, payroll, legal and accounting expenses, and the like. These costs may be fixed or variable. To determine your pricing, take into consideration all of your direct costs and a portion of your indirect costs, and then, add your profit. Here's a very basic example. If your direct and indirect costs are $1,000, and you want a 10% profit, then the cost-plus pricing would be $1,000 cost + $100 profit for a total price of $1,100.

Competitive pricing. This method involves setting a price based on what the competition charges. It relies on the idea that competitors have already thoroughly researched their pricing, and since your product or service is very similar, the price should be comparable to the competitors' prices. This strategy assumes that, by setting the same price as your competitors, you can avoid the trial and error costs of the price-setting process. However, every business is different, and so are its costs. The main limit of competitive pricing is that it fails to account for the differences in direct and indirect expenses of individual businesses. As a result, this pricing method can potentially be ineffective and lead to reduced profits. For example, your competitor may be larger and have lower overhead costs, giving them larger profit margins. Researching a competitor's price can help you see how your pricing lines up, but make sure you take all of your costs into consideration when establishing your price.

Value-based pricing. This method sets a price based on how much your prospective clients believe what you're selling is worth. Instead of looking solely at the cost to provide your products and services or at your competitors' pricing, a value-based pricing strategy seeks to determine how much your prospective clients are willing to pay for your product or service.

Price skimming. This method involves setting a high price for your product or service and lowering it as the market evolves and more competitors enter your space. Remember how much computers and cell phones cost when they first came out? As more competitors entered the market, pricing became more competitive and affordable.

Penetration pricing. This method involves setting a low price to enter a competitive market and raising it later. An example would be Netflix. The company entered the market at a low price, but as demand increases for their services, their pricing continues to increase.

Your pricing strategy can ultimately determine your business's fate. Small business owners can ensure profitability and longevity by paying close attention to their pricing strategy. Many small business owners choose a pricing strategy meant to make them the lowest-cost provider in the market. This approach comes from taking a quick view of competitors and assuming they can win business by having the lowest price. Having the lowest price doesn't guarantee they'll win business and is often not the strongest position for a small business. It invites clients to see their product or service as a commodity and eliminates the perceived value of any value-add they offer. Plus, larger competitors with deep pockets and lower operating costs will destroy any small business trying to compete on price alone. Make sure your pricing is based on the value you offer and the elements that make your business unique.

Develop products or services that are exclusive to your business and create proprietary systems or technology that only your company uses. Create value-added products or services that make you unique in your category. Equally as important, develop your brand name in the market to ensure you create a genuine connection with your target audience.

Develop: Your Message Is Heard Before You're Seen

You're laying a great foundation for your brand by getting clear on your why, your target audience, and your product and service offerings. Now let's use that information to develop the framework for your brand. There are six essential elements involved in developing your brand.

1. Brand name
2. Brand promise

3. Brand positioning
4. Tagline
5. Brand story
6. Brand messaging

Brand Name

A distinct brand name can differentiate you from your competition. Your name evokes emotion and builds awareness about your company. Think about the meaning behind some great brand names, including Google and Amazon. Did you know that Google's original name was BackRub because their search engine searched through backlinks? Have you heard of googolplex? Well, no, because it was left on the cutting room floor back in the late 90s, when Larry Page and Sergey Brin, two graduate students at Stanford, were brainstorming about a business venture. Would you believe that Google is a misspelling of a mathematical term, googol?[15] Lots of business names have similarly interesting backstories. Developing a name for your brand is critical whether it's your business name or a name for a product or service. According to Sticky Branding, there are four primary categories of brand names: descriptive, acronym, invented, and experiential.[16]

Descriptive. Descriptive brand names succinctly describe the business. For example, PayPal is a payment company, and Subway sells submarine sandwiches. These names make it easier for their target audience to identify their products and services. One pitfall of a descriptive name can appear when your company expands and offers products or services outside of the original name

Acronym. Many recognizable brands are acronyms, like UPS, IBM, and HP. Most acronyms are created from descriptive names. For example, it's easier to say GEICO than Government Employees Insurance Company. An acronym can be easy to remember, but the primary pitfall is that it can look like a group of letters without meaning.

Invented name. Some of the most iconic brand names are made-up words, like Google, a misspelling of the mathematical term googol, or Pixar. They're names created specifically to represent a brand. They are very powerful but tricky. Since no one has heard of the word, you'll need a marketing and advertising budget to build brand awareness.

Experiential name. Some brand names build upon the feeling or experience the brand delivers. Twitter allows users to give and receive short bursts of information, and the word "twitter" means a series of short calls or sounds or birds chirping. The experiential name is a positioning statement. It helps your business stand out in the marketplace by setting an expectation of what it's like to choose you. The biggest challenge with an experiential name is connecting the meaning of the name with the brand and customer experience. This requires a substantial marketing and advertising budget.

Naming your business or brand requires strategy because your name is going to be with your business for a long time and should be able to evolve as your products and services evolve. Ask yourself these questions when naming or renaming your business:

- Is the brand name simple to say and easy to remember?
- Is it short, ideally less than eight characters?
- Is the .com domain name available?
- Is it distinctive? How does the name stand out amongst the competition?

- Does the name fit the brand's personality?
- How does it look in print? Does it look as good as it sounds?

Brand Promise

A strong brand promise connects your purpose, positioning, strategy, and client experience. It enables you to deliver your brand in a way that connects emotionally with your clients and differentiates your brand. What promises are you making to your clients? When a brand conveys a promise, it's communicating a guarantee of value to its audience. To motivate clients, a brand promise must achieve the following three goals:

1. Convey a compelling benefit.
2. Be authentic and credible.
3. Be kept, every time.

Many brands struggle to deliver their promise because it's not well-defined. It's important for you and your entire team to be consistent with the promises you make to your clients. Let's take a look at some brand promise examples.

BUSINESS NAME	BRAND PROMISE
Starbucks	To inspire and nurture the human spirit—one person, one cup, and one neighborhood at a time.
Walmart	Save money. Live better.
GEICO	15 minutes or less can save you 15% or more on car insurance.
BMW	The Ultimate Driving Machine

Nike	To bring inspiration and innovation to every athlete in the world.
Apple	Think different.
Coca-Cola	To inspire moments of optimism and uplift.
H&M	More fashion choices that are good for people, the planet and your wallet.
Marriott	Quiet luxury. Crafted experiences. Intuitive service.
FedEx	Your package will get there overnight. Guaranteed.
McDonald's	An inexpensive, familiar, and consistent meal delivered quickly in a clean environment.

The examples above all have the makings of a great brand promise. Marriott's brand promise is about a consistent experience. Whether you stay in a Marriott in Washington, DC, Atlanta, or New York, you will receive the same experience and service. Coca-Cola's brand promise doesn't mention the product, but instead, it aims to position Coca-Cola as a lifestyle brand, which is about more than manufacturing drinks. Walmart offers its shoppers low prices with easy access to personal necessities. Starbucks's brand promise is to serve as a place between home and work for relaxing or getting caught up on work. It's about the experience, not just the coffee. Your brand promise should embody the experience you want your clients to receive every time they interact with your brand.

Brand Positioning

In this busy landscape of businesses competing for your target audience's attention, your number one goal is to stand out. Answer these three questions when considering your brand position:

1. **What is the exact category my brand is in**? It's important to understand what market you are looking to dominate, where the opportunities are, and if there are any gaps you can fill.
2. **Who is my "best" target audience?** You cannot, and should not, be all things to all people. That's why you must narrow your target audience down to your "ideal client" and understand his or her specific needs and pain points.
3. **What sets my brand apart from my competition**? Every brand should look to deliver a unique story in the market. What is it about your brand that makes your business the rock star of your industry? While there may be similar products or services in the marketplace, there is only one you.

Creating a robust brand-positioning strategy involves diving deep into the details of your brand and discovering what you do better than anyone else.

Follow these four steps to create a brand-positioning strategy that's unique to your business.

Step 1. Determine your current brand positioning.

How are you currently marketing your product or service? Do you offer something unique, or are you a copycat of another product or service? It's important to understand your current position before you analyze your competition.

First, identify your mission, values, and what makes you different from the rest of the market. Second, define your target audience. Finally, identify value proposition and your current brand voice.

Your brand position should sound and feel authentic. It should be relatable and easy to understand. Don't use complex lingo or terms that no one understands just to sound impressive. Identify the language of your target audience, and use their language in your brand-positioning strategy.

Step 2. Research your competition.

If you're completing the exercises as you go through the book, you've already researched your competitors. If not, take some time to research and analyze your competition. After analyzing your business, it's important to analyze your competition by performing a competitor analysis to determine what you can do better in your positioning strategy to gain an edge.

Analyze how your competition positions their brand to compete. At its simplest, your research should include:

- Products or services your competitors offer
- Their strengths and weaknesses
- Marketing strategies they're using successfully
- Their position in the current market

Step 3. Identify what makes your brand unique.

Building a unique brand involves identifying what makes you special and different from other businesses. After you conduct competitor research, you are likely to find similarities between their business and yours. As you compare your product or service to your competitors, look for what makes your brand unique. This is the starting point for positioning your brand in the market. What benefits or results does your brand provide relative to your competition (brand promise)? What is the evidence that your brand delivers on this promise?

Step 4. Create your positioning statement.

A positioning statement is a short synopsis that clearly articulates your brand's unique value to your clients in relation to your competitors. Brand positioning statements are often confused with business taglines or slogans. Positioning statements are for internal use. These statements guide the marketing and operating decisions of your business. A positioning statement helps you make key decisions that affect your client's perception of your brand.

Let me pause for a minute and tell you I have revamped my positioning statement so many times I'm surprised I still have a usable whiteboard after all the erasing and rewriting. As your business grows and changes, your positioning statement will evolve. Don't get bogged down in writing a perfect statement. Create one, and modify it as needed. It's easier to steer a plane in the air than it is to get it off the ground.

Let's look at some real-world examples of good brand positioning. JetBlue saw an opportunity to enter the market and position their brand as an airline that provides gourmet snacks and expansive legroom. During my younger years, Taco Bell was well known in the market for Mexican fast food. Chipotle entered the same space by competing on quality instead of price.

I love to make things simple and easy to apply. Here's the positioning statement formula I use with my clients to help them develop a succinct positioning statement.

Positioning Statement Formula

[Brand] + [Category/Niche] + [Target Audience] +
[Point of Difference] + [Reasons to Believe]

Brandwatch provides an excellent example using this formula[17]:

Rhino Energy Drink is a canned energy drink company that provides adventurous millennials with the energy they need to live their busy, active lives. It does this with its special formula of high-quality ingredients.

A strong brand makes all the difference when competing in any market. A unique brand-positioning strategy is critical to making a statement, keeping your target audience's attention, and successfully growing your brand. Take the example of one of my favorite clients, who I met nearly twelve years ago and have been working with for the last five years. She is by far one of the smartest business women I know. Not only is she business savvy, but she's also very strategic in marketing and positioning for her clients. There's only one catch; she isn't as strategic for her own business. She often gets caught up in "shiny object syndrome" and chasing what's next. We've had many conversations about narrowing her niche audience and offering a boutique-style menu of services for her clients. This conversation continues to fall on deaf ears as she chases the money in her business. If the client is willing and able to pay, she'll provide the service they request. Although her business is steadily growing, it will never achieve the success it could until she slows down enough to effectively understand her value proposition and narrow her audience. Just because something is good doesn't mean it's good for you. Stay focused on your core offerings to effectively scale your business.

Tagline

A tagline is an important element of your branding. Insights from your positioning statement can be turned into a tagline, but it's important to distinguish between the two. The positioning statement is for internal use to ensure your team is clear about who you serve, what you offer, and your value over your competition. The tagline is for external marketing use.

Your tagline has one purpose: to attract the right prospective clients and keep them interested long enough to take action. That action could be signing up for your email list, visiting your store, or scheduling a complimentary consultation. A well-crafted tagline can provide more clarity and focus to your overall business mission, but the main purpose is to attract your ideal client.

Here are five reasons why creating a good tagline is important for your business:

1. **Your tagline states benefits.** A great tagline clearly states the benefits your prospective clients will receive from buying your products and services. This is becoming increasingly important as, more and more, we live in a solution-based marketplace. People want what they want, how they want it, and when they want it.
2. **Your tagline differentiates your brand.** Using your tagline effectively will help your brand stand out from your competitors in the marketplace.
3. **Your tagline supports brand recognition.** Some taglines stand out, like "Just do it"; "Can you hear me now?"; "Think different"; and "Because you're worth it." Have you seen a TV commercial or internet ad that stood out because of a catchy or memorable tagline? Of course, you have. One of the major benefits of a tagline is that it creates a memorable connection with prospective clients so they'll not only recognize your brand but remember it.
4. **Competitors can't use your tagline.** When you launch your unique product or service in the market, competitors can copy the design, technology, features, and packaging. However, your tagline should be original and unique to your business and your brand. It should clearly represent your brand and product or service features so that the competitors aren't able to deceive customers by offering them a product or service dressed up to look like yours. Make sure you trademark your tagline once you finalize it.
5. **Your tagline expresses your strategic direction.** The tagline represents the vision and mission of the business

to your clients. It succinctly conveys the problems you solve for your clients and the results they receive from working with you. When customers understand the vision and mission of the business, they're more inclined to purchase your product or service.

Let's look at some examples of memorable taglines.

BUSINESS NAME	TAGLINE
Walmart	Always low prices. Always.
Nike	Just do it.
Coca-Cola	The real thing
Verizon	Can you hear me now?
MasterCard	There are some things money can't buy. For everything else, there's MasterCard.
Target	Expect more. Pay less.
Southwest Airlines	The short-haul, no-frills, and low-priced airline.
Mercedes-Benz	Engineered like no other car in the world.
L'Oréal	Because you're worth it.
M&M	Melts in your mouth, not in your hands.
Apple	Think different.
Bounty	The quicker picker-upper
Lay's Chips	Betcha can't eat just one.
BMW	The ultimate driving machine
Dunkin' Donuts	America runs on Dunkin'.
McDonald's	I'm lovin' it.
Maybelline	Maybe she's born with it. Maybe it's Maybelline.
State Farm	Like a good neighbor, State Farm is there.

It's important to note that there are differences between a tagline and a slogan. A tagline applies to an entire business, and a slogan typically applies to a single product or service or a division of the business.

Here are three simple ways you can develop your business tagline.

Tagline Formula #1: A straight-forward statement directed to your target audience. This tagline is effective because it clearly explains what product or services you provide, and your ideal clients can self-select and decide if they want to work with you.

{Product/service} for {these people}.

Examples:

Digital strategy for small business owners

Chiropractic care for athletes

Tagline Formula #2: A very strong claim meant to influence the purchasing decision. This type of tagline is mainly used by large brands who set the bar very high and are less likely to have to defend their claims. Use with caution.

{Name of Company} – {Strong claim}.

Examples:

Wal-Mart: Always Low Prices

Amazon: Earth's Biggest Book Store

Tagline Formula #3: A straight-to-the-point tagline that features your delivery method for the product or service you offer. This type of tagline highlights your competitive advantage over your competitors.

{This product/service} {in this way}.

Examples:

Fresh groceries right to your doorstep.

Website design done in thirty days.

There's plenty of advice out there about making your tagline catchy and clever. However, your tagline also needs to be concise, clear, and sustainable. You don't want to select a trendy tagline that you'll have to replace within a year. Make sure our tagline will resonate with your target audience and encourage them to learn more about you and become loyal clients.

Brand Story

A brand story is a cohesive narrative that encompasses the facts and feelings created by your business (brand). Unlike traditional advertising, which shows and tells about your brand, a brand story must inspire an emotional reaction. Traditional advertising was based on a one-way flow of information, from brand to prospective client. Now, a brand is a conversation with people who experience the brand (the brand experience). No longer does the power of your brand story rely solely on your marketing team. It's in the hands of your social media followers, clients, employees, interns, and other people who talk about your brand. Of course, you can't control every facet of your brand story, but you can lead it. Add your compelling, engaging story into the mix because your voice matters. Your story should be authentic to your values and relatable. By adding your voice to explain what truly drives your business or brand, you'll build emotional engagement.

Let's look at Apple, a company that tells its story very well. That story is about much more than just the design of their computers; think about the Genius Bar experience, and consider how Apple makes major product announcements. These elements of the business are aligned with Apple's brand story as innovators making beautiful products that challenge the status quo. Apple is successfully leading the conversation about Apple.

Why is storytelling so powerful? A brand story grabs our attention, activates our brains, and stirs our emotions.

A great brand story crafts a narrative in which your product or service solves a problem. Your brand story takes your prospective client on a journey that ideally includes four components:

1. **Problem/Solution:** Describes the pain points your prospective client has and shows how your product or service solves them.
2. **Before/After:** Shows the contrast of the state your prospective client was in before they utilized your product or service contrasted with where they could be after using your product or service.
3. **Edutainment:** Educates and entertains your prospective clients and provides them with tons of value.
4. **Underdog story:** People love to cheer for the underdog, so this is your story of how you overcame an obstacle and can help your clients do the same thing. What lessons did you learn from your failures?

5 Keys to Telling a Powerful Brand Story

Your brand story has to be impactful and should include these five key elements:

1. It's meaningful.
2. It's personal.
3. It's emotional.
4. It's simple.
5. It's authentic.

It's meaningful. Everyone is dealing with content overload. There are thousands of brands vying for attention, and your brand is no different. Therefore, every piece of content you put out should serve a purpose for the target audience you want to consume it. Ask yourself these questions before you start drafting your brand story: 1) What is the purpose of telling this story? 2) What is unique about this story? 4) How will this story provide value to my audience? 5) What do I want my audience to gain from this story?

It's personal. Whether your story is inspirational, educational, motivational, or entertaining, it must be relatable and emotionally connect with your audience. It should be concise and impactful and pique the interest of your target audience. Answer these two questions: 1) How does my product/service (brand) enhance my prospect's life? 2) Why should they stop what they are doing and pay attention to my story? You want people to be able to see themselves in your story. That's the number one reason why they'll pay attention to it.

It's emotional. A strong brand story is all about stimulating emotion and empathy. It's not just about what you do, but also how you affect people. The ultimate goal of your product or service is to make people's lives easier. That's the emotional hook of your brand story; always lead with it. It's important to trigger that emotion immediately with your ideal clients, like the first paragraph of a blog post or the first few seconds of a video, so you can hook them. You can lead with challenges or problems because conflict creates a bit of stress or intrigue. Storytelling elements like personal anecdotes, powerful statistics, or thought-provoking questions can also be effective. You can also end with a satisfying resolution to a problem, which releases the feel-good hormone, oxytocin.

It's simple. One of the most common mistakes in brand storytelling is trying to say too much. Remember K.I.S.S. (Keep It Short and Simple). It's far better to tell a very simple story and maximize emotional attachment than to bombard people with different stories. Make sure your brand story has a singular focus because it's easier to connect to one thing at a time. Focus on one person or one problem at a time so you don't confuse or distract your reader, viewer, or listener.

It's authentic. When you share your brand story, people should know it's *your* story. That means being open, honest, and transparent. It means letting your personality shine through. It also means being consistent. When you're creating a ton of content, it's important to cultivate consistency so that people can not only identify but trust your content.

Today, people have a plethora of information and limited time. Your brand has to make it as easy as possible for prospective clients to say "yes" to your product or service. For this to happen, you must bring right-brained (intuitive) and left-brained (analytical) elements together to bridge the gap.

Strong brands seamlessly bring together purpose, vision, customer service, passion, operational excellence, and strategy to deliver remarkable customer experiences with their brand story. Prospective clients don't beat a path to a company's door because of its marketing. The hype of shiny marketing and advertising campaigns dies down quickly. Customers seek reliable and consistent brands that offer a compelling product or service and a memorable brand experience.

Messaging

Your messaging is such a critical part of your brand, and great messaging requires your words and content to convey your value proposition with clarity and accuracy. Effective brand messaging makes prospective clients emotionally connect with your brand by inspiring them, persuading them, motivating them, and ultimately making them want to buy your product or service.

A brand message is any content that communicates your brand promise to your target audience. No one brand message is going to please all audiences. This doesn't mean you have to be all things to all people. All brand messages should extend from your core brand identity and be tailored to meet the needs of each audience. A brand can appeal to multiple target audiences, each with different perspectives and needs, without changing the brand essence.

You'll use brand messaging throughout your interactions with your target market, including the following:

- Mission statement
- Slogans and taglines
- Brand story
- Elevator pitch (your thirty-second response to "What do you do?")
- Sales and marketing materials (sales brochures, websites, presentations, and marketing campaigns)
- Social media and digital marketing
- The introductory statement in a phone call, voice mail, or email footer
- Press releases (the statement at the bottom of the release that explains what your business does)
- Newsletters and annual reports
- Internal communications

Your brand messaging should be compelling and engaging to encourage your target audience to learn more about you and your business. It should be written in your business's distinct voice and not sound like everybody else. To ensure consistency with your brand messaging, it's important to create guidelines for your team to follow. Once you've created these guidelines, they should be distributed to every member of your team, as well as to any agencies or freelancers you partner with or hire.

Create a brand-messaging document that includes the following:

- Your brand's unique serving/selling position (USP)
- A detailed description of your target audience (or audiences)
- What your business stands for and its goals
- Any slogans or taglines
- Any other messaging that might be used
- Your brand story

Effective brand messaging can strengthen your value proposition, your brand, and the reasons your prospective clients should buy from you. With great messaging, your value is easily communicated and the market gets your messaging very quickly, which speeds up the sales process. Generic brand messaging doesn't help you stand out. Instead, it causes you to miss out on the opportunity to strengthen your position. Without consistent, distinct brand messaging, individual team members create their own messaging, which weakens your market position. Ultimately, poor brand messaging confuses the market.

Your brand messaging informs all of your communication with your market. Use it in your corporate identity, sales literature and tools, your website copy and design, and all of your marketing campaigns.

Design: An Image Is Worth a Thousand Words

The brand design phase consists of three core elements:

1. Brand identity
2. Brand image
3. Brand design

Brand Identity

What is brand identity? Many people think your brand identity is made up of your colors, logo, and business cards. Yes, those items are included, but there's much more to your brand identity than that. So let's dive deep into what brand identity is and why it's important. Simply put, your brand identity is how you want clients and prospective clients to perceive your business. Your brand identity communicates the essence of who you are to your target audience. It's what makes you instantly recognizable to your clients. Your target audience will associate your brand identity with your product or service, and that identity is what forges the connection between you and your clients, builds client loyalty, and determines how your clients will perceive your brand.

Brand identity is the visual message of your brand: name, logo, typography, style, visuals, and messaging. Brand identity is the foundation of your brand. You shape it through your mission, vision, business goals, competitor analysis, target audience, and brand personality. It's how your business wants to present itself and be perceived by others. The brand identity is a blend of the business's name, logo, colors, the visual elements in products and promotions, the message in its advertisements and content, and employee-client interactions. The goal of your brand identity is to cultivate a specific image in the minds of clients and prospective clients.

Brand Image

While brand identity is what you want to present, brand image is how customers actually think of your brand. Brand image is the perception of the brand in the minds of your clients and prospective clients. Brand image develops over time. Your audience forms an image based on their interactions and experience with your brand.

After you've laid the foundation for your brand image, you can start marketing and promotion activities to build a loyal following and generate sales. We will discuss these strategies more in the marketing section of the book, but here are the four components that are necessary to promote your brand:

1. **Public relations (PR).** PR distributes your key messages and business news in trade publications, news outlets, and blogs. By positioning your business as a thought leader and expert source on breaking news and trends, your PR can improve your brand image and raise awareness of your brand.
2. **Content.** Solid content is the key to successfully making PR and digital marketing work for your brand. Get more visibility for your brand profile by consistently creating and publishing contributed articles, blog posts, white papers, podcast episodes, videos, audios, and other unique content.
3. **Social.** Social media is an easy and effective way to share information pertinent to your industry and your audience. It provides an opportunity to interact with clients and influencers in your field. A comprehensive social media presence can elevate your image in the eyes of new and existing clients and increase website traffic.
4. **Search.** Search engine optimization improves your business ranking on search engines like Google. To get

noticed by your target audience you have to rank well for specific keywords and phrases. The goal is to increase the amount of traffic to your business website and other digital media platforms.

Before you start designing your visual elements, you must be clear about your brand identity. All the work you've done up to this point will help you establish who your business is as a brand.

It's important to identify all of these elements before you develop new or updated visuals or messaging for your business. Pull out your notes from previous sections and make sure you've identified the following:

- Your mission (your "why?")
- Your values (beliefs that drive your company)
- Your brand personality (the personality your brand would have if it were a person)
- Your unique positioning (how you differentiate yourself from the competition)
- Your brand voice (how your brand would communicate if it were a person)

Brand Design Building Blocks

Great design continues to be a powerful differentiator. Your brand's visual tone and elements should align with your brand strategy. Your visual elements should invoke a strong emotional reaction from your target audience, attracting them to your product or service. Your design assets are the tangible elements that will determine how your brand is perceived. These assets include things like your logo, packaging, website design, social media graphics, business cards, and the uniforms your employees wear. Before you start creating your design assets, you need to develop the basics of your design structure, which are the building blocks of your brand identity. These include:

1. Typography
2. Colors
3. Form and shape

Typography

Typography refers to the font you choose for your branding materials. There are five major types of typography: serif, sans serif, slab, script and handwritten.

- **Serif** fonts (like Times New Roman or Garamond) are classic, fonts based on a typeface style in use since the 18th century. This font style is great if you want your brand to appear trustworthy and traditional.
- **Sans serif** fonts (like Helvetica or Franklin Gothic) are considered the most economical, efficient, clean, and modern choice. This font gives a sleeker, more modern feel to brands.
- **Slab serif** fonts (like Clarendon or Memphis) bring a vintage vibe to a design and have a rugged look. These fonts work well for brands relating to the outdoors or artsy brands that want a typewriter feel.
- **Script** fonts (like Allura or Pacifico) mimic cursive handwriting. These fonts can be a great way to add a luxurious or feminine feel to your brand.
- **Handwritten** fonts are different from formal or casual scripts. They typically don't have the structure or definition found in the letterforms of a traditional script. They

work well for book covers, posters, and logo design, as they bring a creative and unique touch.

The typography you choose will say a lot about your brand, so choose wisely.

Colors

Developing your brand design involves the art of persuasion. Many different factors influence how and what your target audience buys. A large part of every buying decision is based on visual elements, and one of the strongest and most persuasive of those elements is color. Colors play a pivotal role in a critical decision for your target audience—to buy or not to buy.

According to research conducted by the secretariat of the Seoul International Color Expo, the following statistics exist on the relationship between color and marketing[18]:

- 92.6% of respondents said they put the most importance on visual factors when purchasing products.
- Only 5.6% said the physical feel, via the sense of touch, was most important.
- Hearing and smell each drew a mere 0.9%.

Additionally, when asked to approximate the importance of color when buying products, 84.7% of total respondents said color accounts for more than half of their reason for choosing a product.

The effects of color differ among different cultures, so the attitudes and preferences of your target audience should be a consideration when you think about your brand design. People have specific thoughts and feelings about different colors, so using colors strategically in your branding can have an important impact on how your audience perceives your brand.

Here are some general associations with common colors from a Western culture point of view:

- **Red:** the color of passion, excitement, strength, and speed. It's a perfect choice if your brand identity is loud, bold, youthful, and exciting.
- **Blue:** the most universally appealing color in the spectrum. Blue can help your branding appear more stable and trustworthy. If you want your target audience to trust you, blue is a great color because it represents reliability, belonging, and coolness.
- **Yellow:** represents warmth, sunshine, cheer, and happiness. The cheerful vibe makes it a good choice if you want to feel fun, accessible, and affordable.
- **Orange:** a high-energy color that represents playfulness, warmth, vibrancy, and friendliness. It's used less commonly than red, so it will definitely make your brand stand out.
- **Green:** represents nature, freshness, coolness, growth, and abundance. Culturally, when Americans see green, they normally think of money or nature. If your brand is tied to either of those things, green is an especially good choice.
- **Purple:** the color of royalty, spirituality, dignity, ambition, power, luxury, and peace. If you're going for a luxurious feel in your branding, this a safe bet.
- **Pink:** soft, sweet, nurturing, secure, playful, nice, feminine, and romantic. Pink is culturally tied to femininity. If your brand is targeted to women, pink is a contender for your brand color. It's also a great color for brands with a soft or luxurious identity.

- **White:** represents innocence, goodness, cleanliness, and humility in most cultures. In some parts of the world, it symbolizes sterility and coldness. Some companies, like Adidas, use a white logo on a black background. Many brands that have white as a central color pair it with black or grey.
- **Black:** represents sophistication, elegance, classic, mystery, power, fear, strength, and authority. In contrast, it can also evoke heavy or negative emotions such as sadness and anger. A lot of retailers, such as Chanel and Nike, use black and contrast it with a white background.
- **Grey:** represents neutrality and balance and is a shade between white and black. Grey does carry some negative connotations, particularly when it comes to depression and loss. Its absence of color makes it dull. Apple uses grey in their brand and balances the color with black and white to maintain a clean, neutral look.
- **Brown:** an earthy color. It's the color of the earth, wood, and stone. The color relates to comfort, security, and a down-to-earth nature. The color brown is quickly associated with all things organic.

Market research has determined that color has the unique ability to attract specific types of clients and change buying behavior. Impulse shoppers respond best to red, orange, black, and royal blue. Shoppers who plan ahead of time and stick to their budget respond best to pink, teal, light blue, and navy. It's crucial that your brand colors align with the essence of who your brand is. Choose your colors carefully to ensure they're the right reflection of your business.

Form and Shape

When it comes to brand design, you also want to think about form and shape. These subtle elements can be used to reinforce the desired reaction from the target audience. For example, a logo that's all circles and soft edges will inspire a very different reaction from a logo that's sharp and square. For my brand design, I always lean towards circles and soft-edges because the effect is more feminine.

Let's look at how different forms and shapes can impact your brand design.

- **Round shapes:** Circles, ovals, and ellipses are all about the warm and fuzzies. Brands that incorporate round shapes can create feelings of community, unity, and love. The rounded edges can also be viewed as feminine.
- **Straight-edged shapes:** Squares, rectangles, and triangles make people think of strength and efficiency. These lines create a feeling of stability and trustworthiness. However, if the shapes aren't balanced out with something fun, like dynamic colors, they can feel impersonal and fail to connect with your target audience.
- **Straight lines:** Vertical lines suggest masculinity and strength, while horizontal lines suggest tranquility and mellow vibes.

Great brand visual elements start with foundational building blocks of typography, colors, and form and shape. Let's get down to the nitty-gritty and discuss the visual elements you need to include in your brand design.

Brand Design

All right, all of you controlling, "I can do it myself" business owners. It's probably time for you to loosen the reigns and bring on a designer to create or recreate your brand design. Remember you're not a Jack of all trades, and unless your primary capabilities include graphic design, you need to bring on a professional.

One of the biggest mistakes I've seen many small business owners make when working with a designer is to have no idea about the look and feel they want for their brand. They put all of the power in the designer's hands without providing any real direction. The designer's role is to bring your brand identity to life and translate who you are as a brand into tangible design assets you can use in your marketing. Their job is *not* to create your brand essence; it's up to you to develop your brand design.

I've heard horror stories from clients about their experiences with graphic designers, whether they worked with designers from freelance worker sites, like Fiverr, Upwork, and 99designs, or with an independent freelancer or a design agency. The one thing most of those dissatisfied business owners had in common was an inability to clearly communicate the essence of their brand. I too have had great successes and failures with both the online design sites and design agencies. The key is to establish a brand style guide that clearly outlines your brand identity, typography, colors, and forms and shapes to ensure you and the designer are on the same page about how you want your design to look.

Some of the common visual elements that should be included in your brand design include:

1. Logo
2. Business cards
3. Website
4. Email design
5. Product packaging
6. Social media
7. Print and marketing collateral

Logo. Your logo is the cornerstone in your brand identity. When working with your designer, ensure your logo clearly communicates who you are and what you value as a brand. It should be visually appealing, simple, clean, and uncluttered. Your logo should be classic, not trendy, so you can use it for a long time, and it should be consistent with the industry's standards.

Your logo should make a lasting impression on your target audience and represent your brand well. Once you finalize your logo, make sure your designer delivers it to you in multiple formats, including .png and .jpg, a black-and-white version and color version, and multiple sizes so you always have the logo you need.

Business cards. If you're doing any sort of business development (and who isn't?), you'll want to stock up on business cards. A well-designed card offers the chance to reinforce a positive opinion of yourself in the eyes of potential clients. When it comes to business card design, less is more. Remember to keep it simple. Your business logo on one side of the card and your key personal details on the other side should do the trick. Since just about everything is going digital, you can always create a digital business card on your mobile device. Instead of rummaging through your purse or wallet every time you need a card, have your designer create a digital business card to make it easier to follow up with prospective clients. Long gone will be the stacks and stacks of business cards that start off on your desk and later end up in your drawer, never to see the light of day. There are several apps out there including SnapDat, CamCard, Haystack, and OneCard. Do your research to determine which app is best for you because the apps of today can be non-existent tomorrow.

Website. Your website is one of the most representative aspects of your brand identity. This is especially true if you're running an online business or have a digital product. Your prospective clients will look at your website before deciding whether or not to do business with you, so your brand identity should come through in full force. A website is the most relevant and useful platform to make your business personality known through the design, layout, and content. Your website should tell your brand story. (In the marketing section of this book, I share the exact components your website should include to maximize your sales conversation rates.)

Email design. Email is a great way to engage your clients and increase business. Since most people are on inbox overload, you need to have the right design strategy to make your business stand out from the clutter. First, establish the purpose of your emails. Is it to build a personal connection, or to educate your target audience? Either way, format the email so it's easily readable, and add a few images that are consistent with your overall strategy. If the purpose of your email is to sell a product, include a picture of the product. If the purpose is to build a relationship, have a picture of someone giving a testimonial. Also, make sure you have an email footer with your business logo or a picture of you, whichever is appropriate.

Product packaging. If your product is a physical one, then product packaging is key to attracting the right target audience. Great product packaging design adds value to your clients' experience with your brand and helps to drive both loyalty and repeat purchases.

Social media. Branding your social media graphics matters big time for your business. No matter what social media platforms you're using for your business, you'll want people across all networks to be able to recognize your brand. Branding your social media makes your brand memorable, attracts your target audience, and makes your images shareable. Some tools you can use for your social media graphics include Canva, Photoshop, Adobe Illustrator, PicMonkey, iStock Editor, Word Swag, Snappa, Pablo, Over, and Pixlr. I can personally recommend Canva because I use the program a lot for proposals and graphics. There is a slight learning curve, but when you watch the tutorial videos, it's easy to use.

Print and marketing collateral. It's important to synchronize your online branding efforts with your offline materials, including your logos, letterhead, business cards, envelopes, brochures, signage, newsletter, point of sale materials, and proposals. Your marketing collateral should maintain a consistent brand across all the different channels and mediums. Every touch point your target audience has with you should be representative of your brand.

It's much easier and more cost effective to get your brand design right the first time, when you first start your business, rather than fix it later. However, if you own an established business, you can still rebrand if needed. A rebrand is the creation of a new look and feel for an established product or business. The goal of rebranding is to positively influence a client's perception about a product or service, or the business overall, by revitalizing the brand and making it seem more modern and relevant to the client's needs.

12 Branding Tips to Elevate Your Brand

Here are twelve tips to ensure you stay on track and make the right branding moves to help your business stand out in your industry.

Tip #1. Stay classic. Classic doesn't mean boring. It means not getting caught up in trendy fonts and colors and instead choosing more traditional fonts and colors, such as neutrals and primary colors, that have staying power and will help you develop a brand that lasts. The goal is for your brand to last for decades so you can develop brand recognition.

Tip #2. Match the branding to your business. Let your mission statement and values lead the way. Your brand should align with your business strategy and goals.

Tip #3. Make sure your brand can't be confused with other businesses. When performing your market research, be careful not to take a little bit from competitor A and a little bit from competitor B to develop your brand. Without realizing it, you'll create a brand voice and feel that sounds and looks like theirs. Research, but don't copy. This can be easier said than done. When you inundate yourself with research it's very easy to blur the lines. So make sure you research, step away, and then, come back to brainstorm ideas for your brand identity. Trust me. I have blurred the lines due to information overload and thought something I was saying was an original idea—until someone kindly pointed out that it wasn't. I've also learned my lesson, so I take a break before I act on my research. Consider yourself forewarned. (If you can't tell by now, I'm a research and knowledge junkie and get very excited about new information.)

Tip #4. Ensure it works on multiple platforms. Is your branding, including your logo, going to work in print, on smartphones, on the website, and on promotional items? Your brand imaging needs to have mass appeal and work on multiple platforms.

Tip #5. Stick to no more than two colors. Outside of black and white, only use one or two additional colors. Too many colors can make your design look less professional, and you'll pay a premium price when printers charge by the color (such as T-shirt screening costs). You don't want your brand design to look like a bag of Skittles or Starburst.

Tip #6. Less is more. Less goes a long way with font choices, colors, and length of messaging. Your brand should be minimal, easy to recognize, and clean. When you're designing your brand, you might need to declutter it by reducing the number of colors and fonts that you use.

Tip #7. The name is for life. Your business name, tagline, and other key wording will be with you for life (or a long time if you decide to rebrand). Don't get caught up in trends. Go with something easy to say, spell, design, and remember. Think of it like this: if it's hard for an eight-year-old to say, then go back to the drawing board.

Tip #8. Keep taglines or slogans under seven words. You will hear me use the phrase K.I.S.S. (Keep it Short and Simple) time and time again to reinforce its importance. If you're using a tagline or slogan in your branding, keep it short. Less is more.

Tip #9. Leave plenty of white space. White space is free space when it comes to design. A simple layout, instead of a complex one, is the key to keeping your target audience interested in what you have to say, always with the goal of turning them into clients. Your brand should feel like walking into a newly decorated house. The pillows are fluffed, there's a lot of clean, open space (or white space as they call it in graphic design) and everything has a place.

Tip #10. Steer clear of sharp edges. The lines of your branding should almost always be a little softer and smoother. If you go with sharp lines and edges, your design can look outdated, uninviting, and overly formal.

Tip #11. Choose colors carefully. Color is very important in branding because it directly influences the first impression your target audience develops of you. Colors are more than just a visual aid because colors convey emotions, feelings, and experiences. Do you want your audience to feel excited, passionate, or relaxed and calm? The colors you use will dictate how your target audience feels about your brand.

Tip #12. Include "you" in the brand. Let your uniqueness shine through your brand. Include your personality, favorite color, or words you would say that resonate with your target audience. You are the one unique thing that your competitor can't duplicate, so use yourself in your brand.

When you are developing your professional brand image, don't go at it alone. Find a reputable graphic design and branding expert to help you create a brand that embodies your uniqueness. Your brand identity will set you apart from your competitors. Take the time to ensure that you accurately portray the essence of who you and your business are through all of your brand efforts.

Yes, it's that time again. Let's take a quick pause for an authentic moment. Years back, I hired a top brand strategist. The first time we met, I went to her plush office, where she served me artesian water with a pH balance of 7.0+, and we sat on her white leather couch. I was almost afraid to put my shoes on her white furry rug, thinking my shoes might leave a stain. The day was completely exhilarating. We talked about the goals for my business, my mission, and my vision, and we discussed my brand positioning. We had salmon and spinach for lunch and topped it off with dessert. I was so excited when I left the office that I was beaming ear to ear. I felt accomplished. We met several more times, and within weeks, she delivered my brand strategy.

I could hardly wait to open my email to see what my new brand was going to be. As I read through this twelve-page document, I noticed something was missing. That something was me. The brand strategy sounded nothing like me. What went wrong? I wasn't clear about who I was, who I wanted to serve, and how I wanted to impact my audience with my business. Take this as a cautionary tale. If you don't do the work to figure out the essence of your brand, someone else will assign you a brand image that could completely derail the trajectory of your business.

Do the work, utilizing **the Brand Strategy Map**:

Discover: You are the brand

Define: Clarify your brand to avoid a split personality

Develop: Your message is heard before you are seen

Design: An image is worth a thousand words

Brand Audit

A brand audit is a process through which you take an honest look at your brand to determine what's working and what's not. You want to make sure your brand message is clear and articulates the personality of your brand. You should perform a brand audit at least once a year. This will help you determine if your brand is consistent across all offline and online platforms.

When performing a brand audit, look at each key area in the brand map (discover, define, develop, and design) to determine which areas need to be tweaked or enhanced.

Four benefits of performing an audit:

1. A brand audit helps you to determine the positioning of your business and to plan corrective strategies if required.
2. It empowers you to discover the strengths and weaknesses of your brand.
3. It guides you to align your offerings more accurately with the expectations of clients.
4. It enables you to get an accurate view of your clients' and prospective clients' perception (positive or negative) of your brand.

SCORE published a comprehensive article about how to perform a successful brand audit. The article lists the ten steps below, to which I've added some of my own summary and explanation:[19]

10 Steps for a Successful Brand Audit

Follow these steps for a successful brand audit.

Step 1. Know what you're measuring.

Review your business's mission, vision, unique serving/selling proposition, positioning, and target audience to clarify your brand identity. Get clear about what you think your brand is before you assess the opinions and perceptions of other people.

Step 2. Assess your external marketing materials.

Are you using your brand colors correctly and consistently? Is your tone of voice consistent? Are your design elements cohesive and consistent across all elements of design? Each marketing piece should emotionally connect with your target audience and motivate them to take your intended action.

Step 3. Review your business website.

If designed correctly your website should be generating money for your business. It's not there just to look pretty. Put it to work. How do you know if your website is effective? You can utilize website analytics to measure web traffic and gather pertinent information to assess and improve the effectiveness of your website. Here are a few questions to ask:

a. Where is your website traffic coming from? It's important to diversify and have traffic coming from multiple sources. If all of your traffic comes from one or two places, your online presence is at risk. What if the social media platform directing traffic to your site changes its algorithm, which happens all the time, or what if a website linking to yours shuts down? Ensure that you have multiple sources from which you generate traffic.

b. Is your website attracting your target audience? Attracting random people who would never buy from you doesn't do you any good. Use analytics from your website and email marketing software to determine your conversion rate and where your traffic is originating.

c. Do you have a high bounce rate? If so, this means visitors don't stay on your website long. You need to change your layout and navigation to improve the user experience. What's your conversion rate? Is it increasing or decreasing? Your conversion rate is the percentage of visitors to your website that complete a desired goal, whether that's to opt-in to a newsletter, schedule a free consultation, or download a coupon.

Step 4. Review your social media data.

You don't have the luxury of just posting to be posting. All of your business engagement on social media should be purposeful. Determine what type of people are engaging with your brand, and listen to what they're saying. Is it negative or positive? Is it your target audience? Reviewing your social media data will help you to determine how to modify your online engagement.

Step 5. Survey your clients.

Paying attention to the voice of your customer is important. You can get feedback in various ways, including focus groups, social media polls, and phone, email or online surveys. You want to get inside of their head by asking questions like:

a. What word or words would you use to describe our brand?

b. What problem does our business solve?

c. How do you feel when you interact with our business?

d. Would you recommend our business to your friends and family? If so, why? If not, why not?

e. When you see our business logo what do you think of? How would you describe our customer service? How can we improve the customer service experience for you?

Step 6. Survey potential clients in your target audience.

Once you understand what your existing clients think about you, dig a little deeper to survey prospective clients.

a. Have you ever heard of our business?
b. Have you ever worked with our business?
c. What do you know about our business?
d. How would you describe our business to others?
e. What problem does this business solve for you?
f. How does our business make you feel?

Step 7. Survey your employees and vendors.

Your employees and vendors help to create the client experience that's vital to your brand and business. If your team members or vendors don't understand your brand, they can't convey it to others properly. Use anonymous surveys to ask your employees or vendors some or all of the following questions

a. How would you describe our brand?
b. What is our business vision?
c. What problem does our business solve for clients?
d. How do you deliver on our brand's promise?
e. What keeps you from delivering on that promise to the best of your ability?
f. What one thing would you do to improve our brand?

Step 8. Evaluate your competitors' brands.

Looking at your competitors' brand can provide some key insights to help you make your brand stronger. Start with reviewing your competitors' marketing materials, social media presence, websites, and customer service experience. You can also ask clients, members of your target audience, and even your employees the same questions about your competitors' brands as you asked them about yours.

Step 9. Review your results.

Phew! Once you've gathered and documented all of the information, it's time to analyze the results. What aspects of your brand are working? What areas need some fine-tuning? What components have totally missed the mark? Answer these questions, and create an action plan to better align your brand with your business's mission and vision.

Step 10. Monitor your progress.

Your work doesn't stop with the brand audit. That's the easy part. Once you've updated your brand, periodically review your results. It's imperative that you perform a brand audit every year or two. This will ensure that you're in tune with what your target audience needs and wants. It will also help you keep your brand fresh.

Investing in Your Brand

According to Steve Forbes, editor-in-chief of *Forbes* magazine, "Your brand is the single most important investment you can make in your business." The strongest and most enduring brands result from proper alignment of brand strategies with client requirements. Maintaining a strong brand allows you to:

- Attract your target audience.
- Charge premium prices.

- Attract top talent.
- Set standards for daily operational performance.

Attract your target audience. One of the greatest benefits of having a well-executed and distinguishable brand is attracting your target audience more easily through increased lead generation and closing more sales. A well-defined brand also has a higher rate of satisfied clients who make referrals because your brand is consistent, concise, and credible.

Charge premium prices. In their book *Professional Services Marketing,* Mike Schultz and John Doerr, state that brand leaders in a specific niche can command a higher fee than competitors. On average, that premium is 32%.[20] More money, more money, more money.

Attract top talent. Everyone wants to play on a winning team. An effective brand targets the right kind of employees with messages that speak to their unique needs and desires. An effective brand communicates your business vision, values, and culture so potential employees can decide if your business is a good fit for them.

Set standards for daily operational performance. Your brand helps management understand what level of service and expertise is required to maintain your competitive advantage, fulfill your brand promise, and live up to your business values.

Often, small business owners are so busy managing their executive team or spearheading innovative product launches that they don't have the time, patience, or energy to monitor changing market conditions, new competitors, changing client tastes, disruptive technologies, and other factors that alter the dynamics of their industry. That means in five to ten years any business can find itself out of sync with the marketplace and struggling to stay relevant and compete. Maintaining a strong brand offers a solution to staying cutting-edge and ensuring that you are emotionally connecting with your target audience.

From the Desk of the Decision-Maker

Stephanie Hampton-Best

Vendor Diversity Manager, Corporate Procurement

Synovus Bank

KNOW YOUR BUSINESS. Small businesses just want to get a foot in the door, but I often tell business owners you can't try to be a Jack of all trades. Know your core competencies and deliver on what you do best. Do what you do, and do it very well! Often, if you say you do everything, the company with which you're looking to do work won't know where they can use you. It's too confusing, and then they may not use you at all because you're relying on them to figure out what you can do. Usually, they don't have the time.

KNOW YOUR CAPACITY. When you know your core competencies, you have a better understanding of the projects and opportunities you can go after. Corporations want to know you can handle the opportunity. There is nothing worse than getting the opportunity, and then not being able to deliver. Every opportunity may not be for you. Sometimes, it's better to walk away and identify another more suitable opportunity.

KNOW WHERE YOU STAND. Change is constant, and being a supplier today doesn't mean you'll be a supplier tomorrow. It's important for any business, but particularly for small businesses, to stay abreast of how you're performing after you're awarded the contract. If it's not a standard practice with the company that awarded you the contract, ask to set up a quarterly or a biannual review. This is not only to see how you're doing, but it also gives you the opportunity to gather insights and ask questions about what might be going on with the company. Then, you can identify any potential upcoming opportunities. With regular review, you may realize that you can provide additional services that the company isn't yet aware of, making it a win-win situation.

KNOW THE INDUSTRY. Sourcing and procurement professionals are busy, and things are constantly changing. Sometimes budgets are tight, and decision-makers can't attend the latest and greatest conferences. Be a valuable resource, and share new and innovative information about what's happening in the industry. You can be seen not only as a valuable resource but also as a subject-matter expert. Valuable information is always needed!

KNOW YOUR FINANCES. I always tell people, when they go into business, as elementary as this may sound, to be sure to get an accountant and a lawyer. This is especially important early on, as you begin your business. These professionals will give you advice and guidance. As you grow, they'll get to know your business and become a resource for continued growth. Although finance may not be your strong suit, as a business owner, you need to know and understand the numbers. Don't be afraid to take a finance class. Accountants are good, but as a business owner, you need to be knowledgeable so you can make sound decisions regarding your business.

KNOW YOUR PARTNERSHIPS. Sometimes opportunities are presented when your capacity is limited. That' a great time to form new partnerships or joint ventures to go after projects together. Sometimes it's necessary. However, as much as joint ventures can be mutually beneficial, they also have risks. Do your due diligence when forming a partnership. The joint venture and/or partnership should be seamless. I'm reminded of the phrase "One band, one sound." Make sure it's the right fit. Don't be afraid to walk away or say no if it isn't the right opportunity.

“The best marketing doesn't feel like marketing.”

— Tom Fishburne

CHAPTER FOUR

Marketing

THE ZEN MARKETING ZONE

01

7 Ps of Marketing

- Product
- Price
- Promotion
- Place
- Positioning
- Packaging
- People

02

Zealous Marketing Goals

- Increase revenue
- Brand awareness
- Product or service launch
- Market share growth

03

Evergreen Promotion Strategies

- Inbound vs. outbound marketing
- Digital media strategy
- Website
- Social media
- Customer journey

04

Nimble Marketing Plan

- Common marketing mistakes
- 8 steps to an effective marketing plan
- Marketing automation
- Marketing KPIs

The Zen Marketing Zone

WHEN YOU ARE IN A ZEN STATE, how do you feel? Peaceful, relaxed, and calm are words that probably come to mind. So many business owners go into a state totally opposite of zen when they think of marketing or sales. Their shoulders tense up, and a sense of confusion and dread comes over them. The Zen Marketing Zone is that space where you have clearly identified the unique value your product or service offers and clients are attracted to you instead of you having to hunt them down to work with you. In essence, you are in your marketing flow. You don't feel like a sleazy salesperson; you feel empowered because you're solving your clients' most pressing problems and making their lives a whole lot easier. I know what you're thinking. You want to enter The Zen Marketing Zone but don't know how. Bear with me for a moment.

There are so many new marketing platforms, and social media is constantly changing, so how do you keep up? Businesses that are successful at marketing have a basic understanding of psychology and human behavior. People buy things to satisfy their wants and desires or to meet a need. As a marketer (and yes, if you own a business, you are a marketer), it's important to look at not just what your product or service offers, but also at what motivates your ideal client to buy your product or service. For example, women don't just buy perfume because of the aroma. They're buying romance, love, and fantasy. The new elliptical exercise machine doesn't sell because of the latest features, but because your prospective client is buying a healthier, thinner, or more toned look.

Your marketing should emotionally connect to your audience and address how your product or service will make them feel, look, or act. Keep the clients' motivations in mind when planning your marketing campaigns. There's also a psychological aspect to establishing trust and forming a relationship. Most ideal clients have been burned, treated badly, or disappointed at least once by a product or service. They won't necessarily jump at the opportunity to buy something from you unless they have a sense of confidence in you and your business.

Just like your potential clients, you and I are tired of receiving spam and a surplus of marketing materials. With that being said, your target audience has probably become savvy and somewhat cynical. Only a business with a strong proven reputation will gain their trust, so you want to build a level of trust with a quality product and exceptional service. Both of these should always be reflected in your marketing. Equally as important, to establish and maintain your credibility, your marketing should be authentic, transparent, and consistent.

Let's talk about the practicality of marketing. If it's simply inconvenient for your target audience to purchase from you, or your product or service doesn't satisfy their needs or desires, then don't attempt to fit a square peg into a round hole. Too many businesses lose sales by trying to force people to buy their products or services. This only results in a loss of trust with your prospective client and could potentially end any chance for a future relationship.

Stick to what you're good at, and play to your strengths. Don't try to be everything to everybody. Be genuine about what you can do, and don't over-promise. In the end, you want to sell your prospective clients by gaining their trust and building a relationship based on client satisfaction, mutual respect, and honesty.

Look Before You Leap: The 7 Ps of Marketing

As you may have heard before, "Marketing is putting the right product or service in the right place, at the right price, at the right time." Though this sounds like an easy thing to do, a lot of hard work and research goes into bringing this formula to fruition. Even if one itsy-bitsy element is off the mark, a promising product or service can fail completely and end up costing the business substantially, even to the point of closing or bankruptcy.

Most marketing consultants will tell you that there are 4 Ps of marketing, also referred to as the marketing mix. However, Brian Tracy and Mark Thompson discuss 7 Ps of marketing in their phenomenal book, *Now, Build A Great Business.* I find that list more useful. Here are the 7 Ps of marketing:

1. Product
2. Price
3. Promotion
4. Place
5. Positioning
6. Packaging
7. People

Product. What product or service does your business provide? Be objective as you determine whether or not your current products or services are the best fit for the needs of your target audience. Often, you're so close to your business that you can't look at it from the viewpoint of your prospective client. If you find that your sales team or you are having difficulty selling as much of your products or services as you'd like, honestly assess if your products and services are adequately meeting the needs of your prospective clients. Compared to your competitors, is your product or service superior, in some significant way, to anything else available? If the answer is no, make tweaks until you find the right product and service offerings.

Price. What does your client perceive the value of your product or service to be? Your prospective clients will compare the price with their perceived value of your product or service. If a product or service is priced higher or lower than its perceived value, it won't sell. Does your client accurately perceive the value of your product and service? If not, determine the gap—whether it's your branding, marketing strategy, quality, or customer service—and then close it.

Promotion. How are you going to put your message on surround sound so everybody hears about your business? There are almost limitless promotional strategies you can use, including social media, SEO, advertising, sales promotions, special offers, and public relations. Research to determine which promotional vehicles will resonate most with your target audience. You want to cast a small net to capture your target audience rather than a wide net thrown at anyone who has a credit card or access to a business checkbook. Stay focused!

Place. Is it easy for your target audience to buy from you? Does your prospective client want to purchase from you online, come to your retail store, work with your salesperson, or meet you at a tradeshow? Learn the buying behaviors of your target audience, and then offer your products and services in the exact place where they want to buy from you. Remember a confused mind will *not* buy. So if your marketing message or your place of business is confusing, your prospective client will keep on moving. (For all of you old-school, Soul II Soul fans, I'm singing "Keep on Moving" to reiterate the importance of having the right location so you prospective clients will stay and buy.)

Positioning. Branding takes up a lot of real estate in this book because it's very important to the success of your business. Do your prospective clients get a warm and fuzzy feeling when they think about you, or do they see you as just another business trying to sell them something? Your positioning is how your prospective clients feel about you in their hearts and minds. What three words pop into your clients' minds when they hear your business name? Is it service, excellence, and quality? Or is it over-priced, under-delivered, and late? Your positioning in the market is defined by the specific words people use to describe you and your offerings.

Packaging. Are your products and services wrapped in a shiny red bow? (I mean this figuratively, not literally.) Every visual element of your product or service should be consistent with the brand image you want to portray. People make decisions about you and your business within the first thirty seconds of interacting with you. Are you making a good impression? Small improvements in the packaging or external appearance of your product or service can often lead to completely different reactions from your clients.

People. An empire is not built by one person, but by a team. Your business will grow in direct proportion with the quality of your team. If you have a skilled team that's working on one accord and following your business strategy, watch out. Your business is about to be on fire. Conversely, if you're working with team members who want to do their own thing without considering what's in the best interest of your business, chaos is about to erupt. Your ability to select, recruit, hire, and retain the proper people, with the skills and abilities to do the job you need to have done, is more important than everything else put together in your business. You can have the most amazing strategy, but if you don't have the right people to execute it, failure is right around the corner.

As you analyze and plan your marketing mix, take time to ensure you effectively incorporate all 7 Ps of marketing in your strategy. Doing so now will save you a lot of headaches and money in the end. Planning is half the battle, and the other half is execution. Learn how to do both equally well.

It's time to develop your marketing machine. Marketing is both an art and a science, and it takes a mix of strategy and intuition. I'm going to show you three key elements for developing and executing your bomb marketing strategy utilizing The Zen Marketing Zone. Let's get it!

- **Z**ealous Marketing Goals
- **E**vergreen Promotional Strategies
- **N**imble Marketing Plan

Zealous Marketing Goals

Are We There Yet? Do you remember that movie, starring Ice Cube and Nia Long? The kids kept asking Ice Cube's character, "Are we there yet?" because they wanted to know when they would arrive at their destination and get to see their mother. This question is also incredibly relevant in terms of marketing because if you don't know where you're going, how will you know when you get there? If you don't know what you want to accomplish, how can you determine if your marketing efforts are effective?

Marketing goals define the results you want to achieve with your marketing. Your marketing goals should fit into and support your overall business goals. As with all goals, they should be measurable, specific, and realistic. Your goals are the fundamental building blocks of a well-crafted marketing strategy.

Marketing goals will vary based on the business. Here are some common goals:

- Increase annual sales revenue.
- Expand brand awareness.
- Grow market share.
- Launch new products or services.
- Get the desired ROI on advertising expenditures.
- Use public relations to secure local media coverage.
- Increase the number of new accounts or relationships.
- Increase sales conversion rates.
- Increase customer satisfaction.
- Rebrand or reposition.
- Increase website traffic.

Each of the above goals will need a measurable percent change and a date by which it will be achieved. You might read the list and think all the goals apply to your marketing and should become part of your marketing plan. Although this attitude is courageous, it's not realistic. To do marketing well, your efforts must be focused and measurable. The right number of goals is the number that offers you a reasonably high probability of success over a given time. Success has to be defined by you and your team and be consistent with your overall business strategy.

I want more website visitors, leads, and sales. I want to close more corporate contracts. I want to rank number one in a Google search. These are poorly defined marketing goals. If you want to increase leads, that's a start, but how many leads do you want to generate, fifty, five hundred, or five thousand? Who do you want to close contracts with—Delta Air Lines, Coca-Cola, IBM, Johnson & Johnson, Microsoft? For what search terms do you want to rank number one on Google?

Now, let's take the same goals listed above and turn them into well-defined goals aligned with an overall business strategy.

We need 15,000 visitors, 750 leads, and 10 customers from our marketing launch, within the next twelve months, to achieve our revenue goal of $500,000.

We plan to close training contracts with Johnson & Johnson, Microsoft, and IBM, by the fourth quarter of this year.

In six months, we want to rank number one for the keyword term "business consultant," since we estimate that will generate three hundred visitors to our website per month.

Do you see the difference in the goals? The second set of goals are specific and measurable. At the end of the twelve-month, fourth-quarter, or six-month period, you can evaluate your progress to determine if you've achieved your goals.

Your marketing goals won't be perfect and will evolve over time. Build your marketing strategy around these goals, and measure your progress toward the goal every month or every quarter to see if you're on target. Adjust your goals as needed, and stay current on new marketing trends and best practices to ensure your marketing plan is viable.

Can You Hear Me Now? Evergreen Marketing Strategies

What exactly does evergreen mean? If you're into gardening, you might think it has something to do with leaves or trees. However, in marketing, the term describes systems and processes that are sustainable and can be repeated over and over again. In short, think "rinse and repeat" marketing strategies. Marketing is constantly changing. However, you can create elements of your marketing strategies that can be easily executed the same way every time (with a few tweaks). That way, you can set up the process once and adjust as needed. This is very helpful because it helps you to identify gaps, monitor your progress, and determine when marketing strategies need to be adjusted.

Once you understand your goals, it's time to identify which marketing strategies or vehicles you will use to help you achieve your desired results. Here are some promotional strategies to consider:

- Digital media (social media, SEO, Google, etc.)
- Website that converts visitors to customers
- Content marketing
- Networking
- Direct marketing (sales letters, brochures, flyers, etc.)
- Advertising (TV, print media, directories, etc.)
- Training programs (to increase awareness)
- Blog posts
- A role as a contributing editor
- Direct selling
- Publicity or press releases
- Trade shows
- Channel partners, affiliates, strategic partners
- Customer loyalty programs
- Word of mouth
- Cause-related marketing (links the services and products of a business to a social cause or issue)

Inbound Marketing vs. Outbound Marketing

Inbound marketing is a method of attracting prospects to your business's products or services through the creation of related content and incentives. The content should emotionally connect with prospects and inspire them to identify themselves and take action to request more information or make a purchase.

Inbound marketing closely aligns with content marketing. Content marketing is a strategic marketing approach that creates and consistently distributes relevant content to attract and retain your target audience. The ultimate goal is to drive your prospect to action. In content marketing, you should tell powerful stories, be honest and open, show your brand personality, and use visual imaging. Valuable content should be at the core of your marketing.

With inbound marketing, instead of pitching your products or services, you are providing truly relevant and useful content to your prospects and clients to help them solve their problems. An inbound marketing strategy is both cost-effective and user-friendly and fits well within most small business marketing plans.

Types of inbound marketing include:

- Social media marketing
- Content marketing
- Search engine optimization (SEO)
- Blogging or Vlogging (a video blog)
- Ebooks
- Google AdWords
- Pay per click (PPC)

Traditional marketing, also referred to as outbound marketing, is becoming less and less effective. An outbound marketing strategy requires your team to actively pursue prospects who may be interested in what your business has to offer.

Examples of outbound marketing include:

- Cold calling
- Direct mail campaigns, like postcards or brochures
- Cold emails (spam)
- Interruptive ads
- Door-to-door canvassing of residential and business properties

Brian Halligan, co-founder of HubSpot, a marketing and customer relationship management (CRM) software company, coined the phrase "inbound marketing" and pioneered the concept. HubSpot is the world's number one inbound marketing software. The original methodology of inbound marketing has three phases: attract, delight, and engage. Savvy marketers have expanded the concept to include four phases:

1. Attract
2. Convert
3. Close
4. Delight

Attract (prospects). Attracting prospects is the first step in inbound marketing. At this initial marketing stage, a prospect stumbles across your value-added content by seeing a social media ad, performing an Internet search, or clicking on a link in a blog, website, or press release. The prospect is now aware of your product or service and, based on the value that you offer in your content, will make a decision to take action (sign up for a newsletter, schedule a complimentary consultation, download a coupon, etc.) or not.

Convert (visitors). Once the right visitors have been attracted to your website, the goal is to convert them into leads by obtaining their contact information through an opt-in form on your landing page. To convince them to give you this information, you offer the valuable content they need, at that very moment, in exchange for their contact information. The visitors get the information they're looking for, and you get the ability and permission to market to them in the future.

Close (leads). The closing stage is where you transform leads into clients. This is where your evergreen marketing strategies come in play. Prior to executing an inbound marketing strategy, you must take the time to build your marketing infrastructure, whether it's an automated email sequence, lead-nurturing campaign, webinars, demos, free trials, or coupons. This infrastructure is what moves your visitor from subscriber to client or customer. Regardless of the method, test each strategy, modify as needed, and monitor the performance.

Delight (clients and brand advocates). One core element of inbound marketing is to provide amazing value-added content to both your leads and your clients. That means, even after you convert a lead into a client, you must still engage them through valuable content, social media, follow-up emails, surveys, and trigger marketing. The goal of delighting clients is to solve their problems and to turn them into brand advocates or ambassadors of your business. You can accomplish this through excellent customer service, premium content, signature events, and other special promotions for existing clients. Handled properly, the delight phase builds client loyalty so your client will want to keep buying from you in the future. Happy clients will be more likely to promote your business to their colleagues, which will help your business grow.

Inbound marketing is all about the clients. It's a client-centric, not company-centric, approach. All of your marketing efforts should come back to what your prospects want and need. Remember the more problems you solve for your prospect, the easier it is for them to become a client. The more you wow them as a client, the easier it is for them to become a repeat client. The more your client is a repeat customer, the easier it is for them to become a brand advocate. The more brand advocates you have, the more your business grows. This is a marketing cycle you want to regularly employ in your organization.

The Truth about Digital Media

According to HubSpot, 81% of your prospective clients do online research before making a purchase, and 30% of them wouldn't even consider a business that doesn't have a website. The truth is that only 56% of businesses have a website, giving those that do a distinct advantage over those that do not.[21] However, don't be deceived. Just having a website doesn't mean people are going to be knocking down your virtual door. Unless you've invested time and resources to show up on the first page in a Google search or have marketing and promotions that drive visitors to your website, you'll remain the best-kept secret in your industry.

Investing time and money in digital marketing can help you take your business to the next level, but before you go headfirst into digital marketing, you need to understand what it is and what it takes to use it effectively. Digital marketing, also referred to as online marketing, involves marketing your products, services, business, or organization through online channels. This includes search engine optimization (SEO), email marketing, social media marketing, paid advertising, and content marketing.

Digital marketing can be overwhelming if you're not a marketing professional. If you're looking to build a digital strategy for your business, you'll need to identify your goals, target audience, and target platforms (Facebook, Twitter, LinkedIn, etc.). Once you've established your goals for your target market, you'll be better able to determine which channels will work best for your business.

Key Components of a Successful Digital Marketing Strategy

There are a ton of online marketing channels available, so I'm going to focus on seven. The goal of your digital media strategy is to provide valuable content (blogs, videos, ebooks, white papers, social media content, etc.) to attract new clients, keep existing clients engaged, increase loyalty, and strategically close more sales. If you don't have a dedicated marketing person on staff, you may want to consider outsourcing to a reputable business that can effectively analyze your target audience and turn them into clients.

Here are eight components of your digital media strategy:

1. Website
2. Search engine optimization (SEO)
3. Content
4. Social media
5. Paid advertisement
6. Email marketing
7. Public relations
8. Analytics

Website. A website is the most important component of digital marketing. Having a website means your prospects can find you online and learn more about your products or services. The website must be user-friendly and mobile responsive, and the design should be clean, professional, and easy to navigate. I highly recommend that your website have a blog that offers weekly content to keep your prospects coming back to learn from you, which can help make you an industry expert in their eyes.

Search engine optimization (SEO). Most prospects will search for products and services using search engines. If your website isn't search-engine optimized, you probably won't show up within the first three pages of results. According to Junto, 75% percent of users never scroll past the first page of search results, so you're losing potential clients every day[22]. Search engine optimization requires keyword-targeted content with the proper title, heading, subheadings, tags, meta descriptions, and image descriptions. The process can be time-consuming and complex, and often, it's more effective to outsource it to a specialist to help you achieve your goals.

Content. High-quality content that provides huge value to your prospect is an effective marketing strategy. Posting blog posts, videos, white papers, checklist, tutorials, or photos through your website and social media can help you increase brand awareness. It can also lead prospects back to your website, where you can close the deal on a landing page. Regularly posting fresh, optimized content can help you increase traffic to your site and can benefit your website's search engine position.

Social media. There's no doubt about it; social media is an integral part of marketing. It's an effective way to build an online presence, engage your prospects and clients, and listen to what your clients are saying. It allows you to learn in real time the good, bad, and ugly about your product and service offerings and your overall business practices based on the response you get (or don't get) on social media.

There are a ton of social media platforms to choose from, including Facebook, LinkedIn, Instagram, YouTube, Twitter, and Pinterest. You must research to determine which platform your target audience uses to find products and services like yours. As a rule of thumb, select no more than two or three platforms to use for marketing. You don't want to spread yourself too thin. Use social media to market to your niche target audience.

Paid advertisement. Search engine optimization is very time-consuming and requires a bit of patience before you see results. The best way to immediately show up on the first or second page of search results is through paid ads. Google AdWords, for example, allows you to target certain keywords or key phrases and promote to users who search for them. Additionally, you can purchase paid social media ads. Paid ads enable you to expand your content to the right audience at the right time. Ads can be a cost-effective way to increase your brand awareness and reach prospective clients.

Email marketing. Email marketing is a great way to keep in touch with prospects and existing clients. Unlike social media, you own your email list. If something ever happened to Twitter, Facebook, Instagram, or LinkedIn, you would lose your contacts unless you had them stored somewhere else. Having an email list gives you the ability to make contact with your prospects and clients anytime you want, on your own terms. Attract your leads via social media or other marketing vehicles, and then add them to your email list by using an opt-in form. Email is an effective way to promote specials, create a loyalty program, or get client feedback. When done correctly, you can turn a prospect into a sale and a sale into a loyal client through email marketing. Remember to follow proper email etiquette, including not spamming your list or sending emails too frequently.

Public relations (PR). PR has traditionally focused on generating brand awareness, changing public opinion, and dealing with crises, and digital marketing has generally focused on identifying target audiences and ultimately getting them to convert. PR and digital media marketing complement each other when integrated into a full marketing campaign.

One of the biggest differences between digital marketing and PR are the channels each use to achieve their objectives. Since digital marketing is solely within the online sphere, its marketing channels do not include traditional channels. Digital marketing focuses on pay-per-click (PPC) ads, social media, paid social, content marketing, SEO, creative, and web development.

PR is changing to combine a mix of both traditional and digital channels, including online publications, print publications, and social media outlets. Whether you're sharing an online PR placement through social media as a paid ad or working with SEO to secure quality links within online PR placements, there are numerous ways to integrate digital marketing and PR.

Analytics. I love this quote by management consultant Peter Drucker who states, "You can't manage what you can't measure." He means that you can't know whether or not you are successful unless success is defined and tracked. Analytics track your online promotional efforts and comprise one of the greatest assets in digital marketing. You can analyze the effectiveness of a campaign and make adjustments or changes based on the data. All online marketing channels have analytics you can utilize to help you market more effectively.

Other marketing strategies include affiliate marketing, marketing automation, inbound marketing, online PR, webinars, and more.

Make Your Website Print Money

Long gone are the days of your website being a digital brochure for your business. A business website that can compete effectively in today's marketplace has several responsibilities including the following:

- Create visibility.
- Engender trust.
- Educate and entertain.
- Inform.

- Nurture.
- Convert.

Create visibility. Your website should be optimized for search engines to help prospective clients find your business online. One search engine optimization (SEO) strategy is to organize a website's content by topic, which helps search engines like Google match searches to your site. By optimizing a webpage around topics first, you can rank well for keywords related to that topic. There are many other strategies for search engine optimization.

Engender trust. Your website is a key element for building trust. All information should be current, consistent with your brand, and easily accessible. You need to have elements designed to build trust on your homepage. These include logos or testimonials of current clients, case studies, reviews, or accolades. Make them easy to find as soon as a visitor lands on your website. Your brand promise should also be prominently displayed where visitors can easily see it when they come to your website.

Educate and entertain. Your website should educate and entertain your prospective clients. The content and messaging should let them know you recognize their problems and challenges and are there to provide solutions. Having a blog that's regularly updated or a social feed on your home page is a great way to show your business is active and to keep your content fresh. You also want to educate visitors about the products and services you provide.

Inform. Now that your ideal clients have found you and your brand has started to establish trust with them, it's time to start helping them solve their problems. You can achieve this through storytelling. The story is not about you, but the story is about helping your prospect or customer overcome the challenges and problems they're currently facing and don't know how to solve. You have to immediately let your website visitors see that you know what they're struggling with and that you know how to solve it. Let your value proposition shine. Use your story to show how you are unique and distinct from your competition.

Nurture. Let me ask you a question. If you're unfamiliar with a product or service, how much time does it take you to feel comfortable pulling out your debit or credit card to buy? Do you need to be exposed to the product two, three, or four times? Would you be surprised that it takes a website visitor numerous exposures to your product or service before they're ready to buy? Your website should guide your prospect through the buying process in a non-threatening way. It should be designed to make the next steps apparent and easy for the prospect to take. Make it simple to become a client with an easily navigated customer journey. (Throughout this book, I use the word "client" because it represents a relationship, while "customer" tends to refer to a one-time transaction. However, in keeping with the latest marketing lingo, I'll use the phrase "customer journey." In this case, I'm using the words "client" and "customer" interchangeably.)

Convert. Conversion opportunities should be a part of the customer journey on your website. You'll hear many people say you need to have an opt-in opportunity on your home page or create a landing page for your opt-in form. In either case, an opt-in is a way to get consent from visitors to contact them with further information. With their permission, you are, in essence, putting them in your sales funnel and adding them to your email list. You draw visitors to your opt-in form with an offer of a gift and tell them what to do with a call to action (CTA). A CTA will guide them to the next step you want them to take—to give you their contact information in exchange for a gift of some sort.

Here are a few ideas for effective opt-in gifts:

- Worksheets or checklists
- Mini ebook
- Infographic
- Challenge
- Quiz or assessment
- Video training or tutorial
- Email series
- Resource guide
- Webinars
- Podcasts
- Bonus interviews
- Audio file or audio transcript
- Mini e-course
- Swipe files
- Cheat sheet
- Behind-the-scenes content
- Free workshop
- Live calls
- Free trial or discount code
- Access to a private Facebook group

Your website homepage is often a prospect's first impression of your business. You can make a very good first impression, or things can go really wrong really fast. Your homepage should be visually appealing and easy to navigate. If visitors can't find what they're looking for, they will get frustrated and leave. Don't try to cram everything above the fold (positioned in the upper part of a web page and visible without scrolling down the page). Break the information up so it's easy to find. Limit your navigation menu bar to four to six options. A good rule of thumb is to have your navigation located in the header at the top of every page. Horizontal, top-level navigation is a web-design standard. Search bars are essential, especially for sites with lots of content.

Many businesses feature video on the homepage so prospects can get a real sense of who the owners and leadership are and what they stand for. Through video, visitors can hear your story, feel your energy, and connect with you. This is a great way to engage your audience and begin to establish a trusting relationship with them.

In today's world, prospective clients start their customer journey by researching your business online. Long before you even realize you are being looked at, people are coming to conclusions on their own as to whether or not they're interested in buying from you. Make sure you have a web presence that encompasses all of the necessary elements for an effective website.

Your website should have the following design elements:

- mobile friendly
- easy to navigate
- fast load time
- brand identity design (colors, fonts, images, graphics)
- opt-in opportunity with call to action
- SEO optimized/analytics
- brand promise/value proposition

Your website navigation bar should link to the following:

- "About Us" page (your brand story)
- current content page (blogs, video, social media feeds)

- products and/or services page
- clients/reviews/testimonials page (optional)
- contact/customer support page

Being Social with a Purpose: Social Media

Social media changes rapidly. There are always new platforms and algorithms being added or changed. Imagine spending as little as seven hours a week to increase your business's brand recognition, traffic, and sales with little to no cost. According to Blue Fountain Media, about 90% of marketers claimed that social media generated immense exposure for their business.[23] Most small businesses should utilize social networks as part of their integrated marketing plan to enhance brand awareness and increase customer engagement. Even if your clients don't come directly from social media, you can establish a sound business reputation and position yourself as an expert with social media.

It can be tricky to determine which platforms are best for your business. According to Social Media Examiner, about 96% of marketers are currently participating in social media marketing, but 85% of participants aren't sure which tools are the best to use.[24]

Social Media Examiner lists these ten reasons why you should use social media to market your business[25]:

1. Increase brand awareness.
2. Drive more inbound traffic.
3. Improve search engine rankings.
4. Increase conversion rates.
5. Improve client satisfaction.
6. Enhance brand loyalty.
7. Establish brand authority.

8. Manage marketing costs.
9. Gain marketplace insights.
10. Position yourself as an industry or thought leader.

Increase brand awareness. Social media is one of the most cost-effective digital marketing methods you can use to distribute content and increase your business's visibility. A well-thought-out social media plan can increase your brand recognition with targeted engagement. Engagement should be targeted because you don't want to be on social media without a strategy. You must have the right message, at the right time, on the right platform for it to be effective. You can also involve your entire team, business partners, and even family in your social media efforts by asking them to like, share, and comment on your posts to increase engagement.

Drive more inbound traffic. How do you connect with your target audience? The easiest way is to increase your inbound traffic. Utilize valuable content on social media to drive your target audience to your website or a landing page through various sources including ads, guest blog posts, and your original social media posts.

Improve search engine rankings. Posting on social media can increase your website traffic; however, search engine optimization is very important for achieving higher page rankings. Being able to rank in the top positions for your keywords will increase your website traffic and continue to generate positive results for your business.

Increase conversion rates. The goal is not just to have a bunch of people coming to your website and social media profiles. The goal is conversion, which simply means turning window shoppers (as I like to call prospects) into buyers. Every blog post, image, or video needs to be authentic to your brand, provide value, and ultimately lead the prospect to take action.

Improve client satisfaction. Creating a voice through social media is important in humanizing your business. Clients appreciate knowing that, when they post comments on your pages, they'll receive a personalized response rather than an automated message. Acknowledging each comment shows you're attentive to your followers' needs and aim to provide the best possible experience.

Enhance brand loyalty. Developing loyal clients is important to any business. Considering that client satisfaction and brand loyalty typically go hand in hand, it's important to regularly engage with your clients and develop an emotional bond or connection with them. Social media isn't just a one-sided relationship, in which you market and promote your product or service. It's about building a relationship in which prospects and clients can also communicate directly with you.

Establish brand authority. Client satisfaction and brand loyalty both play a part in making your business a leader in your industry. When prospects see your business posting on social media, replying to clients, and posting valuable content, it makes you appear more credible. Regularly interacting with clients demonstrates that your business cares about client satisfaction. Satisfied clients are eager to spread the word about a great product or service, and they often turn to social media to express their opinions.

Manage marketing costs. I haven't yet encountered a small business, regardless of size, with an unlimited marketing budget. I've worked with start-up clients and clients who have $150 million in revenue, and they all had a cap on their marketing budget. Since you likely find yourself in the same position, it's important to utilize marketing vehicles that are efficient and give you the best bang for your buck. Social media marketing, if used correctly, can help you maximize your marketing budget to increase brand awareness and drive potential customers to your business, and compared to other marketing tactics it has a relatively low financial investment.

Gain marketplace insights. It's important that you hear the voice of your customers. What are the thoughts, desires, and needs of your prospects? One way to find out is to talk directly to your customers via social media via polls, surveys, forums, and targeted engagement. You can monitor the activity on your profiles and uncover prospects' interests and opinions that you might not otherwise be aware of. Using social media as a research tool can provide information that will aid you in understanding your industry and target audience.

Many social media strategies fail because businesses market on the wrong platforms or with out-of-date strategies. Social media changes all the time, and staying on top of the new channels, trends, and current best practices takes a lot of time and dedication. With your to-do list getting longer and your days getting shorter, time is a very precious commodity. If you don't have time for social media, hiring a digital media strategist to help you determine which social media platform your business should use may be a wise investment.

Here are three questions you need to ask yourself before going full steam ahead on social media:

1. Do we sell B2C (business-to-consumer), B2B (business-to-business), or both?
2. Who's our target audience?
3. What's our overall goal?

The answers to those questions will make it easier to narrow down two to three social media platforms where you'll dedicate your time and efforts. Unless you have a large team managing your social media marketing, don't try to be on too many platforms at one time. They each take time and a separate strategy. You won't see results unless you put in the work.

Social Media Platforms Summary

	FACEBOOK	TWITTER	PINTEREST
Demographics	25–55+ men and women	18-49 men and women	18-45 mostly women
Purpose	Building relationships	News and articles	Scrapbooking
Best For	B2C, in some cases, B2B Building brand loyalty	B2B Public relations	B2C Products and services with a female-focused target

	YOUTUBE	LINKEDIN	INSTAGRAM
Demographics	All ages	25–45 men and women	18-35 mostly women
Purpose	Search "how to"	News and articles	Building relationships
Best For	B2C and B2B Brand aware-ness, service industry	B2B, Business development	Lead generation, retail, art, food, entertainment, beauty

Where Your Clients Are: Customer Journey

Do you know all the paths your prospects have taken to become your customers? Did they meet you on LinkedIn, see an ad on Facebook, like an article on Twitter, receive a referral from a business colleague, or did you meet them at a tradeshow and have them fill out a form? In order to monitor your marketing dollars, it's imperative that you know your customer's journey to determine if the marketing platforms you're investing in are working. You can track this process by developing a customer journey map which tells the story of a customer's experiences from initial contact all the way up to customer service. This gives you great insight into any gaps in the process and also helps you to identify your prospects' pain points. Ultimately, it helps you to understand what goals your customers want to achieve and what expectations they have of your business.

The first step in creating a customer journey map is understanding who your customers are. To best understand your customers, you need to develop buyer personas. A persona is a description of a fictitious customer, with all of their demographics and psychographics, to represent your average client. Having a clear persona reminds you to direct every aspect of your customer journey map towards your customer. If you've been doing the exercises as you read through this book, go back to your branding notes and grab your buyer personas. If not, take some time to create them now.

You want to get into your buyers' heads to understand how they behave, what they like or dislike, and the motivation behind why they buy. Buyer personas provide guidance and input for the journey-mapping process. You should create a separate buyer persona for each type of customer you have. Since people interact with your business differently throughout the buyer's journey, you should distinguish between a window shopper, who will be researching for several months, and an active buyer, who's ready to purchase immediately.

One of the most effective ways to conceptualize your buyer personas is to give each buyer a name and description such as Techie Tina, or Micro-Manager Bob. This will help you to personalize each buyer and speak directly to them in all of your marketing messaging. It's also helpful to find a picture of a real person to represent the persona. Keep that photo in front of you to stay focused on your buyer and write more personalized content.

Once you create your buyer persona, make a list of all of your business's touchpoints. These are all the places your prospects can interact with you, including your website, social media, paid ads, email marketing, and third-party reviews. This is an important step in creating a customer journey map because it gives you insight into what actions your prospects are performing. If they're using fewer touchpoints than expected, maybe they're leaving your website prematurely because they aren't finding valuable content. If they are using more touchpoints, maybe your website is complicated and requires them to go through several steps to get to an end goal. Whatever the case may be, understanding the touchpoints will help you understand the ease and objectives of the customer journey so you can improve the experience with your business and any understand roadblocks that are preventing prospects from becoming customers.

Next, develop your customer journey map by visualizing the actions, thoughts, and emotions your prospects and customers currently experience while interacting with your business. The whole exercise of mapping the customer journey remains theory until you try it out yourself. For each of your personas, follow the journey they take.

After you've created your map, it's important for you to analyze the results. How many people are visiting your website but then clicking away before making a purchase? How can you better support customers? Analyzing the results can show you where customer needs are going unmet. Make the necessary changes to provide an amazing experience to your customers.

The Money's in the Nimble Marketing Plan

Let's tie up the subject of marketing with a nice little bow. What do you think would happen if you decided to go on a road trip but didn't have a clear destination or a map to get you there? You'd probably get lost, right? Or you would end up somewhere, but probably not where you want to be. Your marketing plan is your road map. It's the best way to ensure your business will end up where you want it to be.

I often compare marketing without a plan to grocery shopping without a list. If you've ever done this, you know what happens, especially if you also shop while you're hungry. You spend twice as much money and time as you should, and you come home with all kinds of stuff you really don't need or buy things you already have. Operating your business without a marketing plan is sort of like that too. You very often spend twice as much money and waste time on marketing activities that don't yield your desired results.

When you're creating your nimble marketing plan, be very strategic about utilizing marketing vehicles that will drive your ship in the direction in which you want it to go. This will help you stretch your marketing dollars to get the most bang for your buck and attract your target audience. The main challenge for anyone who wants to build a profitable business is a failure to have a platform with an active and engaged audience of people who want to buy your products and services. It's very difficult to make money when no one knows who you are! Your marketing plan should make sure you don't fall into that trap.

Your ideal clients are always thinking, "What's in it for me?" If you're not answering that question, it's possible they'll pass right by your offers. Since words are extremely powerful in convincing your target audience to buy your products or services, you must use powerful words that create an emotional connection and make a positive impression. When you carefully create your marketing message, you can attract the attention you desire and motivate your ideal clients to take action to become prospects and then paying clients. You motivate your target audience by solving a specific problem. The bottom line is most times your marketing messages are not resonating with them because you're not offering them a solution.

I've done quite a bit of research on why people buy. There are both logical and emotional reasons why consumers or businesses pull out their credit cards or cash to make a purchase.

Here are the top ten reasons why people buy:

1. Make money
2. Save money
3. Save time
4. Avoid effort
5. Get more confidence
6. Become more organized and time efficient
7. Improve their health
8. Escape physical pain
9. Attract praise and recognition
10. Increase influence

More often than not, the reason why your customer buys from you is because you are addressing one or more of those desires. It's imperative that you utilize messaging in your marketing that shows them exactly how you do this. As you read through the list of common marketing mistakes, evaluate how many of the mistakes you're currently making in your business.

Mistake#1. Your business name and tagline don't clearly communicate what you do.

Mistake #2. You have no idea who your target audience is, and you're marketing to the wrong people.

Mistake #3. You're stuck in "copy-cat syndrome," imitating what your competitors are doing instead of finding your unique voice.

Mistake #4. Your marketing messages are way too long and boring.

Mistake #5. Your marketing doesn't include key elements, such as your personal story, benefits, and results clients receive from working with you.

Mistake #6. Your marketing doesn't explain in a clear, concise, compelling manner what you do.

Mistake #7. Your marketing doesn't emotionally connect with your ideal client.

Mistake #8. Your business brand and marketing materials don't have a consistent look (colors, look and feel, quality, graphics, etc.).

Mistake #9. Your website doesn't effectively capture leads.

Mistake #10. You don't have a marketing plan, or if you do, you don't stick with it.

Eight Steps to an Effective Marketing Plan

Your marketing plan is a living and breathing document that needs to be cared for and nurtured. It serves as the foundation for all marketing activities. You should monitor the progress of your plan and make adjustments when needed. Follow the steps to create an effective marketing plan.

Step 1. Conduct market research.

Research the market currently buying the products or services you offer. Look at the market dynamics and your target audience demographics. What do they need most from the product and service offerings in the industry? What affects their buying decisions?

Step 2. Define your target audience.

Determine who and where they are, identify their buying behavior, and identify the qualities they value most in your product or service (e.g., convenience, service, reliability, availability, affordability).

Step 3. Describe your product or service.

How does your product or service relate to the market? What does your market need? What does your market currently use? What does your market need above and beyond what is currently available?

Step 4. Describe your competition.

How do you stand out from your competition? What is unique about your business? Develop your unique serving/selling position (USP).

Step 5. Choose your marketing strategies.

Identify the marketing and promotional strategies you want to use.

Step 6. Set a budget.

Money, money, money. How much can you afford? Most marketing strategies will incur a cost even if it's as simple as purchasing a ticket to attend a networking event. Determine what strategies align with your budget. Which ones can you do in-house, and what do you need to outsource? Here are some guidelines for typical marketing budgets:

Lean plan: 1 - 2% of your annual revenue

Target plan: 3 - 5% of your annual revenue

Stretch plan: 6% or more of your annual revenue

Your budget should include all marketing-related costs, including website design, graphic design, software tools, file management, email marketing, analytics, video marketing, social media, automation, customer relationship management (CRM), networking events, tradeshow fees, and any other items that will contribute to marketing your product or service.

Step 7. Create marketing goals and objectives.

Establish quantifiable marketing goals that you can measure in numbers. For example, your goals might be to close a minimum of five new corporate clients per month, sell three hundred products per week, or increase your income by 30% this year. Your goals might include sales, profits, or customer satisfaction. Whatever your goals are, make sure that you can measure them. Utilize S.M.A.R.T. goals to help you with this process:

Specific: real numbers with real deadlines

Measurable: trackable with qualitative or quantitative measures

Attainable: challenging but possible

Realistic: taking into account any obstacles you must overcome

Time-bound: tied to a deadline

Step 8. Monitor your results.

It's important to monitor your marketing activities to ensure you're achieving your desired results. Analyze your results to see what strategies are working, and modify as needed along the way.

Even an effective plan won't work unless you execute it. Remember that talent and skill alone will only get you so far. You have to plan, execute, analyze, modify, and keep on getting back out there. One of the best ways to leverage your marketing plan is to automate as many of your marketing activities as possible.

Clone Yourself Through Marketing Automation

Wouldn't it be nice just to sit back one day and have your marketing done for you? We've all had those days when we have back-to-back meetings from nine until five and we still have a huge to-do list, which includes sending out a bunch of emails to our prospects and getting new blog posts up. Frankly speaking, there's no way we can ever get it all done. That's where marketing automation comes into play. An effective automated marketing system reflects your priorities, creates processes, generates accountability, and measures effectiveness. Once you're clear on your marketing plan, implement a system that ensures consistency, reliability, and results.

Marketing can often appear complex or overwhelming because many small business owners don't have a marketing system or methodology in place, something they can rinse and repeat, something they develop one time and use over and over again to achieve results. This leads to frustration, implementing ineffective marketing campaigns, wasted time, and losing lots and lots of money, which is never fun.

Marketing automation is simply the use of software to put your marketing efforts on auto-pilot. It saves you a lot of time because you sit down and create your marketing system once, test it, and revise as needed. For the most part, it runs on its own. One of the greatest benefits is that you do the work on the front end and reap a huge harvest on the back end. Automation is like adding four additional employees to your team at no additional cost. It enables your business to play a bigger game in the market and strategically scale without a ton of additional capital.

There are many marketing automation software providers in the marketplace, including HubSpot, Infusionsoft, ActiveCampaign, Ontraport, Salesforce, Constant Contact, MailChimp, and GetResponse. Some of these software applications are geared more towards email marketing, while others have a complete customer relationship management system (CRM), payment processing, sales, and detailed analytical tools. It's important to do your research to determine which software is the best fit and can grow with you over time. You want to select software that aligns with your marketing strategy, has a low learning curve, is easy to integrate, and has amazing customer service and onboarding training.

Once you have your automation system up and running, you have to analyze your marketing to determine whether or not it's effective. (Warning: I'm putting on my corporate hat for a quick minute as I talk about key performance indicators.) In my experience, most small business owners who don't have a corporate background may not be familiar with KPIs (Key Performance Indicators), but you should be. (Just because you start small doesn't mean you'll finish small.) Larger or more conventional corporations understand that KPIs let you know if you're on track to meet your business goals in key areas.

Marketing KPIs are an essential part of tracking your marketing investment. Like other forms of investments in your business, you need to understand where your time and money are going and what you are getting out of it.

Marketing KPIs

Do you have any idea what makes your business marketing efforts successful? Understanding what's working and what's not working in your marketing is an important part of your business's growth strategy. Your marketing KPIs provide insight into the marketing efforts that are working well and the ones that have gone horribly wrong. All of your marketing should be measurable so you can make necessary adjustments along the way. To know if your marketing effort is successful, you have to define your goal or objective and then track it.

As you invest money and time in marketing and sales, you should be able to hit certain benchmarks along the way. If you're not hitting those benchmarks, there's something wrong with a part of the system. You need to review and revise. This is where marketing KPIs come into play. Too often, small business owners wastefully spend money on marketing without any thought about the results they'll achieve. Developing smart KPIs enables you to strategically track the return on investment (ROI) for the money spent on marketing.

Some of your marketing KPIs will overlap with sales KPIs, and the KPIs I share here aren't the only ones you should consider. Select the ones that are useful for you or add new ones. The goal is to choose a few KPIs that paint an accurate picture of how successful your marketing is or isn't so you can make adjustments as needed. If you're using marketing automation software, it provides relevant reports. You can customize the reports to pull the KPIs you want.

Sales growth (KPI). The best way to judge your marketing success is by measuring the growth of sales revenue. Over time, this KPI will help you fine-tune your marketing efforts to only include those that drive sales. You can calculate your sales growth on a monthly, quarterly, or annual basis, or over whatever specified period you desire.

Cost per lead (KPI). Numbers don't lie. More leads yield more sales opportunities (prospects). More sales opportunities yield more sales. The importance of viable leads to marketing and sales is comparable to the importance of gas to a car. There are two types of leads you need to focus on: marketing qualified leads (MQLs) and sales qualified leads (SQLs). The difference is a prospect's readiness to buy.

A **marketing qualified lead** (MQL) is more likely to become a customer because they meet your target audience profile and have initiated engagement with you (downloading an ebook, completing an info card at an event, or interacting with you and giving you their contact information). They have identified themselves as a more deeply engaged, sales-ready contact than other leads. MQLs are typically passed on to sales once they have shown an intent to buy.

A **sales qualified lead** (SQL) is a prospect who has been researched and vetted, first by marketing and then by sales, and is deemed ready for the next stage in the sales process. This prospect has indicated readiness to make a buying decision and needs direct sales follow-up.

Understanding the synergy between MQLs and SQLs will help you understand your lead-to-close ratio (the number of leads you've received over a specific period divided by the actual amount of leads you've closed). Regardless of the size of your business, understanding the quality of your leads is vital to the growth of your business. The more qualified your leads are, the more likely you will close a sale. In many cases, a lot of your marketing and sales efforts should be automated in a sales funnel, using marketing automation software. It's important to ask the right qualifying questions during this process to ensure that you correctly nurture each lead.

Unique website visitors (KPI). For most small businesses, your website is your single most important marketing tool. Understanding how well it's attracting traffic is critical, as is understanding how well it's converting visitors into leads. According to the *State of B2B*

Procurement study from the Acquity Group, 94% of business buyers do some form of online research[26]:

- 77% use Google search.
- 84.3% check business websites.
- 34% visit third-party websites.
- 41% read user reviews.

The study also found that 81% of consumers (B2C) research online before making a purchase. Whether you sell B2B or B2C, your website gives you the opportunity to present prospects with information about your business, capture their interest, and convert them into future clients.

Form conversion rate (KPI). If your traffic is steady or increasing, but your traffic-to-lead-to close ratio is low or decreasing, that's a sign that something is missing on your opt-in pages or forms. It's important to track this number to determine if and when a change in your website text, design, form, or other elements may be needed.

Marketing ROI (return on investment). Return on investment (ROI) is the end game. Calculating your marketing ROI will help you assess your monthly and annual performance. It will also help you create effective marketing strategies and budgets. Make sure you're not continuously increasing your budget for marketing activities that aren't yielding results.

Use the formula below to calculate your marketing ROI:
(Sales Growth – Marketing Investment) /
Marketing Investment = ROI

Customer value (KPI). Lifetime Customer Value (LCV) is a prediction of the net profit attributed to the entire future relationship with a customer. One way to increase the lifetime value of your customers is to implement lead-nurturing campaigns that reach out to existing customers offering discounts, loyalty programs, special incentives, repeat purchase programs, referrals, or value-added content featured weekly on your blogs. The goal is to continue to build a relationship with your customer even after the sale has closed.

Learning how to market your small business can be a beast. It requires knowledge of industry best practices, keeping up with industry trends, creativity, and out-of-the-box thinking. Regardless of the size of your business, you have to invest in marketing. Your marketing budget can start very small and grow as your business grows. By establishing goals for your marketing campaigns, you'll have a better understanding of whether or not your efforts and spending are yielding your desired results.

If you want to increase your brand awareness and attract the target audience you desire, it's imperative that you have a strategic marketing plan and an automated marketing system in place. A solid marketing plan can make the difference between your business making $100,000 or $10 million. Old marketing efforts won't help you become an industry leader. You have to roll up your sleeves and learn the needs of your target audience and how to market to them. Having a nimble marketing plan isn't optional; it's a requirement for your business to be successful.

Your marketing plan is a living, breathing document that must be reviewed at least quarterly to ensure that your marketing strategies are achieving your desired goals. As a best practice, my marketing team and I sit down each month to review our goals and analytics, ensure that we are on track, and make the necessary improvements. Every business is different. My team consists of sales and marketing, digital media, public relations, content writing, and graphic design. Each team member brings a unique perspective on how to increase client engagement and brand awareness. Whether you have a team of one, ten, or one hundred, invest the time needed to give your business a solid marketing plan, utilizing the Zen Marketing Zone (zealous marketing goals, evergreen promotional strategies, and a nimble marketing plan), and you will reap the rewards for years to come.

From the Desk of the Decision-Maker

Roz Lewis, CPM, CPSD

President, Greater Women's Business Council

TOO OFTEN SMALL BUSINESSES only want to know what procurement opportunities a company has. However, today's corporate CEOs are looking for innovation. I recommend that small businesses identify a pain point or challenge and provide a S.O.L.U.T.I.O.N. that can make their customer a leader in the industry.

- **S**upplier understands the customer's pain points.
- **O**ut-of-the-box solutions provided.
- **L**ean into the customer's business.
- **U**nderstand your limitations.
- **T**ake time to evaluate your quality control.
- **I**nspire your team to deliver great customer service.
- **O**n-time delivery of the product or service is a priority.
- **N**imble is the ability to be ready at all times.

“Sales are contingent upon the attitude of the salesman–not the attitude of the prospect.”

— W. Clement Stone

CHAPTER FIVE

Sales

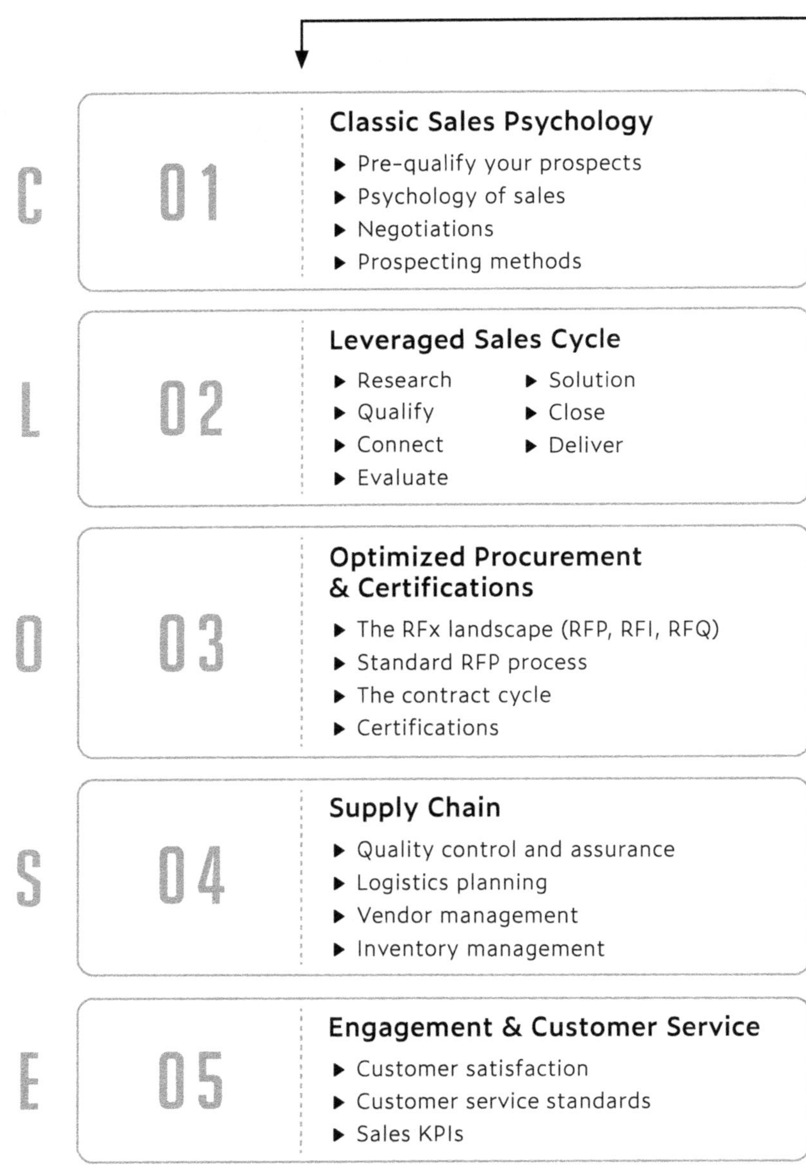
C
01
Classic Sales Psychology
▶ Pre-qualify your prospects
▶ Psychology of sales
▶ Negotiations
▶ Prospecting methods
L
02
Leveraged Sales Cycle
▶ Research
▶ Qualify
▶ Connect
▶ Evaluate
▶ Solution
▶ Close
▶ Deliver
O
03
Optimized Procurement & Certifications
▶ The RFx landscape (RFP, RFI, RFQ)
▶ Standard RFP process
▶ The contract cycle
▶ Certifications
S
04
Supply Chain
▶ Quality control and assurance
▶ Logistics planning
▶ Vendor management
▶ Inventory management
E
05
Engagement & Customer Service
▶ Customer satisfaction
▶ Customer service standards
▶ Sales KPIs

The C.LO.S.E. Sales Method

WHETHER YOU'RE SELLING GOURMET baked goods, technological equipment, or consulting services, you need to learn how to sell. I don't know how many times I've heard a small business owner say they don't like to sell. My response: "Then you don't like to eat!" Even if you're the face of your brand and you have a sales team, you're still in a sales role. You have to sell your vision, your ideas, the quality of your products and services, and your capabilities as a leader. Get ready to adjust your approach to sales, client relationships, and value-based selling. It's time to shift to providing solutions, solving customer problems, creating excitement, and leaving prospects wanting to work with you.

Many business owners still use a one-night-stand type of sales approach. If that's you, learn to commit and move towards courting. A simple decision to be monogamous with your clients and stop cheating can ultimately grow your businesses. Focusing on too many target markets is like dating too many people at one time. It becomes difficult to service your niche and go after one target. Yet, many businesses do it because they're afraid of leaving money on the table. In reality, they actually spread themselves too thin and miss out on sales.

There's a difference between hard work and struggle. If you have to fight and agitate to secure business, it's time to reexamine your products, processes, or prices. Easy and natural acquisitions of clients and business is possible when you reframe the typical overly competitive approach to sales. Go find the hidden money in your business by narrowing your target market to people who understand the value of what you provide. Serve the people, share knowledge, and sell your product or service by emotionally connecting with your audience. Selling is an important part of every business. Sadly, it's also a common challenge for many small business owners. You'll have to master the sales process to succeed in business.

Selling is much easier when you understand the **C.L.O.S.E.** Sales Method:

Classic Sales Psychology

Leveraged Sales Cycle

Optimized Procurement & Certifications

Supply Chain & Fulfillment

Engagement & Customer Service

Psychology of Sales

The secret to increasing your sales is rooted in your understanding of what your prospective clients want. Based on social psychology research, I've created ten sales psychology tips to help you ethically persuade more of your target audience to say yes to your products and services. Remember authenticity and integrity are important, so the goal should always be to under-promise and over-deliver, not to ever over-promise and under-deliver.

Sales Psychology Tip #1: Pre-qualify your prospect.

Your time is very valuable, and you want to make sure you're leveraging it. More often than not, small business owners fail to pre-qualify potential clients. What does this mean? You jump on the phone or meet with people who you haven't properly vetted as viable business opportunities. One way to do this is to categorize the people you encounter as you market your business.

Most of these people can go into one of three categories:

1. **Fans.** They like everything you do. They comment on your LinkedIn posts and invite you to events. You run in the same business circles, but they aren't going to buy from you. They're interested in what you do but will take no action to become a client.
2. **Window shoppers**. They attend your free workshops, read your blogs, and even sign up for a complimentary consultation. They consistently watch what you do and are developing trust in you and your business. Over time, their interest will turn into action, and they will buy from you.
3. **Primed-and-ready clients.** These people have watched you, are connected with you, trust your brand, and are ready to take action. They're ready to make a serious commitment to buy from you. They contact you via your website, email, phone or another avenue to begin working with you.

Pre-qualify a potential client to determine if you're dealing with a fan, a window shopper, or a primed-and-ready client. If it's a fan, continue to offer her great value-added resources. Fans can provide great social proof for you. If it's a window shopper, connect with him because you never know what one thing you can do to turn him into a buyer. If it's a primed-and-ready client, offer her great products and services, and over-deliver.

One way I pre-qualify potential clients is by asking discovery or prospecting questions about their budget, past experience with vendors, procurement process, and readiness to purchase. Practice active listening, ask clarifying questions, paraphrase what the prospect says in your own words, and use open-ended questions. Remember your time is money, and you have to make sure you're investing it where it will yield the highest rate of return.

Sales Psychology Tip #2: Understand the personalities of decision-makers.

That will determine your sales approach. You want to become a trusted strategic advisor for your potential clients. In order to do that, you must resonate and connect with them. If there are multiple decision-makers, assess the personality of each and tailor your sales presentation to address each personality type. In my experience, people fall within one of these four main sales personality types.

The assertive and results-oriented personality is fast paced and energetic. Powerful, driven, goal-oriented, and decisive, these people sometimes appear impatient because they're focused on the bottom line. They want information fast so they can make a decision and move on to the next thing. Professionalism is key in winning over this personality type, so make sure you're always prepared. If you don't know the answer to a question, tell them you'll follow up with them. Show them how your product or service will solve their problems. They aren't impressed with testimonials. Instead, use their competitive streak to show them how your product will help them rise to the top of their industry. Focus on the ROI (return on investment), and keep your statements short.

The friendly and easy-going personality values personal relationships and wants to develop a trusting strategic partnership with their vendors. They like a new challenge. They're enthusiastic and enjoy coming up with creative and innovative solutions, but they don't want to invest a lot of time in research. You'll guide them through the purchasing process by offering valuable solutions that meet their needs, but they need more time to make decisions. Help them visualize how your product or service will enhance their business, and establish a rapport with their team members, as they look to them for advice or approval. They are great listeners and like to get to know you outside of your work role. With the friendly/easy-going personality type, the sales process will take time, so help them to feel comfortable doing business with you. They love testimonials and success stories because they're risk-averse and want to go with proven systems that have guarantees, such as a refund or cancellation policy, to reduce their anxiety.

The humanitarian and philanthropic personality prioritizes personal relationships. They're concerned with the well-being of others, including employees, customers, leadership, vendors, and the community. They want to know how the decisions they make will affect the people around them. They have people-pleaser traits, yet they have strong personalities and will work to convince or persuade others of their convictions. They're out-of-the-box thinkers, creative, outgoing, and spontaneous. They trust their gut and intuition. They value loyalty, trust, friendship, honesty, and mutual respect. The humanitarian-philanthropic personalities want to know you have a proven track record. Present case studies; show how your products or services have positively impacted the lives of others. Focus on building an ongoing strategic partnership and excellence in customer service. You can use some facts and figures, but focus more on the humanity of your product and how it affects others. Summarize throughout the sales process, and continually get their buy-in by saying things like, "So we agree on this," or "We're all on the same page."

The data-driven and analytical personality focuses on facts, figures and hardcore data. They get straight to the facts and love research. When you walk in the door, don't be surprised if they already know a lot about you. They vet everything and don't make decisions quickly. They ask a lot of detailed questions and stick to their deadlines. They focus on facts rather than emotions, and it's unlikely they'll want to know you on a personal level. The data-driven-analytical personality listens intently and is very direct. Don't rush them. They take as much time as they need to make a decision, so expect a fairly long sales cycle. Since they're researchers by nature, they will already know a lot about the benefits of your product. Take time to present customized, innovative, and value-added solutions to them. You'll lose credibility if you make assumptions, so show proof using data. Go with the flow, and don't try to force a relationship with them.

Decision-makers may have one primary trait or a combination of all four. However, once you have an understanding of all four personality traits you can easily adjust your sales strategy to fit any situation that you encounter.

Sales Psychology Tip #3: No one wants to be left out.
Urgency and scarcity are known to increase sales because most buyers have a fear of missing out (FOMO). Scarcity is when a product or service becomes more attractive because of its limited availability or perceived limited availability. Remember when you were younger and your mom said you couldn't eat a certain food because there was only one more left? It made you want it even more. The same applies to sales. Your products and services are often more appealing if they're rare or offered in limited quantity. Time limits create urgency, which also encourages serious leads to buy.

Sales Psychology Tip #4: Bundle more and offer less.
Sometimes less really is more. Providing your prospects with too many different options makes it harder for them to make a decision, which increases the odds they'll walk away without buying anything at all. As I always say, a confused mind won't buy, so make their decision easier. If your business sells a wide range of products or services, research your prospects ahead of time so you know the best solution to recommend. During your discovery phase, ask qualifying questions to build on your knowledge and narrow down the type of

product or service they want. Then, only pitch solutions that match their wants and needs.

Sale Psychology Tip #5: Let others brag on you.

Potential clients want to know you're credible and have provided a wonderful customer experience to someone like them. It's crucial to have testimonials from previous clients who talk about the quality of your products and services, your superior customer service, and your timeliness. If you've worked with any notable brands, it's okay to name drop because that helps to establish credibility. In addition, ask your existing clients to provide referrals to you for potential clients who could utilize your business. A referral establishes instant credibility.

Sales Psychology Tip #6: Overcome that infamous word, no.

When I first started my business, I dreaded hearing the word no. However, as time went on, I realized that no was just a part of doing business. So the word no now means Next Opportunity. If I don't win a bid or a project I'm competing for, I go back and evaluate what I could have done better. This helps me learn from my mistakes and better understand what my ideal client needs, which is very helpful in overcoming objections in the future. If a potential client says no or appears to be on the fence, I ask them what reservations they have. This gives me an opportunity to see if there are any gaps I can fill to get them closer to a yes. Is the timing off, is the price too high, do we need to come up with a different solution, or are they leaning toward a competitor's offering?

Another method is to ask your potential client to rate their readiness to buy on a scale of one to five (with one being not ready, and five being "Let's close the deal today"). Regardless of their answer, ask why they chose the number they did. For example, if your potential client responds with a three, ask, "Why didn't you choose a lower number?" This invites them to explain why they're considering your product or service and often leads them to realize they're more ready to buy than they thought.

Sales Psychology Tip #7: Serve first.

I've heard, throughout my life, that it is better to give than receive, and I'm a firm believer in that principle, even in business. One thing I know for sure is that when you give to people from your heart, and you genuinely serve them, they want to help you in return. Many of my biggest clients have come from volunteering my time and talents by putting on a free workshop, volunteering at an event, or serving on a panel. Regardless of your product or service offering, show potential clients the value first. If you sell software, how about offering a free trial so your prospect can take it on a test drive? If you have a catering business, send a few samples. If you own a promotions company, create a few customized items for your prospect. If your potential customer is able to see themselves using your product or service, it's much easier to get them to a yes.

Sales Psychology Tip #8: Create a common bond.

Researchers at Harvard Business School found that 64% of buyers who have a strong relationship with a single brand do so because of shared values.[27] Think about TOMS, the company which started by donating a pair of shoes to those in need for every pair of shoes sold and now supports several charitable missions. People like to buy from people who get them. It's important to create a common bond or shared values between you and your potential customers. You'll create a community or loyal group of followers who want to be a part of what you're doing because they believe in your values and mission. Think Apple versus Android.

To create shared values, find out what your prospect cares about and emphasize how your products or services honor those values. Before a B2B prospect buys, they consider how their manager, colleagues, and clients will respond. Before a B2C prospect buys, they consider what their friends, colleagues, or spouse will think. Anticipate this, and alter your sales approach accordingly.

Sales Psychology Tip #9: Appeal to the desires of your prospect.

Throughout *The CEO Life*, I've stressed that it's important to appeal to the needs and wants of your customer. This holds true during the sales process. Identify which needs your products or services meet for your prospects, and lead with that during your sales presentation: The primary prospects needs are:

- Money
- Security
- Belonging
- Status and prestige
- Health and fitness
- Praise and recognition
- Power, influence, and popularity
- Leading in their industry
- Love and companionship
- Personal growth
- Personal transformation

Sales Psychology Tip #10: Focus on the customer.

The easiest way to close a sale is to solve the most pressing need or want that a prospect has. Remember you're a solutions provider, a strategic partner, and a trusted advisor. Your job is to focus on the needs and wants of your customer not just the benefits of your product or service. You should become your prospect's ally. They should develop trust in you, knowing you'll always have an innovative solution to their problem. Position yourself through your branding as the only option because you are truly the expert in your industry.

Spend some time studying the psychology behind sales and tailoring your sales presentation to increase buying desire, reduce the fear of loss, and emphasize the ultimate benefit. You'll make more sales and satisfy more clients.

Find Your Target Audience: Sales Prospecting Methods

Prospecting with an inbound marketing campaign method allows you to sell to prospects attracted to you by the high-value content you provide to solve their needs. With outbound prospecting, you reach out to or make initial contact with a prospect within your target audience demographic to determine if they're a viable candidate for your products or services. Outbound marketing is a form of push marketing through which you attempt to get your message in front of a prospect even before the prospect has a desire to or interest in buying the product or service. Push marketing can be considered interruptive. Think about YouTube and television advertising and how they interrupt your favorite shows with ads. Unless you happen to be somewhat interested in or curious about the product or service, you probably don't find these ads to be very beneficial.

If few people know about your product or service, or if prospects simply aren't actively looking for your product or service, then push marketing can be a viable option. However, big push marketing campaigns aren't for the small or medium marketing budget. An inbound marketing campaign may be a more effective route. Inbound marketing takes the opposite approach and is a form of pull marketing, in which prospects are attracted to you. Prospects are actively seeking your product or service, and your job is to present ads and content to emotionally connect with them so they'll enter your sales funnel. Social media, search engine optimization, blogging and vlogging, and pay-per-click ads are just some of the methods of pull marketing.

For pull marketing to be effective, your prospects have to be aware of your product or service category and actively looking for the product or service. When your ad or content shows up, your business is a natural fit because your prospects have been already looking for you—even if they didn't know it. For example, wine, shoes, technology software, accounting services, legal services, hair care, and beauty are products and services people commonly seek. It's very difficult to build awareness with pull marketing for a new product or service category. If your product or service category isn't known, then nobody will be looking for it.

Let's look at some typical prospecting methods.

Referrals. No matter how long you've been in sales, you already know that getting a sale through cold prospecting can be tough. It's always easier when a friend, family member, colleague, or client recommends your products or services to someone else. This is one of the reasons why referrals matter and should be an integral part of your sales and marketing plan. According to McKinsey and Company, word of mouth is the primary factor behind 20% to 50% of all purchasing decisions. [28] Very few small businesses have an automated process or schedule for getting referrals. Develop a system so that, within thirty days of the sale, you follow up with clients to see how you can increase their satisfaction with your product and service and also to ask for a referral.

Twitter. Research to find relevant influencers and decision-makers and reach out to them via direct message. You can utilize tools (free and paid), like Social Oomph, to pick keywords to help with accurately searching for your prospects.

LinkedIn Groups. Identify groups where your leads are active. Get involved, contribute to the conversation, and emerge as a go-to industry expert. You can also utilize LinkedIn tools to gain valuable insights and new leads. If your business sells B2C (business to customer), Facebook groups could provide a similar means to target your audience.

Quora. This site is designed as a place to share knowledge. It's a platform to ask questions and connect with people who contribute unique insights and quality answers. Some forum sites don't seem to have the staying power of social media sites, but Quora continues to be popular in many circles. Thought leaders, like Tim Ferris, author of *The 4-Hour Workweek*, and other top marketers use forums to build their credibility. Search for topics on which you can add value. Your contributions may be seen by influencers in your target industry. These questions and answers are often seen by people who might be your ideal clients.

Cold emails. To successfully implement a cold email campaign, start by researching the right contacts, find out their pain points, and emotionally connect with them by adding value and solving their problems. You can research leads based on several factors, including industry, revenue, and size. Make sure you use a customer relationship management (CRM) and email marketing software to keep track of who you're contacting and how they respond.

Strategic partnership. A strategic partnership is less formal and less time-bound than a joint venture, which is a legal entity between two or more businesses that come together to operate as a single business but still maintain their separate business entity. Instead of going into a legal business entity together, you and another business leverage each other's strengths to create more business opportunities. Each business must add value to the partnership, and it's important to build a relationship with the other business before starting the partnership. The contract I have with Delta Air Lines at the time of this writing is the result of a strategic partnership with a business that has strengths complementary to my own. My strategic partner and I had known each other for over ten years and worked together loosely for about three years before we formed a strategic partnership. Both businesses need to have a similar work ethic, similar values, and a similar vision for the strategic partnership.

Colleague networking. A strategic partnership or joint venture may not always be the answer. However, there's still value in your existing network. Every month, schedule coffee or lunch with a colleague in a complementary industry. You're looking for businesses to establish a win-win relationship with so you can refer leads to each other. This kind of connection is a great way to expand your network. Think about a web design firm connecting with a company that provides digital marketing or branding services.

Direct mail. I know many people think direct mail is antiquated and no longer effective, but don't knock it until you try it. What's in your mailbox? Bills, credit card offers, magazines, and a package or two from Amazon? The art of a handwritten note or small custom package has faded away for a lot of businesses because of the huge focus on social media. A personal touch, such as a handwritten thank you card, could go a long way in helping you start to establish a relationship with a cold lead. B2Bs that do regular creative mailings have a potential to stand out, but don't send these out in a mass mailing. Personalization on physical letters can get expensive when you're dealing with large numbers. Send only to high-quality leads who would appreciate this prospecting method. Send something different, not necessarily fancy. After all, a handwritten note is something that very few people send or receive these days.

Channel partners. The use of channel partnerships can be a high-impact strategy for growing your business. A channel partner is someone who already has access to your target audience. For example, a great channel partnership for me is the local Chamber of Commerce, a membership organization made up of lots of small businesses that need business consulting services. Instead of attempting to identify these businesses individually, I can establish a mutually beneficial relationship with the organization that gives me access to their members. A good partnership is one that can provide access to new clients and referrals that bring you additional business. Look for relationships with partners for whom you can offer a value-add for their current products or services.

Networking. Join networking groups, go to events, and develop relationships. Don't just hand out or collect a lot of business cards. Have genuine conversations and connect with people. Listen and offer value during your conversations. Learn how you can help someone else before pitching your product or service. Be interesting, engaging, and have fun. Research the events you'll attend ahead of time and make sure your target audience will be in attendance at the event. Networking shouldn't be your only form of prospecting, but it should be one of the tools in your sales toolbox.

Webinars. A webinar should be more than a sales presentation. You should provide your valuable expertise to your target audience. The webinar should address the pain you solve for your clients with the methodology, product, or service you use to solve it. Webinars can be a great method to bring a steady stream of leads into your sales funnel.

Old leads. One of the biggest mistakes many sales teams make is a failure to follow up on old leads that never closed. I'm talking about all those qualifying calls or business cards that went nowhere and all the people you already know. Develop a plan, put it on your calendar, and call them already. It's a good idea to add a process to your customer relationship management (CRM) system to track the number of leads, number of follow-ups, and close rates.

These sales prospecting methods will help you start generating more leads, but don't overwhelm yourself. Try implementing one or two of these strategies at a time. Use them, test them, and modify them to fit your selling style. Selling is simply building a relationship, solving a problem for your client, and offering them tons and tons of value. Many people struggle with selling, but you don't have to. Shift your mindset to understand that if you offer an amazing product or service, your client needs you. If you need to strengthen your sales skills, don't hesitate to hire a coach. It will pay off in dividends in the future.

Negotiation: What's in It for Me?

Negotiation is a discussion between two parties to reach a joint agreement about differing needs or opinions. It involves using the art of persuasion to get others to understand and agree with your viewpoint, and it works best when you have a win-win attitude. The key skills involved in a successful negotiation are: communication, sales and marketing skills, basic knowledge of human psychology, analytical skills, basic sociology knowledge, assertiveness, and conflict resolution. No two people are exactly the same. Each and every individual thinks and behaves differently and has different needs, wants, beliefs, and goals. It's important to keep those differences in mind during negotiations.

Here are some good strategies for effective negotiation:

1. Decide on your starting position and how far you're willing to lower what you'll accept.
2. Identify potential objectives and create a solution for overcoming them.
3. Prepare for the meeting by understanding what your objectives are and what you're willing to compromise on to create a win-win solution.
4. Start with what you can reasonably ask for and leave room to negotiate.

Do your research and be prepared with facts, information, and comparable costs. Silence is golden. When you let the other party talk, you can see where they stand on different points of the negotiation. To understand their starting price, ask, "What is your budget?" or "What would you like to invest in this project?" Confirm all the terms that everyone agrees on. This will put both parties in a receptive place to be able to discuss terms that need to be negotiated. Throughout the process, practice active listening. When you identify that the other party is ready to seal the deal and you agree with the terms, execute the contract.

Every negotiation involves a compromise or a change of opinion from one or both parties to reach an acceptable final agreement. It's important to take adequate time to discuss the viewpoints of both the parties and reach an agreement.

Sales Cycle: When Will the Deal Close?

Most small businesses lack a predefined, step-by-step set of interactions to take prospects through to qualify them and convert them to customers or clients. Instead, most small business owners and their teams operate by intuition or happenstance. By taking the time to clearly define your target audience (as you did in the branding section), you can dramatically decrease your investments of money and time. Knowing your target audience will allow you to filter out unqualified leads and increase your sales revenue by significantly increasing the number of qualified leads you convert to clients. Developing a sales system and understanding the sales cycle helps you establish a relationship with your prospects over time. It warms them up by showcasing your business's unique differentiation and the value you can provide.

There are seven crucial steps in the sales process (also known as the sales cycle):

Step 1. Research.

Step 2. Qualify.

Step 3. Connect.

Step 4. Evaluate and educate.

Step 5. Offer a solution.

Step 6. Close.

Step 7. Deliver.

The success of any business, from a local bakery to an international corporation, is based on sales. No matter how great the product or service is or how many millions the company spends on marketing, the primary goal is to increase revenue.

A sales process relies upon the actions a sales team performs to close more deals. Each business model has a unique way to offer and sell products and services based on the clients' needs, the market, and most importantly, based on the sales objectives. It's critical to document your sales process so you can modify it as needed to ensure your sales team is efficient and not leaving money on the table.

Let's look at the seven steps in the sales process.

Step 1. Research.

It's important to establish a set of criteria to evaluate the probability that a lead or prospect will become a client. You should set these criteria during the brand-development phase, when you define the pain points, characteristics, traits, and buying behaviors for your target audience. The more closely prospects meet all or the majority of these traits, the more likely it is that they will convert into clients. During the research phase, you should clearly define who your target market is.

Let me point out that there's a difference between a lead and a prospect. A lead is any potential customer who has expressed interest in your company or services by taking action such as visiting your website, subscribing to a blog, downloading an ebook, completing an info card at a tradeshow, or reaching out to schedule a complimentary consultation. Leads become prospects when you have determined that they align with the criteria you established during this research phase.

To ensure that you have a central place for maintaining your leads, store that information in a CRM (customer relationship management) system. A CRM database enables you to keep track of potential and existing clients and what stage of the sales cycle they're in at any given time. Salesforce and HubSpot are two CRM platforms for both small and large businesses. Make sure you do your research to determine which CRM you can customize best for your business.

From my experience, more than half of sales time is wasted on unproductive prospecting. Prospecting is the process of searching for potential clients or buyers to develop new business. The goal is to move prospects through a sales funnel until they eventually convert into revenue-generating clients. Highly targeted prospecting is more likely to generate contacts who fit the criteria of your target audience. It's imperative that you focus on attracting the right type of prospects who can and will buy your products or services. Take some time to find out where your target audience hangs out. What social media platforms are they on? What networking events, tradeshows, or conferences do they attend? What professional organizations have they joined? Who are their strategic partners? What journals or media outlets do they read, watch, or follow? Identifying where to find your prospects provides you with insight on events you should attend, outlets where you should consider providing content, and strategic relationships you should establish.

When prospecting, focus on communicating directly with the decision-maker or influencing the person who has the ear of the decision-maker but may be serving in the role of a gatekeeper. This could include a receptionist, a personal assistant, the end-user of your product or service, or a direct report to the decision-maker. The goal is to identify the person in charge of making a final decision on procuring your product or service. Often, you'll have to go through a gatekeeper or series of gatekeepers to reach the decision-maker.

Step 2. Qualify.

Once you've identified a prospect, it's time to gather answers to important questions to help you qualify your prospect. This allows you to focus your time and energy on the prospects who are most likely to convert into sales. Sometimes you can gather this information without speaking directly to the decision-maker. If so, do your homework before connecting with them. If not, these questions will be answered during the connect phase. Consider the following to qualify your prospects:

1. **Budget.** Does your prospect have enough money in their budget to buy your product or service?
2. **Authority.** Can your prospect make a purchase decision?
3. **Need.** Does the prospect have a need that your product or service can fulfill?

4. **Timeframe.** Does the prospect have a designated period in which he or she wants to make a purchase?

Once you answer those questions, you can make an informed decision as to whether or not this prospect is worth pursuing. Qualifying your prospects is crucial because it lets you know if it's worth investing your time in pursuing the prospects. This also improves your chances of providing high value to them once they become clients.

In the qualifying phase you want to accomplish three goals:

1. Determine if the prospect is viable.
2. Qualify and prioritize prospects based on the amount of work required to successfully move them through the sales cycle and the likelihood of them closing.
3. Find opportunities to offer value by establishing a connection through personalization, rapport building, and trust development.

When qualifying a prospect, make sure you get two key pieces of information: whether or not anyone else will be involved in the buying decision and whether or not the purchase will come out of the prospect's existing budget. Two objections that may come up during the qualifying phase are time constraints and budget limitations. Before wasting a ton of time on prospects who have either of those limitations, do a little homework to see if you can filter them out. If this isn't the best time, circle back and revisit the prospect at a later date. In the meantime, continue to develop and nurture the relationship so, when they are ready, your business will be their first choice.

Step 3. Connect.

Ideally, you were able to gather some background information that will help you connect with your prospect before your first call or meeting. There are several ways to connect with prospects through email, telephone, a website survey, or a face-to-face meeting to communicate your value proposition. Depending on your type of business, email may be the best and most cost-effective form of communication for early stage prospects. If so, you can nurture your prospects through a schedule of automated emails. If telephone or face-to-face meetings are the best way to connect, you can track this entire process within your CRM.

You'll want to have a series of touch points during your connection phase. One of my clients, who provides Enterprise Resource Planning (ERP) and data management program services for government and corporate clients, uses the following connection sequence: first touch (email, phone, LinkedIn message, or Twitter message), follow-up, demo request, trial request, proposal submission, and closing.

Here's another example from one of my clients who provides technology consulting. This connection sequence is longer because the sales cycle has more steps. Some of the steps may have multiple touch points (calls, emails, or face-to-face meetings). The sequence looks like this: first touch (normally at a tradeshow or referral from an existing client or strategic partner), follow-up (email or phone), invitation to visit technology lab, meeting with prospect's key stakeholders to determine requirements, provide a summary of project requirements and submit a request for quotation, negotiation and quote changes, final proposal, and closing.

Step 4. Evaluate and educate.

Selling requires establishing a mutually beneficial relationship and offering a product or service that solves a problem for your prospect. It's important for you to understand the pain points or challenges your prospects face and educate them on how your product or service solves their problem. During this phase, you should educate your prospect on all the benefits and results they will receive by utilizing your product or service. This helps you to clarify any concerns and remove obstacles that could negatively impact your sales, including budget, time constraints, or specific challenges with your product or service.

Your goal during this phase is to identify the specific needs of your prospect by evaluating their business or personal needs to address any doubts they have, provide value through education, and ultimately move them farther along in the sales cycle. A great way to handle concerns and overcome objections is to include an FAQ section on your website. You can also build trust and authority by providing testimonials, references, and case studies. For prospects who need more time, send regular and valuable content through blog posts or email newsletters to keep your product or service top of mind.

Step 5. Offer a solution.

Once you have a full understanding of your prospects' specific needs and they see the value in your product or service, present them with a proposal that fits their budget, timeframe, and any other requirements. Okay. Let me pause for the cause for just a minute to talk to you about a few best practices on sales proposals and presentations. First and foremost, don't try to fit all of your knowledge and expertise into a proposal. I have seen PowerPoint presentation proposals that looked like an encyclopedia and sales proposal documents that looked like a dissertation. Stop it. Just stop it. Your proposal should be concise and visually appealing (use images, graphs, tables, or charts) and include messaging that targets the correct stakeholder, pricing that's easy to understand, a viable solution that they requested (not what you want to recommend), the process of how you do business, timelines and an execution schedule, customer testimonials, and any other pertinent information. Tailor your proposal for your audience and understand the motivating factors that will drive your prospects to buy. The more your proposal accurately addresses their needs and wants, the easier it is to get them to a yes.

Step 6. Close.

The goal of closing a sale with a prospect is to develop a win-win partnership in which you provide great value to your prospect to relieve pain points in their life or business. When you feel you have nurtured your prospects and alleviated any concerns, *ask for the business* and close the deal. If you successfully close the sale, pat yourself on the back and continue through the steps in your sale process. Your prospect has now turned into a client.

If you don't close the sale, ask the prospect why they chose not to buy your product or service. This information is important for evaluating your sales process and close ratio. Learn from what your prospect says, and make any necessary adjustments within your system to improve your sales process.

Step 7. Deliver.

Hooray! You've closed the sale. Now it's time to deliver. The most important part of any sales transaction is for your business to deliver tons of value. Ensuring your clients receive the product or service they signed up for is critical to business longevity and client satisfaction. The complete process for delivering your product or service should be thoroughly documented, and your sales team should work to ensure an easy transition from close to delivery. Once the product or service has been successfully delivered to your new clients, continue to provide them the highest level of customer service.

Optimized Procurement: Winning the Bid

If you want to do business with large corporations and government agencies, you must know how to break through the red tape and understand the politics involved. Each organization has its own set of documented and unwritten processes and procedures. It's important to learn the culture of each organization you work with. Something that works one way, at one company, doesn't necessarily work that way, across the board, for all companies. Procurement, which plays an important role in these organizations, is simply the sourcing and purchasing of goods and services for business use from an external source. Corporations and agencies set procurement policies that govern their choice of suppliers and products and the methods and procedures used to communicate with their suppliers.

Procurement has changed throughout the years. In the past, procurement decisions focused mostly on price. However, many companies now realize the importance of procurement for both cost reduction and value beyond cost. As a small business, it's important to be competitive on price but also offer value to your clients by improving processes, limiting risks, being fast and agile, or increasing revenue. Your goal should be to positively impact their business while offering a quality product or service at a competitive price.

Evaluating a Bid

Knowing the bid process and common pitfalls is great, and we'll get to that in just a minute. Before we do, it's important to understand that all bids are not created equal. A bid that sounds like an amazing opportunity might not be a good fit for your business. You have to evaluate the bid to ensure you have the right business infrastructure in place and that you can make money on the bid. You don't want to pay a customer to work with them because you didn't accurately evaluate a bid and must assume a financial loss and possibly a negative hit to your reputation. Ask yourself these key questions during the bid evaluation process:

Internal Questions

- Do we meet the insurance and bonding requirements?
- Do we have the infrastructure to successfully implement the project?
- Do we have the working capital to finance the bid?
- Do we need a team/partnership strategy, or can we get the right subcontractors?

Customer Questions

- Do we have a relationship with this customer through meetings or prior contract performance?
- Do we understand the customer's needs and the work to be performed?
- Are we familiar with customer insights and industry trends that affect the customer?
- Do we have a solution that will help the customer achieve its goals and contract objectives?
- Do we have enough information to develop a risk-mitigation plan?

Competition Questions

- Do we know who we're competing against, and can we beat them?

Request for Proposal (RFP) Questions

- Do we have the expertise to assemble a winning bid package?
- Do we know what price we need to bid to win, and can we achieve it profitably?
- Do we have a compelling win strategy?

Taking time to carefully evaluate a bid before jumping in head-first can save your business a bunch of time, money, and resources that might otherwise be wasted.

RFx Landscape

Let's look at five common types of contract proposals.

Request for Proposal (RFP). An RFP solicits proposals from suppliers when a company or government entity is interested in procuring a product or service. The purpose is to determine a supplier's proposed solution and pricing for the requested product or service.

Request for Information (RFI). An RFI is used to gather information from potential suppliers about a product or service. Oftentimes, information gathered in the RFI will be used to help develop an RFP. This is the time for you to shine as a supplier by recommending innovative solutions and showing off your expertise. One of my clients responded to an RFI for a Fortune 100 company and gave them suggestions on potential sustainable solutions that were more cost-effective and great for the company's brand image. These were suggestions that the company had never considered, and as a result of her innovative ideas during the RFI, she ended up winning the bid.

Request for Quote (RFQ). An RFQ is when suppliers are invited to bid on specific products or services. This enables a company to compare pricing for various vendors.

Single Source Bid. A single source bid eliminates the competitive bidding process, and the company selects a single vendor based on price or quality.

Sole Source Bid. A sole source bid is when a supplier is the only one that can provide you with the goods or products you need. This could be based on timing, availability, or because the supplier has a monopoly on the market.

Here are the four steps most corporations and government entities follow in the RFP process.

Step 1. Identify project requirements.

During the planning phase, research will be performed in key areas to establish project parameters, including:

- Scope of work
- Alignment with business strategy
- Potential vendors
- Budget
- Timeline
- Key stakeholders
- Scoring criteria and review process

Step 2. Create an RFP.

Once research has been completed, an RFP will be created to include the following items:

- Introduction
- Statement of purpose
- Background information
- Scope of work
- Budget
- Project schedule
- Contract terms and conditions
- RFP timeline and review
- Requirement for proposals

Step 3. Issue the RFP.

The RFP is issued through various channels, including local and federal government agency websites and corporate procurement portals to businesses that are registered to receive bid notifications and current vendors. Qualified suppliers submit completed bids.

Step 4. Review proposals and award contract.

Once the RFPs are received, the procurement team reviews them and makes a decision with the following steps:

- RFPs scored
- Finalists selected
- Interviews and reference checks
- Best and final offers submitted
- Final negotiations
- Contract awarded
- Other bidders notified

Each organization will have its own procurement process, so make sure you attend the pre-bid conference meetings or discuss the process with the buyer. The steps above provide a high-level overview, but it's essential that you get all the juicy details so you can dot all your i's and cross your t's.

Pricing

Pricing is one element a lot of small businesses struggle with when preparing RFPs. Due to higher overhead, a small business price may be higher than a larger competitor's price. Additionally, a small business may not take into consideration all the factors that impact their costs including:

- Labor
- Equipment
- Technology (software and hardware)
- Insurance and bonding
- Delivery and installation
- Start-up costs (new location)
- Financing fees
- Professional fees (attorney, accounting, etc.)

There's a difference between costs and price. Costs are the items you pay for in order to deliver your product or service before any profit is made. Price is the amount a customer is willing to pay for a product or service. The difference between the price paid and the costs incurred is the profit. Take the time to accurately calculate your costs, including profit and contingency, on all bid proposals.

Make sure you do industry research and competitive analysis to understand market pricing. One way to reverse engineer pricing is to look for government contracts that have been awarded in your industry, since they are public record, and review the pricing schedules. (Corporate contracts are not public record.) You can pull GSA (General Services Administration)Schedules from your larger competitors to see labor and product pricing at www.gsa.gov. A GSA Schedule assists federal employees in purchasing products and services from suppliers at pre-negotiated prices.

Top Reasons Proposals Fail

When I first started responding to RFPs, I was like a deer in headlights. The terminology, pricing equations, and technical specifications had my brain in a fog. One of the first things I did was sign up for several classes at Georgia Tech's Procurement Assistance Center (GTPAC) to familiarize myself with the lingo and procurement process. I took several classes on government contracting, which helped me in the corporate arena as well.

Based on my research and personal experience, here are the top reasons why most proposals fail.

- The proposal is cookie cutter and uses generic text.
- The bid is incomplete or nonresponsive and doesn't address all RFP requirements.
- Inadequate past performance or limited references.
- Product/service offerings don't match requirements.
- Inability to finance the project based on the payment terms.
- Pricing is too high and not competitive.
- Proper market research wasn't performed to understand customer insights or industry trends.
- No distinguishable value proposition or competitive differentiation.
- The implementation team is not qualified and lacks the experience to perform work.
- Project plan, team roles, and implementation strategy aren't clear.

- Project risks are ignored and a mitigation plan hasn't been developed.

Please note if you're working with federal government projects as a prime or subcontractor, you'll need to enroll in E-Verify. E-Verify confirms the eligibility of employees to work in the United States. For more information visit www.everify.gov.

Creating a Successful Proposal

Now that you have a good understanding of why proposals fail, let's delve into some key reasons why proposals are successful

- Proposal adheres to customer's internal processes and procedures.
- Industry trends and customer pain points researched and used in the bid proposal.
- Internal proposal development process is used to track the progress of all team members.
- Strategic partners and team members strengthen the value proposition.
- Team roles and responsibilities are well defined.
- Boilerplate templates are not used; each RFP is customized for each bid submittal.
- A debrief is requested whether you win or lose the contract.

To receive notification of RFPs, register with your local, regional, and federal government agencies and with corporations' supplier databases. When you create a profile, you'll be notified of upcoming bids that match your product and service offerings.

The Contract Cycle: You Won the Bid Now What?

You've won the contract! Yay! Now what? First, you need to review and negotiate the terms and conditions of your contract. Most terms are standard and non-negotiable, but you need to be comfortable with the terms. If not, negotiate. If you're not familiar with standard contract language, hire an attorney.

Common Contract Terms and Conditions

Each contract is unique, but there are some standard contract terms and conditions:

- Insurance requirements and indemnification
- Payment terms and method of payment
- Termination for convenience on behalf of client and termination for cause
- Defined ownership of assets, work product(s), and intellectual property
- Extending terms to subsidiaries and/or equity partners

Contract Types

There are numerous types of contracts utilized in corporate, government, and B2B deals. Here are some of the most common contract types you'll see.

Master Service Agreement (MSA). In this standard agreement, parties agree to terms that will govern future transactions or future agreements. Typical agreement terms cover, among other things, confidentiality, indemnification, warranties, infringement, and insurance.

Time & Materials (T&M). T&M agreements are used a lot in construction and product-development projects. The contractor is paid for the actual cost of direct labor and subcontractors, materials and equipment usage, and a fixed amount for the contractor's overhead and profit.

Fixed Fee Contract (FFC) or Firm Fixed-Price (FFP) Contract. An FFC or FFP is a contract based on a firm fixed price. It does not change based on resources or materials used. When you quote a price for this type of contract, you (the small business owner) assume all the risk. That means if the price goes up for supplies or labor, you must still perform the contract based on the original price you submitted. Make sure you run the numbers several times and include a contingency just in case something unforeseen occurs.

Purchase Order (PO). A PO is a legally binding document that states the services or products to be rendered, quantities or amounts, and the price for the products or services provided.

Cost-Plus Contract or Cost-Reimbursable Contract. A contractor is paid for all approved contract-related reimbursement expenses, plus profit.

Contract Management

Being awarded a contract is only the beginning. It's imperative that you adhere to all terms and conditions within the contract on time and within budget. Successfully executing and managing a contract involves a systematic approach. There are four phases in contract management.

1. Pre-Contract
2. Contract
3. Renewal
4. Close-Out

Pre-Contract

Pre-contract is the period after you are awarded the contract but before work commences. It's a best practice to establish internal policies and procedures to effectively manage the contract and avoid administrative bottlenecks including:

- Ensure all contract documents are consistent and all parties have the correct version, including attachments.
- Define roles and responsibilities assigned to relevant stakeholders.
- Consider whether training is required for contract-management staff.
- Set up workflow for contract-related business processes.
- Establish escalation and alternative dispute-resolution procedures.
- Create a plan to cover implementation, transition, and/or rollout.
- Establish a fiscal monitoring plan based on contract specifications or other applicable fiscal requirements.
- Identify and rate contract risks and determine procedures for dealing with major risks.
- Establish a project-management method to ensure the project stays on schedule and within budget.

During project management, many small businesses fail to perform a risk analysis. Assessing risk is vital to identifying blind spots or potential roadblocks so you can limit unexpected events during the implementation phase. According to Project Manager.com, you should perform a risk analysis on every project to "avoid potential litigation, address regulatory issues, comply with new legislation, reduce exposure, and minimize impact."[29]

There are five steps to evaluating risk.

Step 1. Identify the risk.

Brainstorm with your team to identify potential risks that may affect deliverables, financing, schedules, staffing, or other elements of the project. Document all of these items in a project risk register or a risk log.

Step 2. Analyze the risk.

Once you and your team have identified the risks, determine the likelihood and consequences of each risk. Understand the potential effect each risk could have on the project goals and objectives. Input all of this information in your risk register.

Step 3. Determine the risk impact.

The risk impact looks at the likelihood of the risk happening and the consequence if it does. First, determine the likelihood of the risk: rare, unlikely, possible, likely, or almost certain. Next, determine the consequence of the risk: negligible, minor, moderate, critical, or catastrophic. Document the risk rankings (likelihood and consequences) in your risk register.

Step 4. Develop a risk-management strategy.

Assess the risks that have the highest ranking and develop a risk-mitigation plan, outlining actions and strategies to reduce risks. Your goal is to develop a preventative plan to avoid risks or a contingency plan to minimize risks. Document all strategies in the project's risk register.

Step 5. Monitor the risk.

Use your project risk register to monitor, track, review, and update risks to ensure the project stays on track.

Active Contract

The active contract phase is separated into three parts: internal operations and management, customer relationship management, and supplier relationship management.

Internal Operations and Management. Once all contracts have been executed, upload them to a contract management tool, and set appropriate expiration and renewal notifications to ensure you abide by all the terms in the contract. Record any changes to contract terms, address disputes in a timely manner, and make efforts to resolve any issues.

Review and manage your bid assumptions to document if they were correct or if different actions were taken. Monitor and document changes in scope with change-request orders. If your client doesn't sign off on a change order, you will not be paid for the work performed because it is outside of the approved scope. Monitor, review, and enforce ordering policies and procedures to ensure your project remains within budget. Always strive to improve, and document process-improvement measures to share with your client.

Customer Relationship Management. It's all about the metrics, baby! Most large corporations eat and breathe metrics to monitor your performance. There are two primary objectives for performance monitoring and reporting: financial (creating the value and margin you intended) and operational (delivering on what you committed to deliver). Your clients expect you to deliver your projects on time and within budget. That means you have to ensure that your internal processes and procedures are super tight and you don't miss a beat. They don't want to hear you saying "What had happened was!" or "Um, I forgot to include this in the budget, and now my cost is going to increase," or "My subcontractors aren't performing like they should, so I'm going to need more time."

Your job, as a highly capable small business owner, is to fix the problem, remain on task, and deliver an amazing, high-quality product or service. That's the main reason why I suggest you do so much upfront work on your business infrastructure, way before you get an opportunity to bid on a project. It's too late to tighten up your business after you've submitted the bid proposal.

Managing the incoming and outgoing monetary transactions and the project budgets is called fiscal monitoring. Here are a few best practices your business needs to implement:

- Submit invoices and supporting documentation for prompt payment.
- Ensure all documents and invoices meet contract requirements.
- Review and automate contract price monitoring and price deviations to ensure you adhere to the prices established within the contract.
- Receive approval on any price changes and get a signed change order.
- Monitor payment procedures and maintain copies of any audits.

Vendor/Supplier Relationship Management. Corporations will refer to you as a supplier when your business is awarded a contract. Most of your clients will use periodic business reviews and supplier scorecards to monitor your performance. It's a good idea and best practice to develop internal performance metrics for your business so you can track your own progress and identify gaps and blind spots for process-improvement measures. Your performance is measured in several key areas including:

- **Quality.** Are your product and service offerings of high quality?

- **Delivery.** Do you deliver on time as outlined in the contract?
- **Cost.** Is your pricing competitive and consistent with contract terms?
- **Responsiveness.** Do you respond quickly with viable solutions?
- **Innovation.** Do your deliver value-added and out-of-the-box solutions?
- **Risk.** Have you analyzed potential risks and implemented a risk-mitigation plan?
- **Safety.** Do you comply with all safety standards as outlined by OSHA (Occupational Safety and Health Administration)?
- **Customer Service.** Do you respond to all customer issues appropriately and in a timely manner?

Contract Renewal

Contract renewal is the review and evaluation of the client-supplier relationship to extend or renew the contract. This is the time to look at all the lessons learned during the previous contract period and to review all your process-improvement measures. Look at everything that you didn't include in the contract, the assumptions you got wrong, the costs you didn't include, or the unexpected events that happened to determine what changes need to be made to the contract. First things first, review the contract history, changes, and amendments made since the last renewal to ensure all terms are optimized and favorable for your business. If not, identify areas of opportunity.

Document all recommended changes to present to stakeholders and allow them to review the contract before the renewal date occurs. Ensure all necessary changes have been effectively applied to the contract prior to the renewal date, and set notifications to reflect the new renewal date. The longer you work on a project, the more you should learn, which should be reflected in the terms of your contract.

Contract Close-Out

You might be shedding a tear because the contract is over and you have really enjoyed it, or you may be doing the happy dance because this project has drained your team and resources. Either way, it's important to reconcile outstanding items and close out the contract. It's always a good idea to conduct a post-contract evaluation internally and with the client. A post-contract evaluation, in essence, looks at what went well with a contract and identifies areas for improvement. Typically, there are three areas of assessment: contract deliverables and outcomes, contractor performance, and internal/client contract-management team.

Once the evaluation is complete, gather all required and relevant contract documentation to ensure a clean break. That means all contract deliverables have been given and received, final reports of income and expenses have been generated, invoices have been reconciled, and all financial matters are complete. If you performed well on the project, you can ask for a referral and to be considered for a future project. Your work is done.

Your Business Needs an Edge: Certification

Certifications often give a small business an edge over their competition. There are various certifications based on industry, business size, disability, or minority status. Research to determine what certifications are required for your industry, and pursue them. Here are three popular industry certifications.

Project Management Certification. If your sales strategy is to secure large corporate and government contracts, it will be valuable to have a project management professional (PMP) on your team. Making effective project management part of your business culture will help to drive innovation, cost-savings, risk mitigation, and adherence to contract terms.

ISO 9001 Certification. ISO 9001 is the international standard that specifies requirements for a quality management system (QMS). Businesses use this standard to demonstrate their ability to consistently provide products and services that meet customer and regulatory requirements. If your business is in an industry that requires ISO 9001, get and maintain your certification.

LEED Certification. If your business is in construction or another sustainable industry, you may consider becoming LEED certified. This certification demonstrates a commitment to environmental sustainability and can be a key motivator for clients as they consider your services.

If 51% or more of your business is owned and operated by a United States citizens who is Asian, Black, Hispanic, or Native American, disabled, or member of the LGBT community, you should consider minority certification. Many corporations, such as BMW, UPS, the Coca-Cola Company, Georgia Power, and Delta Air Lines, have diverse-supplier spend goals. They proactively look for qualified minority firms to invite for bid opportunities. Additionally, government entities have set-aside mandates for minority participation in certain contracts. As a result, certification can be a great marketing tool to position your business in the corporate and government spaces, but it doesn't guarantee you a contract. You have to be willing to invest the time to build relationships to get the most out of your certification.

There are numerous MBE (Minority Business Enterprise) and WBE (Women's Business Enterprise) certifications that corporate and government entities recognize. Three of those are the Women's Business Enterprise National Council (WBENC) certification, the

National Minority Supplier Development Council (NMSDC) certification, and the Women's Business Enterprise (WBE) Certification.

WBENC is the largest certifier of women-owned businesses in the U.S. and a leading advocate for women business owners and entrepreneurs. They believe diversity promotes innovation, opens doors, and creates partnerships that fuel the economy. They provide the most relied upon certification standard for women-owned businesses and the tools to help them succeed. Their mission is to fuel economic growth globally by identifying, certifying, and facilitating the development of women-owned businesses. For more information, please visit www.wbenc.org.

The NMSDC Network includes a national office in New York and twenty-three regional affiliates across the country. NMSDC's goal is to help minority suppliers contribute to global supply chains and facilitate win-win partnerships with corporations and government entities. Minority Business Enterprise (MBE) certification with one of the NMSDC affiliates provides emerging firms with invaluable business development resources. With certification, enterprising business owners gain unparalleled access to corporate buyers and executives interested in working with certified minority business. For more information, please visit www.nmsdc.org.

WEConnect International is a global network that connects women-owned businesses to buyers globally. Women's Business Enterprise (WBE) certification is a formal process that verifies for corporations that purchase goods or services from women-owned businesses that these businesses meet universal standards for certification. For more information, visit www.weconnectinternational.org.

If 51% or more of your business is owned and operated by a member of the LGBT community, you may want to consider the **LGBTBE certification**. The National LGBT Chamber of Commerce certifies small businesses that are majority owned, managed, operated, and controlled by LGBT individuals. LGBT business certification shows that the business is a diverse organization that is considered "disadvantaged" by the U.S. government. For more information, visit www.nglcc.org.

Disability-Owned Business Enterprise (DOBE) certification is for small businesses that are at least 51% owned and managed by a person with a disability. Many large corporations involved in national, state, and local supply chains value this certification as a means to meet diverse-supplier spend goals. Certification is performed through the US Business Leadership Network (USBLN). For additional information, please visit www.usbln.org.

If you currently perform work with the government, or are looking to, you might want to consider a certification recognized by government entities.

The U.S. Small Business Administration (SBA) offers the **Women-Owned Small Business (WOSB) certification**, which provides exclusive access to competitive federal contracts for women who maintain at least 51% ownership of a business. You can receive certification through WBENC (www.wbenc.org), National Women Business Owners Corporation (www.nwboc.org), or the U.S. Women's Chamber of Commerce (www.uswcc.org).

Veteran-Owned Small Business (VOSB) or Service-Disabled Veteran-Owned Small Business (SDVOSB) certification can provide access to prime federal government contracts and subcontracts, through set-asides, for a small business with 51% or more veteran ownership. Start by getting certified as a veteran-owned business through VetBiz Registry, a veteran business database. If you are service-disabled, you'll need a disability status letter from the VA during the application process. For more information, visit www.vip.vetbiz.va.gov or www.nvbdc.org.

According to SBA, your small business may qualify for a **HUBZone designation** if it meets the following criteria: "(1) 51 percent of the business is owned and controlled by U.S. citizens, (2) the small business is a Community Development Corporation, an agricultural cooperative, a Native Hawaiian organization, or an Indian tribe, (3) the principal office is located in a HUBZone, (4) at least 35 percent of its employees live in a HUBZone."[30] The HUBZone Program was established for historically underutilized businesses, including those in urban and rural areas. Some government contracts are set aside for businesses that have the HUBZone designation. For additional information visit www.sba.gov.

The Small Disadvantaged Businesses (SDV) certification is for companies with owners who classify themselves as socially or economically disadvantaged. There is no application for this certification. If you are a majority owner who classifies yourself as an economically disadvantaged business you can self-certify. Visit www.sba.gov for further information.

The **8(a) Business Development Program** is for small businesses that have at least 51% ownership by a socially and economically disadvantaged individual. The program lasts for nine years and offers business training, technical assistance, marketing, and counseling to small businesses that have been certified. The first four years of the program are considered the developmental stage. The last five years are the transition stage. The ultimate goal of the program is to graduate 8(a) firms that will scale and thrive in a competitive business environment. To learn more visit www.sba.gov.

Certifications can be a great way to differentiate your business. Once you've obtained your new status, be sure to maintain certification by applying for renewal each year, and let your clients know by advertising your certification on marketing and promotional materials. Be sure to take advantage of perks that come with certification, such as attending member events, participating in mentoring programs, or actively applying for new contracts.

Supply Chain Management: Stop Bleeding Money

Supply chain management (of products) and service chain management (of services) are a struggle for a lot of small businesses. Simply put, supply or service chain management includes all the processes of getting a product or service from you to your client. To compete with the big boys, small businesses have to offer superior quality products and services at competitive prices. Often a small business's overhead is higher because it's harder for a small business to get volume discounts, so you have to tighten up your supply chain to ensure you aren't wastefully spending money.

Every process in the product or service lifecycle has costs associated with it. If you keep your costs low, you can pass on the savings to your clients and the profits to your leaders and employees. Effective supply-chain-management strategies can enhance productivity and cash flow. And who doesn't want a little more cash in the business pockets?

Supply chain management requires the following steps:

1. Document your supply or service chain process.
2. Build relationships with several vendors.
3. Implement quality control and assurance measures.
4. Create a solid plan for logistics.
5. Manage your vendors.
6. Control your inventory.

Document your supply or service chain process. The concepts of supply chain and service chain may be a little foreign because the topic is usually only dealt with when discussing global enterprises. However, if you really want to grow your business, you can't afford to ignore this element. Initially, my business only provided services, so I didn't think supply chain management was relative to me until I learned about service chain management. It took me a long time to implement a service-chain-management process. I documented all of the suppliers involved in helping me deliver my products or services, which included trainers, business consultants, salespeople, project managers, digital media experts, web developers, CRM specialists, printers, videographers, and customer service representatives.

When I mapped my supply chain process for each product and service I offered, I realized how many suppliers were involved. I identified gaps, bottlenecks, and areas of risk. I also realized I was overpaying my vendors, the delivery time to my clients was too long, and I didn't have the right systems in place to manage quality. Clearly outlining each step of your supply or service chain will help you strengthen your delivery method, reduce costs, and improve quality.

Build relationships with several vendors. Most small business owners have established relationships with one or two great vendors. You build strong relationships over time and establish a level of trust. However, if the vendor goes out of business or is unavailable, the small business owners can be left unable to fulfill an order or provide a service. It's vital that you build relationships with multiple vendors to ensure delivery as agreed to your clients. Also, as you scale your business, you will require additional vendors to fulfill the obligations of your new projects.

Implement quality control and assurance measures. Quality, quality, and quality—it's all about the quality. You don't want to supply your clients with low-quality or faulty products or inferior services. Your supply chain needs internal and external quality-control measures to ensure products and services are delivered according to contract terms and companywide standards. This starts with vetting every vendor to be sure they can deliver on time and within budget.

Regardless of the product or service you offer, ensure that you have a signed vendor contract that explains what's expected of each party.

What happens if a vendor doesn't deliver a product or service on time? Will they reimburse you for a loss? Research thoroughly to select the right vendors. Take time to vet all vendors, checking references, verifying capabilities, understanding their internal processes, and ensuring they have the financial stability to execute on your projects. Take your time to get to know them and build a solid relationship. Additionally, establish quality control or quality assurance metrics for each vendor to review their performance regularly. Implement an internal quality control or quality assurance policy to standardize your processes and ensure every customer receives the same level of service, every time.

Create a solid plan for logistics. Logistics is the process of goods and services moving through your service or supply chain. How do your products or services get from point A to point B? If you're providing consulting services, logistical planning may include travel and accommodations. If you're providing products, logistical planning may include a freight delivery schedule and shipping costs to customers. It's important to have supply chain software that manages your processes. If your company is large enough, you may invest in software like SAP, or if your company is smaller, research to find the best software application for your business. Software Advice, a software review company, does an annual ranking of supply chain software. This year, their top picks included Logiwa WMS, Infoplus, Spendwise, and SpendBoss.[31]

Manage your vendors. Proper vendor management helps you control costs, enhance customer service, and mitigate risks. Have a solid contract for each vendor, spelling out the terms of the engagement from scheduling and delivery to cost and discounts. Include a contingency plan, and spell out ramifications for missed deadlines.

Manage contracts for each vendor, and establish performance metrics for periodic reviews.

Control your inventory. I recently met a small business owner with an amazing product for the beauty industry. The brand packaging was on point, the testimonials were great, but the business had one major problem—inventory control. The business couldn't keep up with the orders. They were selling out of product faster than they could restock it. There was no inventory control process in place, and as a result, the company was losing money. On the flip side, I met a fashion designer, several years back, who started a high-end online boutique. When they launched, they stocked their warehouse full of products without testing the market. They had an overstock of inventory. Your business loses money if you have too much or too little inventory. You have to develop the right formula to keep enough inventory in stock without overstocking and ensure you have a steady sales flow while maintaining cash flow.

Look at the trends and patterns in your sales cycle to determine the appropriate amount of inventory to stock. Your supply chain software will enable you to pull reports and perform trend analysis to better estimate your inventory needs. Make sure your inventory control software integrates with your accounting software. Research best practices in supply or service chain management to determine which ones to implement in your business. Proper supply chain management increases efficiency, helps to control inventory, and improves cash flow, which all lead to happy clients. If you need help fine-tuning or implementing a robust supply or service chain management system, bring in a consultant. Your number one goal is to create a system that has redundancy and provides the highest level of quality and customer service.

Always Deliver What You Promise: Customer Service

Providing a wonderful customer service experience for your clients can dramatically impact your business growth. Sadly, customer service often takes a back seat to the daily demands of running a business. Great customer service should include delivering on your promise, exceeding customer expectations, and responding to all concerns in an expeditious manner. Keeping loyal customers happy is far less expensive than acquiring new ones. I can't tell you the number of restaurants I've visited that had delicious food but poor customer service. I didn't return because I didn't have an overall great customer experience. Just providing a stellar product or isn't enough. That' only part of the experience. You have to be meticulous about the details of your business, which includes every interaction with your customer from acquisition to nurturing a loyal client, who will refer you to business colleagues, family, and friends.

If a client isn't happy, a business owner isn't happy. Clients often become frustrated over small problems that aren't addressed, such as unclear communication, slow follow-up on questions, or ignored requests. Building competencies around customer service and continually improving your customer relations is one of the best ways to grow a small business. Keep in mind that your support process should be a part of your marketing and sales process within your CRM system so you and your team can track everything.

Customer Service Standards

What is customer satisfaction? It's a measure of how products and services supplied by a business meet or surpass customer expectations. In every encounter with your client, you want to ensure they have a positive experience with your product, service, employees, and anyone who represents your business.

There are six steps to providing excellent customer service. Include these steps in your customer service process:

Step 1. Listen actively and patiently to your client.

Step 2. Understand their concerns and validate them.

Step 3. Mitigate the risks of escalating the concern.

Step 4. Communicate effectively and honestly.

Step 5. Act immediately to resolve the problem.

Step 6. Remedy the issue with a win-win solution.

One of my favorite things about Amazon, besides the Prime two-day shipping and not having to go into a store, is the company's return policy. If I am not satisfied with my item, I simply get on my computer within thirty days of purchase, print out a shipping label, and return the item. Talk about customer satisfaction! Think about staying at a high-end hotel. There's water with fresh lemons and limes in the lobby, plush comfy seats, a bellman to take your bag, and a concierge at your beck and call. Now, that's good living and good customer service.

You don't have to run a billion-dollar company or a fancy hotel to have great customer service. You need to have a customer-centric approach, which simply means providing a positive customer experience before the sale, during the sale, and after the sale. This enhances your brand loyalty, increases profit through customer retention, and helps you gain a competitive edge.

Becoming more customer-centric requires a strategy that includes knowing your customers' needs and offering a reward structure that prioritizes customer service over simply generating revenue. Let's talk about some steps that will help you to start becoming more customer-centric.

Listen to your customers. Knowing more about your customers makes it easier for you to satisfy their needs and desires. Gathering thorough information about each customer makes it easier to sell to them and service them, which increase the chance that they'll continue to work with you. Ask your customers what they think, need, and want, and why. Once you have this information, act on it.

Enhance your customer's perception of your business. A customer's perception is much stronger than the reality. You may believe you're offering an amazing customer experience and addressing the needs and concerns of your customers, but if the customer doesn't agree, there's a notable gap. Talk to your customers to get feedback about what you can do better, and then, do it. This will help to ensure your desired customer experience is aligned with your customer's perception.

Make your customers part of the solution. Don't just guess about what your customers might want or need without considering their point of view. Tailor your product or service solution to meet the customers' needs.

Map your customer's journey. Creating a customer journey map is important in marketing and sales, but it's also important in customer service. This map allows you to walk in your customers' shoes by traveling with them as they interact with your business. Do your research and focus on desired outcomes from the customers' perspective. This enables you to see your customers' needs at each interaction with you, understand how well you meet those needs, and identify opportunities for improvement.

Monitor customer interactions. Listening to and monitoring your customers is critical because only you know all your touchpoints. Set key performance indicators (KPIs) based on customer expectations.

Monitor to see how well you meet and exceed goals, or identify areas that you fall short in and make improvements. These are the most popular methods for interacting with your customers:

- **Customer service portal.** It's helpful if you have a help-desk, FAQ, or support chat option on your website so clients can get the answers they need without help from your staff.
- **Social media.** Bring your social feeds directly into your CRM software so your staff can monitor the feeds and reply to customer service questions as needed.
- **Phone support.** To save on labor, minimize the need for a live support line as much as possible. In some cases, however, there's no way around it. Most CRM solutions will empower support staff by putting customer information at their fingertips.
- **Email.** People still email a lot, so set your emails up to be automatically created as needed.
- **Phone sales.** Some clients will call your sales department because that's who they know. Make sure your salespeople can manually log customer service cases into the CRM if need be.

Collect data. Most companies don't have one central location for all of their data. Sales data is in one system, marketing data in another, product and service information somewhere else, and digital data may not even be tracked. Ideally, all of your customer data should be integrated into one system and accessible for all departments within the organization. That way, employees can clearly see the relationship between you and your customers and make decisions accordingly. This is one of the most important systems to establish for your business.

Digitally engage with customers. Every transaction between your business and your customers generates data or information about that transaction. Carefully look at this data to gain insights into their buying behavior and improve the overall customer experience.

Develop a customer experience strategy. Review your customer journey map to understand your interactions with your customer, and then decide what you want the customer's experience to be. Create a customer experience strategy that clearly outlines these expectations, and train your entire team on it for successful implementation throughout the organization.

Recognize and reward your employees. Everybody likes a pat on the back or to be recognized for a job well done. Empower your employees to offer excellent service to your clients, and recognize them for their efforts. Create a corporate-wide incentive program that rewards your team for consistently implementing your customer experience strategy. Something very small could go a long way to show your team how valuable they are to you. When TruGreen came to treat my lawn, the technician gave me a survey to rate my experience. If he received a score of 10, which meant a customer was completely satisfied with the service, he would receive a $10 gift card. The company had instituted a corporate-wide 10X10 Customer Satisfaction Experience. For every 10 rating technicians received, they would receive a $10 gift card.

A customer-centric focus is crucial to your business's success whether you have a B2C or B2B model. Either way, there's always a customer on the other end. Determine the profile of your customer, establish key metrics and performance indicators for success, and restructure company departments if required to ensure proper alignment. When the customer feels involved and important, you'll know you've reached your goal of becoming customer-centric.

Sales KPIs

Developing sales KPIs (key performance indicators) for your business can be a bit tricky because there is no "one size fits all." When developing your sales metrics, the most important thing is to set metrics that will help you achieve your business sales goal. Sales KPIs are measurable values that indicate the performance of various sales processes. When developing sales KPIs, think about the method you used to set S.M.A.R.T. goals. The metrics should be specific, relevant, measurable, actionable, and timely. Historical data and trends will help you create your KPIs.

Here are five steps to help you define your sales KPIs.

Step 1. Develop corporate-wide sales goals.

This includes goals for revenue, growth, customer acquisition, and customer retention. You can break down these goals, such as by department, but you need to have overarching corporate goals. Most companies will have one primary objective with one or two secondary goals that support the primary objective. Everyone in the company should know these goals. For example, here is a corporate-wide sales goal:

Primary goal: Increase annual revenue to $10 million.

Secondary goal: Grow 5% month over month.

Step 2. Break down the goals.

Make the goals attainable by breaking them down into bite-size pieces. How much monthly revenue does your business need to make in order to achieve $10 million in sales? Let's do the math.

$10,000 ÷ 12 months = $833,333.00 per month

Primary sales goal: $833,333.00 in monthly sales

Secondary sales goal(s): 5% growth month over month

Average contract size: $175,000

Average sales cycle: 3 months

Cost of sales: $4,500

Opportunity-to-win ratio: 80%

Step 3. Create an action plan.

Take the goals and metrics you outlined in step 2 and determine what sales strategy you need to reach those goals. Work backward to determine how many contracts you need to close to reach your goals. How many sales meetings, emails, or calls are required to obtain your prospect goal? How many leads or contacts will your sales team need to generate to fill your pipeline? Keep drilling down until you understand all of the sales activities required to reach your revenue goals.

Whether you have a new business with $0 in revenue or an established business with millions in revenue, follow this process to ensure that you have a systematic process of monitoring the overall effectiveness of your sales process.

Step 4. Review your metrics.

Look at your numbers. Are you on track to reach your sales goals? What is your close ratio? Are your conversion rates increasing or decreasing? Are you receiving a return on investment from your marketing efforts to fill your pipeline? Review your metrics monthly to determine if you are on track.

Step 5. Monitor your metrics.

Once you have your sales metrics in place, it's important to monitor them so you can recognize trends, see what's working, and identify areas of improvement. Keeping the key metrics in front of you and your team will help you track your progress and make changes as needed.

KPIs are living and breathing metrics, meant to be shared and monitored regularly. A great way to monitor your metrics is to use a sales dashboard that combines informative graphs and actionable metrics and gives you a quick overview of your company's sales performance. There are a ton of software applications that offer integrated dashboards, reporting tools, and data analytics. You can search Google for top-performing dashboards for small businesses to get a list of software applications with pros, cons, pricing, and customer reviews.

To get you started, here are several common sales KPIs.

Monthly sales (KPI). Compare your actual monthly sales to projections and goals over time.

Lead flow (KPI). The number of leads your salespeople work on each month. This measures the current month's new leads against previous periods to see whether the money and time you're spending on marketing is justified. It will help you spot trends and adjust your marketing and sales activities accordingly.

Lead response time (KPI). The rise of inbound marketing means companies are focusing more on online methods to generate leads. Research has shown that the lifespan of an online lead can be quite short. Speed of response is crucial.

Activity metrics (KPI). Review all activities (email sequencing, complimentary consultations, LinkedIn, Twitter, prospecting, tradeshows, etc.) to determine which are providing the best quality leads. Set a monthly target, and focus on the activities that yield the greatest results.

Lead-to-sale conversion rate (KPI). This is important because you want to know the quality of your leads. For example, if 10% of your new leads convert into paying customers that means that 90 leads out of 100 bring in no business whatsoever. There's always a reason why new leads don't become paying clients. Find the cause, and improve the sales results by tackling the problem (providing better sales materials, offering a greater benefit to the prospect, improving the customer experience in the buying process, or offering promotional pricing).

Cost per lead (KPI). Everything your team does to attract new leads costs you money. To calculate your cost per lead, add up all of your monthly marketing-related costs and divide the total by the number of new leads for the month. Include a portion of the marketing team's salary for time spent on lead generation. Decrease your cost per lead by improving the customer experience and increasing brand awareness. If your cost per lead keeps rising, you may need to revisit your marketing strategy and focus on more profitable channels.

Cost per conversion (KPI). In reality, only a small number of your leads will actually convert to paying customers. That means the cost per conversion can be incredibly high. To calculate the cost per conversion, add up all your monthly marketing costs and divide the total by the number of new customers or sales for the month.

Customer attrition/turnover rate (KPI). This metric shows how many clients decide to stop using your service or product. To grow, the number of new customers has to exceed the attrition rate. Customer attrition rate is calculated as a percentage of clients who have stopped using the service during the previous one-year period. For example, if 4 clients out of 25 stop subscribing to your service, the attrition rate is 4 / 25 x 100 = 16%. It's normal to lose some clients, but a high attrition rate often indicates problems in the sales process that need to be corrected.

Sales cycle length (KPI). This is the time between the client's first contact and the client's first payment. A sales cycle that's too long can hurt your business. Use your CRM system to track the average time between a lead becoming a prospect and when the sale is closed. Enhance your process to shorten the sales cycle whenever possible.

Average contract length (KPI). Businesses that offer time-based contracts or sell subscription services can measure the average length of contracts. Take a simple average of the lengths of all the contracts signed in a month and ensure the trend is going upward rather than downward.

Team spirit (KPI). For a sales team to be as productive as possible, team spirit and morale need to remain high. Sales culture demands consistent productivity and high energy to drive sales. To measure the morale of your team, use a mix of surveys and qualitative discussions with sales team members. Measure employee happiness and see how it correlates to sales performance.

Marketing collateral conversion rate (KPI). Your branding and marketing teams are busy creating brochures, videos, and social media postings, but are these tools converting sales? To identify a possible disconnect between your sales and marketing teams, measure the percentage of sales closed using a piece of marketing collateral. When you make a sale, survey the client to find out what marketing methods were used.

Sales are the heartbeat of a business. If the business isn't making money, then the doors will eventually close. An effective sales process includes more than just sales goals. Make sure you invest the necessary time to implement the C.L.O.S.E. Sales Method in your business.

The **C.L.O.S.E.** Sales Method consists of the following components:

- **C**lassic sales psychology
- **L**everaged sales cycle
- **O**ptimized procurement and certifications
- **S**upply chain
- **E**ngagement and customer service

Not only will your sales increase but you will enhance your overall customer experience.

From the Desk of the Decision-Maker

Vickie Irwin-Avery

General Manager, Supplier Diversity Electric Operations

Southern Company

SMALL BUSINESSES OCCUPY a relevant space in the supply chain of major corporations; however, they must demonstrate the mutually beneficial value and innovation they offer. Small businesses should "own" their value proposition and demonstrate that they're the subject-matter experts in their field or industry.

Research a corporation's business and approach them with solutions that provide increased benefits to their customers while meeting the corporation's cost, efficiency, and quality and reliability standards. Understand the current and future state of the industry and any new trends and breaking technology. Familiarize yourself with the corporation's values and mission. Learn how the corporation/industry's pricing model works. (How does this company make a profit?) Understand the business's key drivers for operational and financial success.

> “A bad system will beat a good person every time.”
>
> — W. Edwards Deming

CHAPTER SIX

Systems

	01	Scale Your Business with Systems
	02	Delegation and Implementing Systems
D	03	Diversified Marketing Platforms
E	04	Expansive Sales & Client Management
L	05	Leveraged Technology
E	06	Empowered Human Capital Management
G	07	Game-Changing Operations Procedures
A	08	Action-Oriented Customer Service
T	09	Trusted Legal Counsel
E	10	Efficient Financial Processes

The CEO D.E.L.E.G.A.T.E. System

MOST SMALL BUSINESSES FAIL not because of a lack of talent, hard work, and effort, but because of a lack of systems and processes. Many coaches, strategists, and thought leaders often say work "on" your business not "in" your business. However, when you're working sixty to ninety hours a week to service existing clients and constantly networking to get new ones, it can be hard to find time to work "on" your business. I know all too well what it's like to be so immersed in building or growing your business that you dive straight into putting out fires, adding new products and services, and creating strategic partnerships. You don't make time to create well-thought-out systems that could scale your business and save you a lot of heartache, money, and time.

The importance of creating systems hit home hard for me when one of my clients died of a massive heart attack in his early fifties. His death shook me to the core because he delivered my youngest son and we had developed a great business relationship over the years. A very successful ob-gyn, best-selling author, and philanthropist, he gave his all to his practice, which was more like his calling. Even though he'd grown his practice to a successful, multimillion-dollar business, this achievement came at a high cost to his family and his health. He worked more than eighty hours a week, pouring everything he had into his business. We often talked about the need for him to slow down, bring on other doctors, and systemize his processes. He even made some strides in two of the areas, but he still held on too tightly to his business, doing way too many deliveries and seeing an unhealthy number of patients. It likely cost him his life.

One of the best ways to have harmony between your life and business is to implement systems that enable you to leverage your time, finances, and resources.

Get Unstuck with Systems

Business systems are documented procedures and processes that enable the business to run without you. By consistently using these proven methods of running your business, you avoid having to reinvent the wheel over and over again. You can duplicate successes, identify areas of inefficiency, and make improvements. Regardless of the size of your business and whether you are in the start-up, sustaining, or scale-up phase, systems will help you grow your business over time.

Start with the end in mind. Do you want to grow your business to sell it? Do you want to have a team of people running your business while you oversee the entire operation? Do you want to build a business you can leave as a legacy for your family? Regardless of your answer, efficient business systems will enable you to scale your business properly and achieve your goal.

Many small business owners hold their business so close to the heart that they aren't able to make the best business decisions and they fail to put into place the systems that would let them take a step back. Without systems, you don't own a business; you *are* the business. If you want to double your business revenue, you have to work double hours, which limits your revenue opportunities because there are only so many hours in a day. If you want to take a vacation or you get sick and need time off, your business shuts down. On the flip side, if you have systems in place, then you *own* the business because the business will continue to run with or without your direct involvement.

If you want to experience financial success and freedom (whatever that means to you), you have to shift your mindset on how you operate your business. You need documented systems in every key area, including marketing, sales, accounting, talent management, and other operational functions. Remember that systems are the difference between *being* your business and *owning and running* your business. That little distinction will make all the difference in the world to your financial and personal freedom. Simply put, systems will **S**ave **Y**our **S**elf **T**ime **E**nergy and **M**oney, personally and professionally.

Scale Your Business by Implementing Systems

I've had my share of business failures. However, since I learned something from each experience, I call them lessons instead of failures. In my more than twenty-five years of business experience, my greatest stress came from operating without a business strategy or systems in place. Many, many years ago, when a business partner and I started a new media company, we focused on developing websites and digital media products. We started with a bang, networking and securing new clients. Unfortunately, neither of us had a background in the services we provided. So when we started getting clients, we had no idea how to deliver. I was unprepared, stressed-out, and overwhelmed.

Today, it would be easy to go to YouTube and take a quick tutorial on WordPress or some other DIY web-development software, but this was back in the day of coding and HTML. Our business grew much faster than we had prepared for, and we had no systems in place to deliver our product or fully service our clients. The story turned out well because we ended up partnering with very experienced web developers, but we also lost money because we underbid for a lot of projects and underestimated the work involved to provide high-quality products and extra value to our clients.

Businesses often grow at a rate faster than anticipated, and when the train starts moving, it's hard to catch up. It's much easier to build systems from the start of a business; however, it's never too late, even if your business is in crisis mode. There are many benefits of having systems in your business.

Systems build a valuable asset. One of the most valuable assets in a business is the set of systems that makes the business run like a well-oiled machine. In that case, the business doesn't have to rely on one or a few key people for its success. In essence, the business can continue running without you. I read an article in which Warren Buffet said he loved to invest in boring businesses that were easy to understand and had repeatable systems and processes in place. He said he didn't invest in high-risk businesses but preferred easy-to-understand products and businesses with well-documented processes. You are the visionary for your business, and you want documented systems in place to ensure your vision is executed.

Systems help you leverage and scale. When your business has documented and repeatable processes in place, you can expand and scale more easily. As an example, look at Chick-fil-A. It doesn't matter if you're in Atlanta, Miami, or Houston, for the most part, your experience at a Chick-fil-A restaurant is going to be the same. Why? An "operations and franchise" manual spells out everything from how the restaurant looks to what the staff will wear, how the customers are greeted, and the way the food should be prepared. All the systems are documented to ensure the business can scale and doesn't depend on one person or even a few people. If these processes weren't spelled out, then every time a new restaurant opened, the operator would have to re-create each aspect of the business, which leaves room for error, wasted labor cost, and unnecessary expense.

Systems provide consistency. One of the most important things you can do to build customer loyalty is to ensure a consistent, positive customer experience. With pricing, customer service, product or service delivery, technical support, or accounting, a customer should know that you'll always deliver on time and with high quality. To ensure this type of consistency in your business, it's imperative that you document your processes step by step.

Recently, I visited Massage Envy to finally use a gift card that had been in my purse for the last few years. I was a little embarrassed when I made the appointment because I thought the gift card might have expired. When the receptionist told me it was still valid, I scheduled a ninety-minute massage. When I arrived, the young lady who greeted me had a very bubbly personality, and she gave me a booklet that explained the services I'd be receiving. She also provided me with a packet of paperwork that explained the Massage Envy "system." In essence, regardless of which massage therapist I worked with, I would receive the same level of service. They'd all been taught a particular method for massages and how to deliver them. This system enables Massage Envy to offer a consistent client experience independent of how much experience individual massage therapists have in providing the service.

Systems lower labor cost. One of the biggest expenses for many small businesses is labor cost. I had a recent conversation with a thought leader who operates a multimillion-dollar branding and marketing business. She explained that one of the biggest shifts she had to make in her business was taking time to thoroughly think through her processes (systems) and develop a clear five-year business strategy. During this process, she realized she was overstaffed. She had a lot of employees operating inefficiently and performing redundant functions. Once she and her leadership team took a step back to document their systems, she was able to consolidate her team and hold team members more accountable for their productivity by ensuring they executed based on the systems.

Once you and the necessary team members sit down and think through and document your processes, you'll understand where the human bottlenecks are, which might include you. Then you can determine what labor you need to run your business efficiently. Systems allow employees to do more in less time, which can inevitably lower your labor costs, increase morale, improve efficiency, and positively add to the bottom line.

I've highlighted four, but there are numerous benefits to implementing sound systems in your business. If you're ready to save time, energy, money, and countless headaches, start implementing systems in your business today. In the next few pages, I'll provide you with a high-level overview of some key systems you should have operating in your business to help you scale and increase productivity, but first, let's look at the steps for creating a system.

Delegate Is Not a Bad Word: Seven Steps to Creating a System

Business owners, you cannot clone yourself, but strong and effective systems truly are the next best thing. Are you ready to stop reinventing the wheel? Strong systems make it so you don't have to do that anymore. As your business grows, test, modify, and tweak your systems as needed. My rule of thumb when it comes to systems is to decide if you need to "Do it," "Delegate it," or "Delete it." As a CEO, you should be spending 80% of your time working in your "sweet spot" and deleting or delegating everything else. (Your sweet spot is made up of revenue-generating activities.)

Effective systems in your business give your freedom. They give you personal freedom because you don't have to be tied to your desk to ensure your business runs successfully, and they free you to grow your business with the help of others. I discovered the brilliance of systems when I started creating products in my business. I decided to add products as an additional revenue stream to generate passive income. Most of my consulting clients were on retainer. In addition to providing services, I wanted to package my intellectual property in products.

My core consulting business is scalable because I have project teams who perform a great deal of the consultative work. In the same way, I wanted to develop a scalable model for delivering products. My goal was to develop products one time and then sell them over and over again. This started my quest to learn everything I could about online marketing, product development, protecting my intellectual property, sales funnels, and more.

During this journey, I realized that online marketing success is rooted in systems. From product development and launch to social media marketing and everything in between, you must have a system. Thought leaders who reached the multimillion-dollar level all had systems in place to market and sell to other people in their specific industry. Although the titles and methods were different, everyone who was successful had created a framework or system for how they did business and attached a price tag to it. Very smart, and I wanted in.

I enrolled in two of the top programs for building an online business. The expense was hefty but well worth the investment. I didn't stop there. I continued learning by investing in certification for Lean Six Sigma, which strives to improve performance by systematically removing waste and reducing variation. I began developing strategic systems in my business and helping my clients implement lean systems in their daily operations.

As a wife and a mom, my house can sometimes be a little chaotic with so much happening at one time. I utilize these same steps to help me create routines and systems for my family so we all stay sane, happy, and in a peaceful place. Here are seven steps to create a system.

Step 1. Name the system.

Determine what system needs to be created and name it (lead generation, customer service, order fulfillment, accounting, etc.).

Step 2. Create your goal.

Establish the result you want your system to accomplish by creating a specific objective or goal. For instance, in your accounting system, you may want to ensure that all invoices are paid within fifteen days. Your specific steps in the system need to lead to this objective.

Step 3. Document the process.

Document the current process, step by step. Identify and write down the major components needed to perform each step in the process. Write the processes in a manner that allows your staff to easily read and follow every step without having to ask you any questions. Make sure your process doesn't have any ambiguity in it. If your staff has to interpret the information, it leaves room for error. Each team member responsible in the process should be involved in documenting it to ensure complete accuracy.

Remember, the goal is to remove you from the system and make it implementable by others so whoever has the task of executing the system can easily follow the steps and achieve the desired result. The system should also be written in a step-by-step manner because, if you don't achieve your desired goal, you can to go back through the system to determine what step was missed. This process should be followed for new and existing systems.

Step 4. Review the process.

After you and your team have thoroughly documented the process, check each step for accuracy and make sure they're in the right order to achieve your desired goal. Collaborate with your team to make any necessary changes.

Step 5. Create a visual map.

It's very important to have your process presented in an easy-to-read format. There are several methods you can use, including a checklist, flowchart, process map, or an infographic. Select an option that will be easy for you to update if needed and easy for your staff to follow. Include all of the steps of your process in your visual map.

Step 6. Execute your system.

Once you document your system, determine if it will need to be systemized, automated, or delegated. Systemized means you will do it yourself but follow a standard process. Automation uses technology to execute a particular process, like your online marketing, to increase reliability and efficiency. Delegation is entrusting a task or responsibility with specified guidelines of expectations, results to be achieved, and performance measurements to another person.

Step 7. Evaluate and continuously improve your systems.

One key to successfully scaling your business is to ensure that you perform ongoing and continuous improvement to your systems, products, services, and processes. Once you've implemented your systems, periodically review them to ensure that you're consistently achieving the desired results. If the system needs to be changed or enhanced, you and your team should invest the time and resources required to make your business operate as efficiently as possible.

It's Time to Boss Up: Systems Your Business Must Have

Before I had systems in my business, I couldn't accurately track my results. For instance, there was no system in place to track the return on investment from the money I spent to acquire new customers from networking events, social media, sponsorship, advertising, and tradeshows. Once my team and I sat down to document the actual steps in each one of these areas, attached a dollar amount, and then did the analysis to determine our success rate, it helped me realize I acquired most of my clients through strategic partnerships and referrals, instead of advertising or tradeshows. Without this information, I could have kept spinning my wheels and spending money in areas that didn't yield the highest level of return. Instead, I established my marketing system to leverage the avenues that yielded me the greatest return on investment for my marketing dollars.

There are many specific systems your business will need to have based on your industry, the products and services you offer, and your desired method for operating your business. However, there are eight systems you should have in place regardless of your industry or business. I have already addressed some of these systems, and I will summarize them here. Others, I will discuss in more detail.

The CEO D.E.L.E.G.A.T.E. System is made up of eight essential processes:

1. Diversified marketing platforms
2. Expansive sales and client management
3. Leveraged technology
4. Empowered human capital management
5. Game-changing operations procedures
6. Action-oriented customer service
7. Trusted legal counsel
8. Efficient financial processes

Diversified Marketing Platforms

Often, your sales and marketing-management tools overlap and are packaged in the same software, like Infusionsoft, Ontraport, or HubSpot. A marketing-management system monitors the process for how you market or promote your business. This includes customer relationship management and promotional strategies, like email marketing and social media ads, that you use consistently in your business.

Expansive Sales and Client Management

A sales and client-management system includes software that manages your entire sales funnel, from pre-sale to post-sale, and maintains and monitors customer service and client engagement, including refunds, exchanges, and complaints. Sales management software enables your sales team to stay organized by tracking customer information and reducing data entry for calls, emails, texts and documents. Your team is able to focus on selling rather than worrying about administrative tasks such as updating databases, scheduling calendar events, or creating follow up reminders. The software automates reminders for follow ups, schedules tasks necessary to the sales process, and creates assignments for relevant team members.

Leveraged Technology

Technology changes at the speed of lightning. There are so many technological advances, from artificial intelligence and blockchain technology to the Internet of things (IoT) and cybersecurity. It's a best practice to review technology trends a few times a year to identify shifts within the technology landscape that affect your business. To remain competitive and offer innovative and value-added solutions, you need to know technology industry trends.

In a recent strategic planning session, the relevant trends for the construction industry were artificial intelligence, robots, smart cities, connective construction sites, and drones, to name a few. My client had to tweak their current service offerings to incorporate two of these elements that were cost-effective and viable solutions to integrate into their business model. To remain competitive, they have to ensure their business is able to scale with the appropriate technology. Several of the other new technologies were very costly and wouldn't yield a substantial return on investment because of the size of their business, so they decided not to invest in them. A word of caution, research and thoroughly review and analyze the cost of any technology investment to determine which should be implemented in your business. Some of your research may yield a greater understanding of what's happening in your industry with no further action required on your part. All new technology should be incorporated into your strategies and align with your business goals.

Four technology applications should be at the center of your business: a customer relationship management (CRM) platform, a financial software tool, an application for mass communication for marketing and sales, and data protection software. These technology components will allow you to stay organized, manage cash flow, rapidly communicate, and protect your business from cyber threats. I've addressed the CRM, marketing, and sales systems in earlier chapters and will discuss the financial software tool later in this chapter. Now, let's take a look at data and cybersecurity.

Data or cybersecurity is the number one technology small businesses need to seriously consider in today's world of malware and security breaches. Any business of any size, which has confidential and proprietary information, needs to ensure their data is not vulnerable. Cybersecurity refers to protective digital privacy measures applied to prevent unauthorized access to computers, databases, and websites and to protect data from corruption. All of your computers should be protected against viruses and spyware by installing antivirus software and antispyware that is updated regularly. Protect your internet connections by using a firewall and encrypting passwords and other pertinent information. Also, make sure your Wi-Fi network is hidden.

Establish corporate-wide security practices and policies to protect all sensitive information. Educate employees about your cybersecurity practices and hold them accountable. Work closely with your banks and credit card processors to ensure all transactions are secure. Back-up all systems regularly, and ensure important data is also stored off-site in a cloud environment. Maintain an SSL (Secure Sockets Layer) certificate for all public-facing websites.

Whether you offer a product or a service, technology is a key factor in growing and scaling your business. It helps you to operate lean, be more efficient, and increase productivity. Review your current infrastructure to ensure you have a customer relationship management (CRM) platform, a financial software tool, an application for mass communication for marketing and sales, and data protection software. If you need to, hire an information technology (IT) consultant to help you build a solid technology infrastructure that is scalable and helps you achieve your business goals.

Empowered Human Capital Management

A human capital or talent management system is an integrated software suite that addresses the four pillars of talent management: recruitment, performance management, learning and development, and compensation management.

You're an amazing leader. You're innovative, courageous, and compassionate, but what about your team? Have you had problems with employee retention, recruitment, and management, or issues with building a strong corporate culture? If you have employees, the answer is probably yes. Whether you have one, one hundred, one thousand or ten thousand employees, there are some human resources best practices to which you should adhere.

When human capital management is done right, employee performance, commitment, and loyalty increase. This helps the business accomplish its mission and ultimately achieve its business goals. There are several components to effective human capital management. To simplify, let's group them into three main categories: administration, talent management, and employee relations.

Administration

1. Employee documents policies
2. Job descriptions
3. Business compliance
4. Standard Operating Procedures (SOPs)
5. Payroll and benefits

Talent Management

1. Recruiting
2. Hiring
3. Onboarding

Employee Relations

1. Training and development
2. Performance measures
3. Progressive discipline
4. Retention
5. Termination

Administration: Employee Documents

Do you have all of your employees' paperwork in a nice file, or is it scattered somewhere in the office or saved in random folders on a computer? Human resources (HR) team members are, in essence, the bookkeepers of your staff. They maintain all the paperwork keeps your business compliant with labor laws and protected in the event of a dispute.

If you have W-2 employees, you should have the following paperwork on file for all of them:

- **I-9 form:** ensures an employee has authorization to work in the United States
- **Medical file:** copies of medical insurance and life insurance enrollment documents and disability information if applicable
- **Employee file:** job description, offer letter, IRS Form W-4 (the Employee's Withholding Allowance Certificate), payroll details, signed acknowledgment of employee handbook, performance reviews, training verifications, employee benefits forms, next-of-kin and emergency contacts forms, and any other pertinent documentation related to the employee's tenure with your organization

Administration: Employee Policies

In addition to these standard forms, your business should have a current employee handbook that outlines the expectations and protocols for your business.

At a minimum, your employee handbook should include:

- Business mission, values, and objectives
- Code of conduct
- Anti-discrimination policy

- Non-disclosure agreement (if needed)
- Safety and security policies
- Job descriptions
- Organizational chart
- Compensation and benefits descriptions
- Schedule, vacation, sick time, and leave policy
- Recruitment and hiring policy
- Discipline policy

Administration: Job Descriptions

A note of caution, make sure your job descriptions are detailed and document the exact requirements of a job. Too many small businesses skip this step, and it wreaks havoc later when dealing with employee-relations issues. Whether it's a full-time or part-time position, each job description should include the following: job title, location, role objective, responsibilities, desired experience, company description, salary range, benefits, work hours, travel requirements, and company compliance-required information (if applicable).

Administration: Business Compliance

One of the most important functions of an HR department is ensuring that the business is compliant with local, state, and federal rules and regulations that impact all aspects of the employee relationship, from hiring and benefits administration to termination and workplace safety. Small business owners often fail to take the required time to learn about laws that impact their business, such as the Fair Labor Standards Act (FLSA), the Immigration Reform and Control Act, and the Equal Pay Act. If you have one W-2 employee, you need to become aware of labor laws and workplace rules and regulations that impact your business including, but not limited to:

- **Anti-discrimination laws:** including Title VII, the Americans with Disabilities Act (ADA), and the Age Discrimination in Employment Act (ADEA)
- **Wage and hour laws:** the Fair Labor Standards Act (FLSA) and individual state laws pertaining to minimum wage
- **Leave laws:** the Family and Medical Leave Act (FMLA) and relevant state laws
- **Immigration laws:** the Immigration and Nationality Act (INA), Immigration Reform and Control Act (IRCA), and the Illegal Immigration Reform and Immigrant Responsibility Act (IIRIRA).
- **Benefits laws:** various required benefits, such as social security and workers' compensation, that employers must provide and which may vary based on the size of your business and the state you do business in
- **Safety laws:** Occupational Safety and Health Administration (OSHA) laws
- **Union laws:** compliance with the National Labor Relations Act (NLRA), even for non-union businesses

In addition, the Department of Labor (DOL) requires that certain labor law posters be displayed in the workplace. You can download your workplace posters on the DOL website. I know this is a lot to remember especially since many of these laws change often. Outsourcing to a third-party HR provider can assist you in remaining compliant.

Administration: Standard Operating Procedures (SOPs)

Standard operating procedures are written, step-by-step instructions describing how to perform specific tasks. The purpose of SOPs is to ensure employees complete the exact tasks, the same way, every time to ensure consistency. Standard operating procedures help maintain efficiency and safety. They should be brief, easy to understand, and updated periodically to ensure they are relevant and applicable to the business. SOPs enhance communication, increase efficiency, save time, mitigate risk, and improve accountability. You should have SOPs for every function in your business, including but not limited to: sales, customer service, human resources, finance and accounting, product launches, and legal.

Administration: Payroll and Benefits

Many small businesses may not be able to offer comprehensive benefits packages like larger companies, but there's still benefits-administration work to be performed, including payroll.

Payroll processing and benefits are complicated responsibilities that also fall under the umbrella of HR. Payroll refers specifically to the money paid to employees by the company and involves tax deductions and withholdings. If you need assistance with payroll, you can always check with the bank that houses your business accounts or utilize a payroll service, such as Intuit Payroll, Paychex, or ADP.

Providing comprehensive benefits to your employees is equally as important as payroll management. There are two types of benefits, those required by law and those that aren't.

Benefits required by law include:

- Social security tax
- Workers' compensation
- Unemployment insurance
- COBRA insurance
- Family and medical leave

There are exceptions to providing these benefits, depending on the size of your business and the state in which your business is based.

Benefits that are not required by law, but which are often offered as part of a benefits package include:

- Health insurance
- Dental and vision insurance
- Commuter benefits
- Paid time off
- Paid holidays
- Work-from-home flexibility
- 401(k) plans
- Employee discounts
- Employee assistance programs

The process of deciding what benefits to offer to your employees can be fairly involved and is another reason small business owners outsource their human resources. Employees will typically select benefits during the onboarding process or during an open enrollment period.

Talent Management: Recruiting and Hiring

Recruiting and hiring can be stressful, especially if you don't have a good process in place. Hiring a good employee requires matching a candidate's skills, expertise, and abilities with the culture of your business and the job requirements. In addition to having the experience, they must be the right personality fit and have the potential to develop and grow within your company. When hiring a candidate look five to ten years into the future to determine if that person will still be a good fit for your team. If you're looking for an employee to be a part of your team for the long run, you need to take into consideration what matters most to the people you're hiring.

A recent Care.com article, "Retention by Generation," addresses the needs, values, and expectations that are unique to each generation.[32] For Millennials/Generation Y/Gen Next (born between 1980 and 1994) engagement, meaning, and purpose in their work is crucial. They want to be aligned with companies that represent their values, have flexibility, and offer leadership opportunities. Generation X (born between 1965 and 1979) have gained valuable experience, knowledge, and expertise throughout their careers and want to pursue leadership roles. They have an intraprenuer spirit—that of an employee with entrepreneurial skills and leanings—and don't want to be micro-managed. They want independence, recognition, and support. Baby Boomers (born between 1946 and 1964) are rapidly approaching retirement. They value a higher salary, security, benefits, a retirement plan, and advancement within the company. Of course, these are generalizations, and every individual is motivated by different factors. Take the time to thoroughly get to know the candidates you're hiring to make sure they're the right fit for your business.

Ask open-ended questions in your interviews to determine how a candidate has responded or will respond in specific situations. Ask them to provide examples and walk you through the process they've used in the past.

Here are some examples of open-ended questions that can be asked during the interview process.

Tell me about yourself.

What is your greatest strength?

What is your greatest weakness?

What motivates you, and why?

What are your five-year professional goals?

How do you handle workplace conflict?

Why are you the most qualified person for this job?

Describe an innovative solution you provided for your previous employer.

How would you describe your leadership style?

Tell me about something that isn't on your resume.

How do you foster team collaboration?

How do you evaluate success?

Tell me about a time you handled a stressful situation at work.

Why are you leaving your current job?

Recruiting and hiring can be a heavy lift because it has a lot of moving pieces, including writing a persuasive job description, identifying the right vehicles to recruit talent, interviewing, and preparing a competitive offer. Additionally, you have to adhere to Equal Employment Opportunity (EEO) laws throughout this process.

Effective HR management includes developing and administering processes and systems that minimize the likelihood of a bad hire. Additionally, those systems help to reduce the risk of discrimination claims based on inappropriate questions asked during the interviewing process or negligent or unethical reference checking.

A CareerBuilder survey found that "the average cost of a bad hire is $17,000 annually in lost productivity, time, and cost of hiring and training a replacement."[33] Additionally, they found that some candidates go to great lengths to embellish their resume with facts that are inaccurate, including where they went to school, degrees they obtained, skillsets they have, places they worked, and references. As best practices, you should perform a criminal background check, confirm identity and employment history, verify education, check licensing, and perform a drug or credit check if applicable for your business. Since your employees may potentially have access to critical data, it's important that you verify that they are who they say they are. Unfortunately, the days of sealing a deal with a handshake, accepting everybody's word as the gospel, and borrowing a cup of sugar from your neighbor are pretty much gone.

Do your due diligence to ensure you're hiring the person who has the skillset, personality, and work ethic that's compatible with your culture. Taking a little extra time during the recruitment and hiring process can prevent you from having to fire a bad hire. The CareerBuilder survey mentioned above summarizes the top reasons companies had to fire a bad hire, including: the employee negatively impacted morale, lack of quality in work product, productivity issues, attendance problems, inability to work well with other employees, and an exaggeration of skillset and expertise.

Talent Management: The Onboarding Process

"Onboarding process, what is that?" You would be surprised how many small business owners have asked me that question. Onboarding is not just for large corporations. It's required for any business that wants to successfully integrate new employees into the business culture and the way you operate. An onboarding process can last a few weeks or up to a year depending on the role and responsibilities.

Here is a checklist of several things to complete during the onboarding process:

- Employee must complete W-4 and I-9 forms.
- Employee must provide their social security number.
- Employee must provide bank account information and a voided check (if they desire to get paid via direct deposit).
- Employee enrolls in company benefits (optional).
- Employee must provide emergency contact information.
- Employer must provide employee with equipment needed to do their job (such as a computer or phone).

On your employees' first day, they should be given a copy of the employee handbook and a job description that explains the responsibilities and expectations of their new role. During their first week, they might receive training from their manager, shadow several team members, and have one-on-one meetings to gain a deeper insight into the business culture and processes.

As they ease into their roles over the next few months, it's important to provide them with constructive feedback, coaching, and mentorship. The onboarding process will vary from company to company. The most important thing is having a structured process that prepares them with the information they will need to be successful.

Employee Relations: Training and Development

Training and development are critical to small businesses, which often operate with a lean staff, making cross-training employees to perform multiple job functions essential. Additionally, small businesses have to be creative in identifying low-cost to no-cost training opportunities for both soft skills and technical skills.

Employee Relations: Performance Development

You have invested money and time in hiring employees, which is a great first step. In order to retain employees, you must have a formal plan in place for employee development, including:

- Training, coaching, or mentoring employees for growth and development
- Administering quarterly or annual performance reviews
- Resolving workplace conflicts and disputes
- Handling discipline and termination
- Communicating companywide updates
- Arranging workplace events

- Ensuring a safe work environment
- Promoting health and wellness services

Management and HR should establish companywide policies and procedures for the aforementioned items, all of which should be clearly outlined in the employee manual.

Employee Relations: Performance Reviews

Performance reviews should be done quarterly, or at a minimum annually, based on the number of employees each manager has. The goal of the review should be continuous growth and development opportunities with constructive feedback to the employee. The review should be objective and based on the responsibilities outlined in the job description and goals set by the leader and employee. There should be a companywide performance review system that outlines the process and expectations.

I encourage my clients to perform a 360-degree evaluation on all of their employees to receive a holistic view of employee performance through a process of collecting feedback from peers, direct reports, and the employee's manager. The 360-degree review enables the employee to leverage strengths and identify blind spots. If the employee performs well on the review, great! If there are areas that need to be developed, create an individual employee development plan with goals; skills to be developed; recommended training, coaching, or mentoring; and an implementation and review timeline.

Employee Relations: Progressive Discipline

Progressive discipline is the process for handling job-related behavior that does not meet expected performance standards, which have been clearly communicated to an employee. The primary purpose of progressive discipline is to assist the employee with understanding performance issues and help them develop a plan for improvement. The process is not intended as a punishment, but to assist the employee in overcoming performance issues to satisfy job expectations.

The first time you notice an employee performance issue, you may have a conversation with your employee to discuss the changes that need to be made. The second time, you may give a verbal warning. The third time, you may write up the employee with a performance plan. The final time may lead to termination. If you have standard operating procedures that must be followed, the first time may be a verbal or written warning, based on the severity of the issue. Your culture will determine the appropriate progressive discipline, but there should always be a formal progressive discipline policy in place that is followed.

Employee Relations: Employee Retention

Regardless of the size of the organization, leadership should maintain a current organizational chart so employees can identify a career path and growth opportunities. If there aren't a ton of growth opportunities, leadership should identify creative ways to retain employees, including rewarding great work with money and fringe benefits, flexibility, recognition, a fun working environment, a culture of open communication and transparency, tools and resources for employees to perform their job more easily, and development opportunities for growth through increased responsibilities and more complex projects. If you have key employees who are invaluable to your business, you may look at profit-sharing, including bonuses tied to performance or a small ownership stake.

Hiring and retaining the right employees is an investment in time and money. Research, preparing, and hiring employees who are the right fit for your culture, assembling teams that complement each other, and creating an environment where employees feel valued and appreciated are all essential to your business success. I always say growing a business is a lot like flying a commercial airliner. Just as it takes more than one person to fly that plane, it takes more than one person to build a successful business. You have the pilot (the

CEO), navigating the plane,the flight crew (employees), taking care of the customers, and the aviation department (leadership), taking care of employees, and researching the industry, to course-correct as needed. Make sure that your team is equipped with a flight plan that leads your business to success.

Employee Relations: Termination

"Parting is such sweet sorrow," but sometimes it's necessary. You've done all you can do. You've trained, mentored, coached, and thrown a lifeline to your employee, but nothing worked. What do you do? Well, make sure you fire the employee the legal way. You might be wondering if there's an illegal way. Oh, buddy, yes, there is, and I've seen way too much of it.

First things first. Know your employer rights. In most states, if there's no employment contract, employment is on an "at-will" basis. This means, in most cases, employers have the right to fire employees for any reason, at any time, and employees have the right to leave the business, at any time, for any reason. If the employee is under contract, the terms of the contract will most likely apply. A written contract may clearly state the reasons you can terminate the employee. However, an oral contract may be your word against the employee's. Second, do your due diligence to ensure no discrimination or violation of contract clauses by the owner, leadership team, or fellow employees has taken place. Speak with your attorney regarding any questions in reference to employment law.

Be upfront, transparent, and clearly communicate your expectations to an employee. It's way easier to discipline an employee if you have clearly communicated your expectations in writing, starting with a good job description that lists specific job requirements, a detailed handbook, consistent performance reviews, individualized employee plans, and progressive discipline. If you fail to implement these measures, you might be setting yourself up to pay unemployment or be hit with a wrongful termination lawsuit.

If you and the employee part on good terms, perform an exit interview to understand their reasons for leaving the organization, their experience while working there, and changes that can be made to improve the overall work culture. On the other hand, if the relationship ends on a sour note, wish your employee well, and cut your losses. In either case, remain professional and honest, and walk in integrity.

If everything I've described in this section seems like a lot of work, that's because it is. Small businesses typically need to use some combination of staff and outsourcing to handle human resources. HR outsourcing means handing over some or all HR responsibilities to an HR firm or using HR software to administer certain tasks. Human capital management is a priority for small businesses. You know the old saying about a happy wife making for a happy life. Well, a happy employee equals a happy business, which means increased profitability and productivity. Your human resources department, whether it's made up of one or one hundred people, should operate like a well-oiled machine with documented processes and procedures to limit liability and enhance the corporate culture.

Game-Changing Operations Procedures

Your operational management system refers to how you manage the day-to-day operations of your business. This includes scheduling, keeping track of log-ins and passwords, project management, and ordering supplies. It also includes management of your business administration documents, including incorporation and business license renewal, annual board and shareholder meetings, and the like. One foundational element of your operations is the employee manual or handbook. At a minimum, your handbook should include the following policies or procedures: onboarding, code of conduct, communication policies, compensation, benefits, performance reviews, sick leave and paid vacation policy, safety and security, non-discrimination policy, and new hire and separation policy.

Another key element is your project management software, which helps you organize, plan, and manage all of your projects. Are you tired of searching for emails about a project or rummaging through files to get organized? As your business grows, you will need software, preferably cloud-based software, for all of your team members to access to make collaboration and completing tasks easier. There are tons of free and affordable options, including Basecamp, Trello, Asana, Bitrix24, and ActiveCollab. As always, do the research to determine the best fit for you based on learning curve, price, scalability, and features.

Action-Oriented Customer Service

A proactive customer service system pulls together several components of your business, including business strategy, marketing, social media, sales, technical support, and customer service. Sadly, many small businesses don't have a system in place for managing customer relationships. A customer service system is software that enhances the overall customer service experience. It tracks the journey of the customer from prospecting all the way to engagement after the sale. When customers face issues, they want a fast resolution.

As we discussed in the marketing and customer service section, a customer relationship management (CRM) system is key to documenting customer interactions. Your system can be customized to track customer requests by creating a ticketing system for all emails, calls, social posts, or chat messages. Having one centralized system to gather all of this information makes it easier to resolve issues in a timely manner. Customer service represents your brand image, values, and mission. Additionally, happy customers are more likely to refer people and remain loyal to your brand. Customer retention is easier and less expensive than obtaining a new customer, and customers are more willing to pay premium costs for exceptional service.

Trusted Legal Counsel

A legal management system or process ensures your business is protected legally in terms of contracts, liability, potential risks, insurance coverage, trademarks, patents, and copyrights. Way too many times, I've seen a small business owner invest countless hours in developing intellectual property and patent-worthy products and ideas and fail to protect them with trademarks or a patent. Make sure you trademark your intellectual property and secure your domain name and social profiles.

When you incorporate your business with your state, you have not trademarked the name. If you want to trademark your business name or any name, you must do so with the U.S. Patent and Trademark Office (USPTO). The first step in securing a trademark or patent is performing a free search on the USPTO database at www.uspto.gov. Next, you will want to hire a trademark attorney to perform a comprehensive trademark search and prepare the application or a patent attorney to prepare your patent application. The preparation of these documents requires expert knowledge and expertise to ensure you're legally protected. If you don't have an attorney as part of your business team, now might be a good time to ask your business colleagues for a referral to make sure all your intellectual property and trade secrets are protected through trademarks, copyrights, and patents.

It's important to have a business insurance advisor help you determine what type of coverage you need, which may include general liability and business property insurance, professional liability, workers' compensation, commercial auto, business income, commercial umbrella, commercial flood, or other types of insurance.

Equally important, have legal advisors on your team to develop and review contracts to ensure all terms and conditions are favorable for your business.

Efficient Financial Processes

This is a big one. Your financial management system is the software or system you use to manage your revenue, expenses, and cash flow. What is your profit margin goal, and how will you ensure that you achieve it? How do you manage accounts receivable and accounts payable? You should track all of your financial information in one system. If managing finances for your business has you feeling completely overwhelmed, no worries. Let's break it down.

Financial management includes:

1. Budgeting
2. Bookkeeping
3. Financial statements
4. Financing

Effective financial management lets you see whether or not you're making a profit. It helps you decide what you can afford to spend on your office location, inventory purchases, employees, equipment, and more.

Business Accounting Terms to Know

Regardless of the stage of business you're in, there are essential accounting terms you must know. This section will cover the basics.

Gross Revenue. The total amount of all monies received from clients in exchange for your product or service, before any deductions or expenses.

Expenses. Everything you must pay to stay in business, such as rent, payroll, costs of materials for goods sold, taxes, interest on debt, utilities, and other operating expenses.

Net Profit. The actual profit you make once you deduct your expenses from your gross revenue. If your revenue is greater than your expenses, then your business is profitable.

Cash Flow. Cash flow means that you have enough cash in your bank accounts to pay all your expenses. Cash equals proceeds from sales, investments, sale of assets, loan proceeds, and the like, used to pay for operating and direct expenses, servicing debt, or purchasing assets.

Break-Even. Many small businesses operate at a loss for years, which means their expenses are greater than total revenue. The break-even point is achieved when total revenues equal total expenses. For most businesses, this is a turning point because profitability is right around the corner.

Budgeting

You might be surprised to learn how many small businesses are operating without a budget. Owners are running numbers in their head, bouncing checks, and paying obscene amounts of money in overdraft fees. I'm not just talking about start-ups. Some of these small businesses are making several hundred thousand or millions of dollars per year. Why is this happening? They don't have a business budget as the foundation for their financial management system. They're operating on a wing and a prayer.

A budget is a list of all your monthly or yearly expenses, organized by categories. A budget is a tool that helps you:

- Track all your business expenses.
- Plan for the future.

- Forecast.
- Plan for expansion.
- Make a profit.

Once you create a budget, use it to compare what you've forecasted or budgeted with your actual expenditures.

Budget Categories

Here's a brief list of typical budget categories. Make sure you customize your list for your specific business.

- Rent
- Utilities
- Telephone and internet
- Insurance
- Employees
- Contractors
- Payroll taxes
- Office supplies
- Inventory purchases
- Permits and licenses
- Dues and memberships
- Subscriptions
- Income taxes
- Owner's draw
- Travel
- Interest
- Bank service charges
- Postage
- Legal and accounting
- Marketing and sales
- Continuing education
- Other

Bookkeeping

How are you currently tracking your income and expense transactions? Hopefully, with QuickBooks or other financial software. Effective bookkeeping helps you make more informed business decisions regarding financing, taxes, business expansion, and retirement. If you try to manage everything manually, keeping track of your accounting documents can become overwhelming. I've been using QuickBooks and QuickBooks Online for more than twenty years, but there are several other options on the market. Find accounting software that's easy for you to use, and identify an accountant who can review your books at least annually and prepare your business taxes.

There are a few bookkeeping steps you should take to manage your finances correctly, including:

1. Separate your business and personal checking accounts.
2. Reconcile your business checking accounts each month.
3. Invoice your clients through your accounting software.
4. Track online and offline sales.
5. Deposit all sales with appropriate invoices.
6. Utilize a business check or business debit or credit card for all expenses.
7. Pay business expenses on time to maintain a good business credit score.
8. Document every owner's draw if the company isn't profitable.
9. Pay yourself (the owner) a salary if you're profitable, and pay appropriate taxes.
10. Run a profit and loss (P&L) statement every month to look at the financial health of your business.

Business Financial Statements

The paper trail continues. It's obvious that managing a small business involves a ton of paperwork. It's important that your financial documents are in order because you will need them to file your business taxes, to apply for business financing, and to track revenue, expenses, and profitability. These are the four main financial statements every small business owner should maintain and review regularly:

1. Balance sheet
2. Income statement
3. Cash flow statement
4. Revenue forecast

Balance Sheet. A statement that details the assets, liabilities, and equity of a business for a specified period of time.

Income Statement. Often called a profit and loss statement, it shows the business revenues and expenses over the course of a year.

Cash Flow Statement. Sometimes referred to as a statement of cash flow, it reflects the inflow of revenues from the selling of products and services and the outflow of expenses from paying operating expenses for a specific time.

Revenue Forecast. Often called a sales forecast, this is a calculated assumption of the amount of revenue or sales you expect the business to have during the upcoming year.

Hiring an Accountant

Using an accounting software will definitely help you to establish a strong financial foundation for your business. However, I strongly recommended you hire a professional accountant to review your books for errors, at least annually, to help with business tax filings, and to make recommendations for major financial decisions. Verify that the person you hire is a certified public accountant (licensed to practice in your state), has competitive fees, and has an impeccable track record.

From the Desk of the Decision-Maker

Valerie S. Nesbitt, C.P.M., CPSD

Airport Director, Business Diversity

Hartsfield-Jackson Atlanta International Airport (ATL)

THE BIGGEST MISTAKES I see small businesses make when they want to do business with corporations and government entities are: 1) not following instructions on the bid documents, and 2) not becoming familiar with the corporation's business model and needs before approaching them.

Don't try to be everything to everyone or a Jack of all trades. Find your niche and master it, and don't expect to get the contract just because you run a small business. Expect to get the business because you are the *best* at what you do. Don't be afraid to join forces via a joint venture or strategic alliances.

To ensure you are a corporate/government-ready small business, know your potential customers' needs before you walk in the door. In other words, do your homework. Hire the right professionals for marketing, accounting, and sales. Train your team and keep abreast of technology.

“Leaders instill in their people a hope for success and a belief in themselves. Positive leaders empower people to accomplish their goals.”

— Unknown

CHAPTER SEVEN

Leadership

360°
AUTHENTIC
01
Leading Your Organization
▶ Alignment with business strategy
▶ Unique innovation
02
Self-Leadership
▶ The A.C.C.E.S.S. leadership framework
▶ Honest leadership assessment
▶ Engaging personal brand and executive presence
03
Leading Your Team
▶ Navigating change
▶ Transforming your employees and creating a high-performance culture
▶ Intentional succession and exit planning
▶ Creative diversity & inclusion
LEADERSHIP MODEL

360º Authentic Leadership Model

DO YOU THINK BEING an effective leader is only for executives in large corporations? If so, then think again. Leadership starts at the top, and developing a team of confident leaders is a critical component in managing a high-performing enterprise. Business owners must hire to complement the areas of weaknesses in the company. But first, do you know your own leadership style and what you need to round out your team? How are you managing yourself? Most business owners don't focus on their development as leaders. It's important to know the type of manager you are so you can make the necessary adjustments to your leadership style to get the most out of your team. There are all types of leaders, and the ones running a small business must be decisive and strategic.

The good news is leadership skills can be learned over time. One important quality a decisive leader must have is authenticity. I don't mean saying everything that comes to your mind in the form of brutal honesty. That could be counterproductive. Authentic leadership means remaining true to your values and mission, personally and professionally.

Let's take a look at my 360° Authentic Leadership Model, which consists of three critical components to establish a firm foundation of leadership within your business:

1. Leading your organization
2. Self-leadership
3. Leading your team

Leading Your Organization

Today's fast-paced world of innovation and technology requires leaders to be critical and strategic thinkers and to align their leadership with their business strategy. The first step is thoroughly understanding that strategy. How can you hit a target when it's not clearly marked? Sadly, that's what a lot of small businesses owners try to do. They attempt to lead a team with everyone going down different paths because they don't know the ultimate destination. It's important to go back to the fundamentals of business strategy I shared in earlier chapters. Align your leadership with the "why" of the business, lead based on the business culture you want to build, define what success looks like for all team members, establish goals with accountability, and have an executable action plan.

Innovation should be embedded in your leadership culture. As you develop yourself and your team leaders, innovation within your company and the industry can help you increase revenue, lower employee attrition, and the overall customer experience, all while lowering costs. Innovation for small businesses can be simple and cost-effective. Regularly meet with your team to discuss process-improvement methods for your products and services. Get feedback from your employees, customers, and partners on how you can do things better and faster. You never know where the next big or great idea will come from.

It's important for you and your team to develop an innovation mindset, which includes continuous learning. You don't want to get stuck in old routines. Attend workshops, conduct research, read books and articles, and attend industry events. Make sure you're on top of cutting-edge trends and developments that pertain to your business. Develop a culture of innovation and calculated risk-taking. Some ideas you test will work, and others will fail. Embrace a fail-forward culture, in which you learn from the mistakes but you keep striving to innovate.

The new buzzword for innovation is "design thinking" (even though the concept originated more than seventy years ago). Design thinking is a methodology or framework for developing and delivering innovative ideas to solve problems. It requires teamwork and collaboratively creating innovative solutions. There are five to six steps in this process. After working with many small businesses, I've narrowed the process down to four steps to make it easier.

1. Identify the problem.
2. Brainstorm viable solutions.
3. Test your ideas.
4. Get feedback and modify.

Innovation is essential to gaining a competitive edge for your business. It helps to improve processes, enhance products and services, increase efficiency, and grow revenue. Make innovation a part of your culture and your personal leadership style.

Self-Leadership

The most effective leaders possess a strong sense of self-awareness and cultivate a personal leadership mindset. It's difficult to give to others what you don't have. One of my clients, with whom I recently started working, is going through a very difficult time in her personal life. She's in the process of getting a divorce, which is placing a huge strain on her three young children and on her health. She isn't sleeping or eating well, and she feels like her life is in total chaos. As you can imagine her business is suffering. She's disengaged, making irrational business decisions, missing deadlines, and placing the stability of her business at risk. Just this morning, before sitting down to write this, I had a difficult conversation with her about the next steps of her business. Thankfully, it was well-received because she understands that she's a leader, and regardless of personal situations, she has to establish the strategic vision for her business. She has to rally her troops and give them their marching orders. Fortunately for her, my team can step in and help develop and facilitate the strategic plan and establish processes while she takes some much needed time off for self-care and preparing for her next chapter. This story could have gone a totally different way if she didn't understand the importance of her leadership at such a critical time.

Being an effective leader requires you to embody certain competencies and skillsets. It requires you to know who you are and the value you bring to the people you lead. I teach a class for corporations called Navigating the C-Suites, which discusses principles required to gain A.C.C.E.S.S. and a seat at the table. These same principles should be applied with your team to strengthen your business as you seek to gain a seat at the table with new corporate, government, and business-to business-clients.

A.C.C.E.S.S. means:

Assessment

- Who are you, and why do you deserve a seat at the table?
- What are your experience, knowledge, and skillsets?
- What is your personality style, and is it a fit for your culture?
- Are you self-aware and cultivating emotional intelligence?

Clarity

- What's your value-add to the business and clients?
- Is your communication style effective and does it foster win-win conflict resolution?
- Do you manage your time and delegate appropriately?
- Do you understand corporate politics and how to navigate the maze?

Confidence

- Do you look the part and have executive presence?
- Are you likable, fun to be around, and easy to work with?
- Do you know when to speak and when to remain silent?
- Do you have a good reputation and respected professional and personal brands?

Excellence

- Do you operate with a spirit of excellence and integrity?
- Do you have an impeccable worth ethic?
- Do you bring high energy to the team?
- Can you be trusted?
- Are you loyal?
- Do you take on highly visible projects and perform well?

Strategy

- How do your personal mission and values align with the business strategy?
- Do you positively or negatively contribute to the business culture?
- Do you contribute innovative ideas to help develop a sound business strategy?
- What out-of-the-box ideas do you offer to help the business grow?

Solution

- How do you help the company perform better, faster, and more cost-effectively?
- Are you a problem-solver or a problem-maker?

- Are you a team player, or do you have a reputation for flying solo?
- Do you coach, mentor, and train your team to perform at their highest level?

In order to be granted access to the next level of clients, you have to flow in what I call "the Alignment Zone." You need to develop the character traits and competencies needed to uplevel your clients. Larger clients want leaders who and have proven themselves by leading their companies well. They want stand-out leaders, who are innovative, cost-conscious, and provide an exceptional customer experience. You can have the most amazing product and service, but if you can't lead your team and yourself effectively, your business won't survive.

Review the A.C.C.E.S.S. leadership framework and ask yourself each one of the questions. Be honest about areas in which you need to improve, and then make a plan to enhance those areas because the success of your business depends on it. As you are assessing yourself, think about your personal leadership style. There has been so much research done on the different types of leaders that it can be a bit overwhelming to process.

I've simplified it to three types of leaders:

1. Micro-manager
2. Hands-off
3. Strategic

Micro-manager. This leader is on you like white on rice. They manage every task you take on and want to know about your actions before you take them. This leader wants to help you come up with the plan and the actions required to execute the plan. They can be a bit overwhelming and can drown out creativity. This type of leadership will work best with someone who isn't self-motivated, gets off task easily, requires managing, and has a hard time focusing. This leadership style will not work well with self-starters, innovators, or intrapreneurs who like managing their own projects and coming up with solutions to their own problems.

Hands-off. This leader trusts you to be self-motivated and get your work done on time. This leader believes that, if you have a question, you will ask it. They discuss the project expectations with you and trust you to deliver. Rarely, do they check in with you for status updates because they expect no news to be good news. This leadership style works best for someone who is self-motivated, creative, an out-of-the-box thinker, a strong leader, or someone driven to meet deadlines. This leadership style does not work well for someone who is often off task, needs clear directions on what to do, or has a hard time managing and prioritizing tasks and projects.

Strategic. These leaders align their leadership style with the business strategy. They are democratic and want to hear the opinions of others. They work with their team members to help them come up with goals, and they discuss possible solutions on how to execute and achieve the goals. They trust that their team has the necessary skills and capabilities to perform tasks, but they're available for coaching and advice if needed. They establish clear boundaries and expectations and check in with team members periodically to ensure that they're on track. They foster an environment of collaboration and teamwork. This leadership style works well when team members perform cross functions, wear many hats, and are deadline driven.

Knowing who you are as a leader makes it easier for you to lead your team. Be clear about what your personal brand is, what you stand for, and how you treat your team. Remember your personal brand encompasses the essence of who you are mentally, physically, spiritually, and emotionally. It's how you treat people, your character, keeping your word, and showing up on time.

A strong leader must embody exectuive presence and step into the CEO role. Too often, small business owners show up more as an employee rather than as the owner. They're so used to working in the business, serving clients, performing administrative tasks, and providing customer service, that they don't show up as the visionary inspiration behind the business or the politically savvy CEO. Having executive presence means being self-aware and understanding how people perceive you, being an active listener, communicating with clarity and integrity, cultivating a network of influencers, and operating like a boss under stressful situations.

Don't expect your team to do anything different from what they see you do. Parents who tell their children do what I say do not what I do are ineffective. The same is true for leaders in business. You're a role model to everyone that you lead. Lead by example not by words.

Leading Your Team

Phew! I'm sure you're exhausted from all that assessment and self-evaluation. Well, the next step is to take all the wonderful leadership qualities you have and pour them into your team. There are a set of leadership competencies you need to lead your team. (A competency is a skill that equips you to perform a specific task.) Leadership competencies equip you to lead your organization. Just as a mechanic requires a precise set of skills to fix cars, leaders require a certain array of competencies to lead effectively.

Leadership is often misunderstood and difficult to define. Every time I turn around, it seems like there's a new leadership model, framework, or theory. To simplify things, I've grouped the leadership competencies into four core areas:

1. Lead people.
2. Lead change.
3. Communicate and build coalitions.
4. Be results driven.

Lead people. This competency is both an art and a science. It involves lots of trial and error and requires you to develop and implement strategies that maximize employee performance to achieve your business's vision, mission, and goals. The competency of leading people includes team building, cultural awareness, integrity and honesty, and conflict management.

As a leader, your role is to inspire, motivate, and guide others toward the accomplishment of your business goals and to encourage and facilitate cooperation within the business to develop a common focus. You do this through coaching, mentoring, training, rewarding and guiding employees. Great and effective leaders also champion cultural diversity in the workforce, not because they have to but because they want to and it's the right thing to do.

It's important that you're not just talk. Lead by example, with integrity and honesty, and foster a high standard of ethics to instill mutual trust and confidence in your team. That trust will be particularly useful in times of conflict. Some conflict is unavoidable. As a leader, you are responsible for limiting the negative aspects of conflict while increasing the positive aspects.

Lead change. The only thing that stays the same in business is, well, nothing because change is always right around the corner. Whether it's technology, industry trends, the entrance of new competitors in the marketplace, or marketing strategies, there will always be change. You have to learn how to navigate and ride those waves. Leading change requires you to develop and implement your business vision and to incorporate that vision into the organization's core values.

It also requires you to foster a work environment that encourages creative thinking and the ability to maintain focus, intensity, and persistence, even under adversity.

Leading change is the most difficult competency to master. Most people like tradition and consistency and have an attitude of "We've always done it this way." However, in the digital age and our microwave society, where everything is constantly changing, this thinking won't work. There are two keys to leading change: 1) Demonstrate openness to doing things differently so you create an atmosphere of continuous learning. Apply new ideas and technology, or apply traditional technology and traditional thought processes in new ways. 2) Recognize and understand external forces that impact your business and remain innovative and competitive.

Communicate and build coalitions. You and your business are stronger when you collaborate and work with others rather than trying to do everything by yourself. Leaders need to be able to explain facts and advocate for ideas in a convincing manner while communicating and negotiating with individuals, teams, and other businesses.

Be results driven. All talk and no results will lead to business destruction. Being results driven requires accountability and continuous improvement. It includes the ability to make timely and effective decisions and produce results through strategic planning, implementation, and evaluation of results.

Transformational Employee Development

As a small business owner and leader of your team, you should always make personal growth and development a priority for you and your team members. One great way to discover growth opportunities is through a personality assessment. There are several industry standard assessments, including the DiSC Assessment, The Myers-Briggs Type Indicator (MBTI), and the Riso-Hudson Enneagram Type Indicator (RHETI). These tests give a non-biased perspective on how team members interact with others, process information, make decisions, and perceive the world. The reports received from the assessment can be used to develop individualized training, coaching, and mentoring plans for each team member. The goal is to provide each employee with the tools and resources they need to help you develop a high-performance culture.

High Performance Culture

All right, you're rocking and rolling and moving right along. You've assessed your leadership style, you've hired the right team, and you've performed personality assessments on your team members to help them create their growth plans. What's next? As a business owner, you're probably a high achiever, so it goes without saying that you want your team to perform at the optimal level. To achieve that goal, you need to create a high-performance culture.

Creating a high-performance culture is a journey that doesn't happen overnight and has the potential for many pit stops and breakdowns along the way. Your culture is individual and unique to your business but here are a few insights on principles to embrace as you create a high-performance culture.

1. Remain true to your values and mission.
2. Inspire innovation and be unique.
3. Embrace failure as a part of success.
4. Invest in developing your leaders.
5. Create a culture of coaching and mentoring.
6. Train your team on emotional intelligence.

7. Empower people to make decisions.
8. Take calculated risks and learn from mistakes.
9. Institute a process of continuous improvement.
10. Celebrate small and big wins as a team.

And most importantly, have lots of fun and grow together.

Intentional Succession and Exit Planning

A lot of small business owners are so focused on growing the business that they don't think about succession planning or an exit strategy. Succession planning is essential to scaling the business you've invested blood, sweat, and tears into,—whether your intention is to sell it or leave it as a family legacy. Proper succession planning helps you to identify critical leadership roles that are essential to the success of your business. It also helps you to hire properly, groom your team members, and have qualified and capable people ready to fill the leadership role when needed. There are five key steps in succession planning.

Step 1. Assess.

Accurately assess the current and future needs of the business based on an organization chart, strategic plan, and goals. Prioritize key positions to determine which roles require a successor (someone to fill the position).

Step 2. Define.

Clearly define roles, responsibilities, and expectations for each position. Create and implement an objective (not subjective) performance-management process. Develop a succession plan to align managers and employees with strategic objectives.

Step 3. Identify.

Identify high-potential leaders within the business. Evaluate their strengths from current performance, assessments, and 360° feedback.

Step 4. Train.

Train employees based on specific areas of improvement that align with the business needs. Conduct ongoing training and development and include mentoring, coaching, and relevant job rotation.

Step 5. Monitor and evaluate.

Perform annual audits to ensure succession planning is effective and objective. Continuously work with leaders to identify internal talent to replace key positions as needed. Maintain strong partnerships to identify external talent if required.

Creating a pipeline of qualified leaders is imperative. You don't want to be caught off guard by an unexpected departure of a key team member or a long-time employee who retires sooner than planned. Create a culture of developing leaders and cross-training them in various departments to maintain the needed talent to fill in gaps when required.

On the other hand, if you're looking to sell the business, then you need to have a sound exit strategy. If the business is profitable, an exit strategy gives you an opportunity to make a nice profit. If the business is not profitable, it can help you to limit losses. An important element of an exit strategy is business valuation. A business valuation specialist will help the business owner and the buyer examine the company's financials to determine a fair value for the business. Having a solid business infrastructure, including processes and systems and a well-developed leadership, increases the value of your business.

Creative Diversity and Inclusion

What does "diversity and inclusion" mean? Depending on who you ask, it can mean a lot of different things. At a basic level, it means including all people, regardless of ethnicity, race, gender, gender identity, social class, age, physical ability or attributes, religious beliefs, sexual orientation, value systems, ethical beliefs, national origin, or political beliefs. That's a long list, but in essence, it means everyone should have an opportunity to sit at the table. Diversity and inclusion isn't just a conversation to be had in the board rooms of large corporations. It should be woven throughout the fabric of small businesses as well.

Research continues to prove that there are many benefits to diversity and inclusion, including improved retention rates, stronger workforce performance, and higher employee engagement rates. Don't get overwhelmed at the thought of incorporating diversity and inclusion within your business strategy.

Start with small diversity and inclusion initiatives such as those that follow.

1. **Define what diversity and inclusion mean to your business, and educate everyone on it**. Recently, I was working with one of my technology clients on their three-year business strategy. As we reviewed the organization chart, the owner realized all of his leaders were men. He decided he wanted to diversify his leadership team and committed to a 10% increase of diverse women leaders. He defined what diversity and inclusion looked like for him and educated his team so they could adjust interviewing and hiring policies to reflect the new goal.
2. **Enable employees to create corporate-wide programs that support diversity**. One of my clients instituted a corporate-wide program that gives employees one paid

day off per year to volunteer at a charity or non-profit organization of their choosing. The owner encourages his team to select programs that are diverse and inclusive. This small business owner defined diversity and inclusion to include community outreach and philanthropy.

3. **Diversify your recruiting efforts**. If you want to truly have a diverse and inclusive team, you have to start with your recruiting and hiring efforts. Are you sourcing candidates from resources that have diverse candidates? Are you implementing a "blind resume" policy to avoid bias in the early hiring stages? (A blind resume means removing a candidate's name, current company, and school from the hiring process to prevent your team from making a judgment about a person based on the information presented in the resume.) Make the necessary changes in your hiring process to increase diversity and inclusion in your company.
4. **Train your team on "unconscious bias" and diversity and inclusion.** Everybody, whether we admit it or not, has unconscious bias. How you were raised, what school you went to, your personal experiences, friends, societal stereotypes, and cultural experiences all have an influence on how you make decisions and respond to situations. Unconscious bias occurs when your brain makes a quick assessment or judgment about someone based on who you are and what you've been exposed to. Training your team to recognize and check their unconscious bias helps to create a more inclusive culture.
5. **Reflect diversity and inclusion in your branding and marketing messages**. Does your brand represent diversity? Is it inclusive? Can a person of a different race, ethnicity, or gender see themselves working with you?

> If you don't include diverse people in your marketing campaigns, then the answer to all of those questions is probably no. If you really want to embrace diversity and inclusion, it's important to share a diverse culture in your branding and marketing efforts.

Creating a more diverse and inclusive culture will take time and consistency. You can't force your team to embrace diversity and inclusion, but you, as a leader, can embrace the uniqueness of your employees, vendors, strategic partners, and clients to set a positive cultural tone. While most business owners have the best intentions for diversity and inclusion, they don't have a strategy in place. It's often easier to hire for specific sets of skills or experiences without thinking about diversity or different backgrounds and experiences. This may be easier in the short-term but could cost you in the long-run. According to a recent McKinsey & Company report on diversity, there is a direct link between gender and ethnic diversity and increased company financial performance. "Diversity and inclusion is not only a competitive advantage but a key enabler of growth".[34]

From the Desk of the Decision-Maker

Lissa J. Miller

First Vice President, Supplier Diversity

SunTrust Bank

BEING A CORPORATE-READY SUPPLIER is a must for any small business looking to scale and grow. Competition is fierce with innovation, cost savings, and constant changes in technology and industry trends. As a baseline, a small business must do the following:

- Research your target corporation(s)/organization(s) and understand their services, footprint, leadership, customer base, and procurement process.
- Know who your competitors are and differentiate yourself.
- Understand how your costs and pricing compare with your competitors.
- Make sure your business has sustainable practices, infrastructure, and leadership.
- Don't put all of your eggs in one corporate basket; diversify your revenue streams.

Pull the Trigger: Your Next Steps

CAN YOU BELIEVE IT? You did it. You were committed, and you made it to the end of the book. I am so super proud of you. I'm sure the journey has been bumpy, filled with some pit stops, dead ends, and detours. There are so many facets to growing a successful business that the journey seems endless at times. My intention was to provide you with a blueprint of the exact steps you need to build a robust business. There are so many moving parts as you navigate the start-up, sustainability, or scale-up phase. Utilize this book as a reference manual and refer to it as you grow your business. Use the B.U.I.L.D. framework to establish a solid infrastructure for your business while reaping the financial and personal rewards of your hard work.

Business Strategy

Unique Branding

Integrated Marketing and Sales

Leveraged Systems

Decisive Leadership

I've covered each of these important aspects of growing a business in the pages of *The CEO Life*. I've also given you specific strategies to enhance your quality of life while you step fully into your role as CEO. So what's next? You're on fire, ready to scale up the quality of your business and personal life. You know it's possible, and now it's your turn. You've decided this is your year to grow and expand your business and achieve more. You're ready to maintain meaningful relationships and get unstuck. It's time to find your passion and live your best life.

Women from Madam C.J. Walker, one of the first black millionaires, to Janice Bryant Howroyd, the first black woman to own a billion-dollar business, are true testaments of the power we all have to build something great from little or nothing. What I know for sure is that you can't do it alone. Whether you're a man or a woman and regardless of your race or ethnicity, it takes a village, a team, and a nurturing community to create your successful CEO life. So I invite you to join me on this journey of building a rich legacy by investing in yourself and your business. I look forward to meeting you personally at one of my seminars or virtually at www.theceo.life. Until then, remember to create and implement your strategy, and then expect success.

Business Start-Up Checklist

STARTING A BUSINESS IS VERY EXCITING, but it can also be overwhelming if you don't know the proper steps to establish a solid foundation. Save money to fund your business, do your research, and get professional legal and financial advice as needed.

Here are ten steps to guide you during this process.

Step 1. Research the industry you want to start a business in to determine if it's viable.

Step 2. Select a business name (perform a U.S. Trademark search to ensure the business name is available).

Step 3. Decide on a legal structure (Partnership, LLC, S-Corporation, C-Corporation).

Step 4. Register your business name with the Secretary of State.

Step 5. Obtain a federal tax ID number (EIN Number) with the Internal Revenue Service.

Step 6. Open a business bank account.

Step 7. Obtain a business license (for the city/state you will be doing business in).

Step 8. Get a sales tax permit (if you're selling a physical product).

Step 9. Establish an accounting/record-keeping system.

Step 10. Reserve your website domain name.

“The road to success and the road to failure are almost exactly the same.”

— Colin R. Davis

If you enjoyed reading *The CEO Life,*
please leave a review on Amazon.com!

Connect with me on social media:
@coachtrenee

Connect with me on the web:
www.theceo.life
www.isuccessconsulting.com
www.treneesmith.com

Endnotes

[1] Association, A. (2018). How Does Stress Affect Us?. [online] Psych Central. Available at: https://psychcentral.com/lib/how-does-stress-affect-us.

[2] Sba.gov. (2018). Small Businesses Drive Job Growth in the U.S. | The U.S. Small Business Administration | SBA.gov. [online] Available at: https://www.sba.gov/advocacy/small-businesses-drive-job-growth-us.

[3] Waring, D. (2017). Small Business Failure Rates: Why All The Stats Have It Wrong. [online] Fit Small Business. Available at: https://fitsmallbusiness.com/small-business-failure-rates.

[4] THE 2017 STATE OF WOMEN-OWNED BUSINESSES REPORT. (2019). 7th ed. [ebook] American Express, p.12. Available at: https://about.americanexpress.com/sites/americanexpress.newshq.businesswire.com/files/doc_library/file/2017_SWOB_Report_-FINAL.pdf.

[5] CB Insights Research. (2018). The Top 20 Reasons Startups Fail. [online] Available at: https://www.cbinsights.com/research/startup-failure-reasons-top/

[6] Harvard Business Review. (2015). Only 8% of Leaders Are Good at Both Strategy and Execution. [online] Available at: https://hbr.org/2015/12/only-8-of-leaders-are-good-at-both-strategy-and-execution.

[7] Phegan, B. (2017). Benefits of a Good Company Culture - Enlinx. [online] Enlinx. Available at: http://enlinx.com/benefits-good-company-culture.

[8] Morrison, M. (2010). Published History of SMART Objectives. [online] RapidBI. Available at: https://rapidbi.com/history-of-smart-objectives.

[9] Sec.gov. (n.d.). EDGAR Search Results. [online] Available at: https://www.sec.gov/cgi-bin/browse-edgar?CIK=0001288776&action=getcompany.

[10] McIntyre, G. (2019). Free Business Credit Report: 5 Places You Can Find One. [online] Fundera Ledger. Available at: https://www.fundera.com/blog/free-business-credit-report.

[11] NOW Corp. (2019). product-now-account » NOW Corp. [online] Available at: https://nowcorp.com/product-now-account.

[12] OptinMonster. (2019). 32 of the BEST Value Propositions (Plus How to Write Your Own). [online] Available at: https://optinmonster.com/32-value-propositions-that-are-impossible-to-resist.

[13] Fabrikbrands.com. (2017). Memorable or forgettable? What your brand personality says about you. [online] Available at: http://fabrikbrands.com/what-your-brand-personality-says-about-you.

[14] MBA Skool-Study.Learn.Share. (n.d.). Brand Personality Aaker Definition | Marketing Dictionary | MBA Skool-Study.Learn.Share. [online] Available at: https://www.mbaskool.com/business-concepts/marketing-and-strategy-terms/1863-brand-personality-aaker.html.

[15] Instead, T. (2019). The Horrible Name that Google Was ALMOST Called—And How They Came up with Google Instead. [online] Skillcrush. Available at: https://skillcrush.com/2013/11/12/horribly-google-called-google.

[16] Miller, J. (2015). Brand Naming Process: How to Make a Brand Name Resonate. [online] Sticky Branding. Available at: https://stickybranding.com/brand-naming-process-how-to-make-a-brand-name-resonate.

[17] Brandwatch. (2016). How to Write a Brand Positioning Statement. [online] Available at: https://www.brandwatch.com/blog/write-brand-positioning-statement.

[18] Advertising, T. (2018). *Importance of Color Theory in Advertising/Pod Blog/ Home - ThePodAdvertising*. [online] The Pod Advertising. Available at: http://www.thepodadvertising.com/Pod-Blog/Importance-of-Color-Theory-in-Advertising.

[19] Score.org. (2017). How to Do a Brand Audit. [online] Available at: https://www.score.org/resource/how-to-do-brand-audit.

[20] Schultz, M., Doerr, J. and Frederiksen, L. (2013). *Professional Services Marketing*. Hoboken, N.J.: John Wiley & Sons, Inc.

[21] Hubspot.com. (2018). *2018 Marketing Statistics, Trends & Data - The Ultimate List of Digital Marketing Stats.* [online] Available at: https://www.hubspot.com/marketing-statistics.

[22] Junto. (2019). 25 Mind-Bottling SEO Stats for 2019 & Beyond | SEO Insights | Junto. [online] Available at: https://junto.digital/blog/seo-stats.

[23] Medium. (2018). ADVANTAGES OF SOCIAL MEDIA MARKETING. [online] Available at: https://medium.com/@crescenttech555/advantages-of-social-media-marketing-45f56dde9938.

[24] Blue Fountain Media. (n.d.). 10 Advantages of Social Media Marketing for Your Business | Blue Fountain Media. [online] Available at: https://www.bluefountainmedia.com/blog/advantages-of-social-media-marketing.

[25] Blue Fountain Media. (2019). *10 Advantages of Social Media Marketing for Your Business* | Blue Fountain Media. [online] Available at: https://www.bluefountainmedia.com/blog/advantages-of-social-media-marketing [Accessed 18 May 2019].

[26] Tour, F., Pricing, P., In, S. and FREE!, S. (2017). Digital Marketing Statistics, Trends and Data for 2017 | DailyStory. [online] DailyStory. Available at: https://www.dailystory.com/digital-marketing-stats-trends-data-2017.

[27] Sugarbird Marketing. (n.d.). What brand purpose is and why it is important to buyers. [online] Available at: https://www.sugarbirdmarketing.com/brand-purpose

[28] ReferralCandy — Give Any Ecommerce Store a Referral Program. (n.d.). 2: How Powerful Is Word-of-Mouth, Exactly? – The Definitive Guide To Referral Marketing. [online] Available at: https://www.referralcandy.com/referral-marketing-guide/2/how-powerful-is-word-of-mouth-exactly.

[29] Bridges, J. and Bridges, J. (n.d.). How to Analyze Risks on Your Project - ProjectManager.com. [online] ProjectManager.com. Available at: https://www.projectmanager.com/training/how-to-analyze-risks-project.

[30] HUBZone program. (n.d.). HUBZone program. [online] Available at: https://www.sba.gov/federal-contracting/contracting-assistance-programs/hubzone-program.

[31] Softwareadvice.com. (2019). Top Supply Chain Management Software - 2019 Reviews. [online] Available at: https://www.softwareadvice.com/scm.

[32] Erdmann-Sullivan, H. (2017). Retention by Generation — What Matters Most. [online] Workplace.care.com. Available at: http://workplace.care.com/retention-by-generation-what-matters-most.

[33] Resources.careerbuilder.com. (2016). 75% Of Employers Have Hired the Wrong Person, Here's How to Prevent That. [online] Available at: https://resources.careerbuilder.com/news-research/prevent-hiring-the-wrong-person.

[34] McKinsey & Company. (2017). Delivering through diversity. [online] Available at: https://www.mckinsey.com/business-functions/organization/our-insights/delivering-through-diversity.

www.ingramcontent.com/pod-product-compliance
Lightning Source LLC
Chambersburg PA
CBHW071539210326
41597CB00019B/3052